Understanding Organizations

Understanding Organizations

Howard Lune

polity

First published in 2010 by Polity Press

Polity Press
65 Bridge Street
Cambridge CB2 1UR, UK

Polity Press
350 Main Street
Malden, MA 02148, USA

ISBN-13: 978-0-7456-4427-1
ISBN-13: 978-0-7456-4428-8(pb)

A catalogue record for this book is available from the British Library.

Typeset in 10.5 on 13 pt Swift
by Servis Filmsetting Ltd, Stockport, Cheshire
Printed and bound by MPG Books Group, UK

The publisher has used its best endeavours to ensure that the URLs for external websites referred to in this book are correct and active at the time of going to press. However, the publisher has no responsibility for the websites and can make no guarantee that a site will remain live or that the content is or will remain appropriate.

Every effort has been made to trace all copyright holders, but if any have been inadvertently overlooked the publisher will be pleased to include any necessary credits in any subsequent reprint or edition.

For further information on Polity, visit our website: www.politybooks.com

Contents

Figures and Tables

Figures

Tables

Acknowledgments

I am indebted to many careful readers, without whom there would be even more errors than the ones you might find. Particular appreciation goes to Katherine Chen, Jacqueline Johnson, Victoria Johnson, Kevin Leicht, Jacqueline Olvera, and Gwen Dordick, the anonymous reviewers, and all of the production staff at Polity.

Introducing Organizations

What is an organization?

IT is no longer possible to study modern industrial society (or post-modern, post-industrial society) without the study of organizations. Virtually everything we do as members of a society or community, and vast amounts of what we do as individuals, occurs within organized settings. Even our personal lives and intimate relations are structured by organizational constraints. Colleges and universities, for example, draw together students who are far more similar to each other than they are to the rest of the population. Of course there are age similarities, but also geographic factors, economic issues, and personality issues shaped by the less tangible aspects of the reputations of the schools. Yet consider how the practice of bringing together large numbers of relatively similar young adults at the start of their independent lives for several years of close living defines our worlds: your expanding social and political awareness is shaped in large measure by conversations and experiences in college; your career is shaped by what you study and with whom, including your friendships and other social networks that will stay with you; and a great many marriages begin as college relationships.

Who knew that when you decided on the school that allowed you to keep a car instead of the one that didn't, or when your second-choice school offered you better financial aid than your first-choice school had, such significant pathways to your future were opening or closing? Of course, this organizational alignment of your social future did not just begin here. Parents compete to get their kids in the "right" pre-schools to help track them to the best colleges (or, at least, I have read that in "lifestyle" articles in news magazines). Similar factors are at work when communities invest in junior league sports or music programs, or raise property taxes to improve science education in the high school, so you may well have been on this path from organization to organization – school to team to university to workplace – for a lot longer than you realize.

Does all of that matter? Wherever you go, you meet some people and not others, or learn one skill instead of a different one. Does the organizational setting make such a difference? The answer, of course, is yes, though it will take a few chapters to show you why. But, first, we need a little vocabulary and a brief bit of history.

For the moment, let's say that an organization is a group with some kind of name, purpose, and a defined membership. For any given organization, you are either part of it or you aren't, and you know which. This is in contrast to other kinds of groups, such as groups of friends or members of a neighborhood community. With groups like that it's possible for some people to consider themselves members, or to be considered as members by most participants and yet have other participants disagree. An organization, therefore, has a clear boundary between its inside and its outside.

An organization can be more or less formally organized. A formal organization tends to have roles or jobs or ranks within it, and guidelines, rules or by-laws defining how things get done within it. A less formal or informal organization might not specify that much detail. And then there are semi-formal organizations that lie in between. I once belonged to a food co-op, for example, which was technically a formal organization but so loosely run that very few people had much idea what their exact responsibilities were supposed to be. Most of us just showed up around the time we were expected and asked someone what needed to be done.

Another useful term is *institution*. An institution may be thought of as a collective entity or any way of organizing relationships that is widely familiar and routinely practiced. Many organizations are institutions, and many institutions are organized. An institution is defined by the unwritten rules that everyone understands about some kind of organized behavior. Marriage is an institution, but not an organization, while the military is both an institution and a set of organizations. Things are done in particular ways in institutions not necessarily because of rules but because those ways of doing things are "taken for granted." Similarly, when certain ideas or ways of doing things become so taken for granted that people mostly stop thinking about alternative ideas, we say that those ideas have been *institutionalized*. Once things become institutionalized in an organization, you'll find that the organization's members can come and go, but the organization still keeps functioning the same way, following the same procedures without having to stop and rethink everything each time there is a change in personnel. This is called *institutional memory*. There is more to say about institutions, but this will do for a start.

As a student, you had, or have, a defined social role, a purpose, and a clear set of social relations with others. Other students are your peers, though some might belong to a class ahead of you or behind you. There are people you answer to in some way, people who provide you with help or resources, and people whose roles there do not directly relate to yours. School is a formal organization. There are rules and roles, members and non-members, and goals.

The higher education system, on the other hand, is an institution. Through years of standardization and the efforts of professional societies, we can now pretty much assume that a bachelor's degree from any college in any state or nation is functionally equivalent to any other, even though the details of the underlying education and even the fields of study might be different. So the individual organizations that make up that institution – the degree-granting colleges and universities – are each "certified" members of the higher education system, and each has its own role within it.

Within your family, you also have an identified role in a social structure. Parents and grandparents, children and siblings, and aunts and uncles form a stable and fairly well-defined group, the contours of which repeat with minor variations from family to family, city by city, nation by nation. Since families are not formally organized, each family is free to be as unique as the individuals who form it wish. But that doesn't easily happen, as anyone who has tried can tell you. The family is a social institution. The family as an institution also has rules and roles that are widely recognized even if they are not written down or, for the most part, officially enforced. It is partially governed and protected by laws, regulated, taxed differently than individuals, and extensively measured. Such social institutions are not organizations, but their place in society is both organized and taken for granted.

Now here is a trick question. When was the last time you did anything for any length of time outside of the boundaries of organizations and institutions? Most residents of the "industrialized nations" are born in hospitals, and many die there, or in hospices or other nursing facilities. We spend our early years in school or with family, occasionally getting out to participate in team sports or other organized leisure activities, organized classes, and organized trips. (Apparently, many people go bowling alone, but most sports are organized.) We may be affiliated with an organized religion through which each of life's major transitions will be formally observed with an organized ceremony. We may spend time in the military, summer camps, possibly jails or otherwise under "institutional" care. We move about as free individuals through highly organized traffic systems, or ride on mass transit systems along with the rest of the masses. Most of us seek full-time, or more than full time, legitimate work for a formal work organization. (But don't assume that illegitimate work isn't carefully organized as well.) If we're lucky, our workplaces have routine inter-organizational relations with pension systems and insurance companies, providing us with benefits such as health care. Some of us also have unions. In each of these cases, the social roles, the behavioral rules, the criteria for membership, and the costs and benefits of membership were all worked out and formalized long before we came along. The choice offered to us as individuals is whether to participate or not. But the costs of not participating are often quite severe, so most of us make the same choice.

Our relationships with formal organizations run much deeper, however, extending far into our personal lives and leisure time. We may shop in malls with identical, interchangeable branches of the same global retail corporations, knowing little about the individually owned alternatives available to us. We buy food the same way, favoring supermarket chains and fast-food outlets over local markets. While only a minority of people contributes to charitable causes, most do so through large, formal organizations. (The routine exception to this involves contributions to religious organizations.) Our money is mostly held in one of the branches of a handful of international banking corporations, and we make a majority of our purchases using one of the major credit cards instead of cash, yielding end-of-year summary statements that define our spending profiles. These profiles may be used by us to change our habits, if we wish. Versions of them are also routinely sold to marketing companies, which helps explain why we receive mail-order catalogs that we never asked for. Our consumption patterns are analyzed, yielding consumer profiles that estimate the sorts of things we're likely to buy in the future. Many of us conform to the predictions by purchasing from those catalogs.

Few of us actively participate in democratic politics, beyond occasionally voting; preferring instead to leave such things in the hands of formal political parties, organized interest groups, and professional lobbying firms. Those who are more active typically join social movement or community advocacy organizations (chapter 8). The ethnic minorities among us may support or belong to ethnic cultural associations, some of which organize for greater access to the political system. While those professional political organizations do whatever they do, the majority of us who receive our news almost exclusively from one of the five largest news corporations in the US see and hear little of it. (This is less true in comparable nations outside the US, but the worldwide trend is in the direction of the American model.) We depend on our formal system of police, courts, and prisons to manage crime and social control, and we often vote in favor of strengthening those institutions, though most of us are not quite clear on what they do and how they operate. We perceive them as "our" institutions, working on our behalf, and we want them to have the resources they need to operate effectively. As a culture, we trust our organizations.

At the same time, we don't trust them (Chanley, Rudolph, and Rahn, 2000). We distrust government, complain about our jobs and companies, denigrate organized communities as "special interests," and use the word **"bureaucracy"**[*] as an insult. We also greatly value our individualism and our liberties, which stand in contrast to "big government," "big business," and other large, organized systems. To paraphrase Homer Simpson, formal organizations are the cause of, and the solution to, most of our problems.

These examples and encounters can help us to broaden the definitions that we have been developing. Organizations have goals, names, and boundaries. They also have different roles or expectations for different kinds of members, such as owners, employees, volunteers, and staff, which translate in specific conditions to students and workers, managers, writers, cooks, designers, custodians, etc. The differentiation of tasks, responsibilities, and titles is referred to as the "division of labor" within an organization. We can characterize and study organizations according to their levels of differentiation. Informal organizations where all members share responsibilities are said to have very little differentiation. Formal organizations tend to be highly differentiated. Examples of highly differentiated organizations would be multinational firms or government agencies in which some units of the organization exist to oversee other units which coordinate still other units, all of which is far removed from the people who create or provide the goods or services for which the organization was created.

Organizations also act on behalf of specific groups. Corporations work for their investors and shareholders. Schools work for their students. Teams play for their members (and fans, sometimes). Unions represent their members, but also act on behalf of their industries and potential future members. We can refer to the groups whose lives are directly affected by the organizations as *constituents*. Clearly political organizations have constituents, as the term is often used as a synonym for voters.

Some constituents are clients. Some are members or participants. Some could be customers, although organizations that have customers are more likely to be representing the groups whose goods they sell rather than those who buy them. Co-ops are organized similarly, except that their members are the customers. From just these few characteristics, a vast array of organizational forms is possible.

Organizations also have what we might call "settings," although the terms environment, **niche**, field, domain, and industry are also

---

[*] Terms in bold throughout the text appear in the glossary at the end of this book.

used to describe the context in which an organization operates. Frequently, though not universally, the setting for an organization can be understood as a kind of social institution. Firms are embedded within industries; the industries are defined by their place within the economic system, which is a kind of social institution. Schools are organizations within education systems that are institutionalized. Competitive sports teams operate within the institutions of competitive sports. Social institutions aren't always larger than organizations, and they don't always define the context for organizing. But it is worth keeping an eye on this relationship.

Political and economic institutions, in particular, shape formal organizations such as corporations and political parties. What do I mean by "shape?" Let's say the institutions create the paths along which the organizations can best travel. The major institutions define how things are done and how the parts connect. When we talk about whether some action or other makes sense, it is often the institutional context that determines what is sensible or not. We can say that the institutions create meaning and the organizations in those institutional settings work with the given meaning system.

Consider this example. I have often heard it said that Americans are litigious, which is to say that we like to sue each other. Somehow this doesn't seem to be the sort of thing that many people would like. Yet we do have a lot of lawsuits. One explanation is that there is an institutionalized relationship between our courts and our other large institutions. Within any given workplace, school or other formal organization, there might or might not be a procedure for stating grievances. There might be a way of raising problems, and it might, sometimes, lead to things being fixed. This is all very haphazard and unpredictable. On the other hand, we have a set of clear legal mandates for certain forms of organizational behavior. In terms of discrimination, the US has a series of federal laws forbidding discrimination on the bases of race, age, religion, sex, or nationality, as well as federal regulatory agencies responsible for occupational safety and health, food and drug safety, fair and safe housing, environmental protection, and so on. If an organization creates a safety hazard or discriminates against its members or fails to deliver on contracted services, then they are in violation of rules that have been determined by courts. You can sue them, and if you win, the organization will be legally obligated to change their behavior while some vast institution out there somewhere will become responsible for making sure that they do it. That's a result you can't get by filling out a suggestion card. So it makes more sense to sue in many cases, and less sense to pursue less formal channels. This is because of the institutional context – the connection between courts, regulations, and organizations.

The legal-institutional context of business in the US has also encouraged organizations to routinely create and publicize codes of conduct and rules for ethical behavior. In contrast, formal organizations in Germany tend to avoid explicit rules and discussions over ethics, which some business leaders there consider "public moralizing" (Palazzo, 2002). In the German case, ethical behavior within an organization is frequently seen as the personal responsibility of individual leaders, and not a matter of rational-legal behavioral "checklists." In this context, it makes sense for those who have grievances against an organization to try first to handle it internally. It would not make sense to turn to the courts for help until other options had failed.

Returning to the language of the field, institutional changes over time have made it easier or more profitable for groups and individuals to do things in certain ways more often than doing them differently. Institutions influence one another, and organizations respond to them in similar and often predictable ways. We've already noted that there are a lot more formal organizations in modern industrial society than there were before. That means more of us act through such organizations than through other means, and we do so because that's what works best in our society.

Organizational theorists Edward Laumann and David Knoke (1987) have argued that for over a century – since the rise of the modern industrial state – governments and large corporate entities have shared in pressing for the social and political changes that created these conditions. That is, large formal organizations have actively shaped the international institutional context in which we have come to depend on large formal organizations. This shift has supported the massive growth of both business and government. The authors do not suggest that generations of corporate and political leaders have acted this way simply to make money, or that they are merely "the capitalist class" operating on behalf of class interests. Rather, the practices that have gained favor and become institutionalized and taken for granted are those that support a "business-friendly government," thereby allowing and encouraging the continued authority of people who work best within this sort of environment. Our major institutions support the rise of large, complex formal organizations, from which emerge the people and coalitions that define our major institutions. The result is some combination of great continuity and a lack of attention to alternative ways of thinking and acting. We have institutionalized the idea of building institutions.

Numerous writers have referred to this condition as the "organizational society" or "organizational state" (Laumann and Knoke, 1987; Perrucci and Potter, 1989; Scott, 2004; Zald and McCarthy, 1987). Generally speaking, those terms indicate that participation in modern society is primarily shaped by participation in formal organizations, for both better and worse. The broad changes in the organization of modern society that have given rise to this arrangement have been praised almost as often as they have been decried. The point of the sociology of organizations is not to fear or prevent the organized foundation of our lives, but to see and understand it. Whatever our specific areas of interest or concern, we need to know more about organizations.

The organizational society

This book is concerned with the sociology of organizations in the United States and "comparable" societies. But which societies are those and what makes them comparable? For the most part, I will be referring to contemporary industrial democracies, although a more technically accurate phrase might be "advanced capitalist societies." These nations are sometimes also referred to as the "Western industrial democracies," the "Northern states," and the OECD member-states. While many of them share some cultural histories or overlap of religions or languages, the key feature holding them together is their relationship to global industry and the market economy. That is, the political and economic institutions that shape the organizational contexts of the OECD (Organisation for Economic Co-operation and Development: <www.oecd.org>) nations are comparable and routinely interact with one another, as they have throughout the expansion of industrialization. Thus the social processes and developments that most concern us begin with the industrial revolution in Europe and the US.

The sociology of organizations as a field of study was born out of what we now call economic sociology, and has its theoretical roots firmly in the massive social changes brought about by the Industrial Revolution. Actually, we can distinguish two industrial revolutions. The first, fueled by massive new coal-based power generation capabilities, transformed the productive systems in the decades around 1800, beginning in Great Britain. The second industrial revolution began about 100 years later, and this is the period with which the whirlwind of organizational transformation really started. The term "revolution" is probably over-used; but in this case it seems to fit. It was out of this second revolution that pre-industrial social relations were overthrown and the organizational society was born. Prior to that time, almost all of the functions that we attach to bureaucracies existed outside of the boundaries of large, formal organizations. Now, some have almost no independent existence at all. In order to understand what these organizations do, and what their impact is, we need to review the rise of the bureaucratization of nearly everything.

A brief and highly selective history of the modern age

This chapter has argued that large, formal organizations play a huge role in almost every aspect of our lives. The following questions are among those raised by this argument. How did this come to be? How does this affect us? And – so what? I have promised that this book will answer the last question eventually. We've looked at some of the answers to the second question already. At this point, I wish to address the first question.

One of the grand narratives of the modern age is the increasing interconnectedness of the major institutions of social, political, and economic life. This development required a sharp break from the conditions of pre-modern life, which were more or less shaped by local traditions. Large social, cultural, political, and economic shifts necessarily also included significant organizational changes. It is therefore hardly possible to review modern history without giving attention to the organizational processes that accompanied, and sometimes drove, these other developments. Highlights include the following.

From at least the seventeenth century through much of the nineteenth, most of the manufacturing in Europe and the US was either family based or managed in relatively small, independently owned businesses. Changes in ownership structures supported changes in economies of scale, and hence, technologies of production. The term "economies of scale" usually refers to larger corporate entities or collections of investors being able to build bigger facilities with more equipment in order to produce more things, faster, thereby lowering the cost per unit. Large-scale production is therefore usually cheaper and faster than small-scale production, assuming that one can invest enough up front to create a large-scale production facility. With early industrialization, emerging manufacturing companies introduced technologies of mass production to challenge craft manufacturers who worked largely by hand and often out of their homes. The new organization of investment, coupled with greater transportation capacities and long-distance communications, altered the organization of production (Chandler, 1992).

This made possible the creation of factory production on a mass scale, or "Fordism," in the early twentieth century. But even before that, the reorganization of ownership and investment enabled the kinds of capital investment necessary for a single corporate entity, or firm, to start up many large operations at once. Early industrial firms had been run by their owners and foremen. The expansion of firms into large diverse operations fostered a need for professional managers who worked for salaries, thereby creating large organizations with many layers of authority and a complex division of labor. Similarly, with ownership increasingly removed from operations, personal and family ownership gave way to our contemporary models of collective investment in which numerous stockholders own shares, and CEOs report to shareholders (Fligstein, 1985).

The early years of mass production had a considerable impact on the production of all "durable goods," from clothing to tools to furniture. Changes in fashion and styles followed these changes in production. Whereas individual craft manufacturers could boast that each item they created was unique, inexpensive mass production and transportation popularized the idea of identical, interchangeable goods. Shopping malls, however, had to wait until the invention of air conditioning.

Changes in economies of scale and technologies caused a shift in the place and organization of production. Rural forms, including craft and agriculture, yielded dominance to urban factories. Among other changes, this accelerated the movement of populations from the country to the city, and the growth of cities. This trend has recently achieved a milestone, as the majority of the world's population now lives in urban areas.

But the industrializing world's rural populations didn't just volunteer to move to the new urban frontiers. The governments of most of the industrializing nations created new laws to regulate unemployment, promote individual land ownership and pressure rural peasants into joining the new industrial working class, changes which forced people off the land and into the cities to look for work. For the most part, these coercive laws were met with resistance from newly formed associations of industrial workers or peasant communities. But, generally, the actions of these private organizations were deemed illegal, and therefore put down by organized state agencies (i.e., the police). The development of this new conflict between the police and "the unemployed" led to a variety of legal responses aimed at further pressuring non-landowners into hiring themselves out to others. In Great Britain, for example, the state introduced laws against loitering (hanging out in one place without purpose) and vagrancy (moving about without purpose). This formally mobilized state and police power against citizens who, literally, were just minding their own business.

As work moved to the cities, and into factories, family units became smaller and more mobile, ushering in that uniquely modern form: the nuclear family. The reorganization of work created new family structures that were more isolated from each other, in which two parents had to divide the responsibility for tasks that once involved several generations working and living together.

As extended families faded, and smaller families lived and worked apart from any sort of large rooted communities, people began to rely on new organizations to provide services and support that had once been provided by family and neighbors. This required serious changes in the organization of social services and the relationships among government, individuals, and philanthropies. Charities that had once been based in particular communities, parishes, or neighborhoods now found that: (1) the need for their services was growing everywhere; (2) parts of their work were being done by new government agencies; and (3) they could receive public funding to do some of what they were doing before, thereby creating new forms of public–private partnerships. Over time, these new arrangements began to coalesce into what we now call the "Welfare State" (Hasenfeld, Rafferty, and Zald, 1987).

As the Welfare State model became institutionalized within the industrializing Western democracies, the social organization of citizenship and relationship between states and citizens changed dramatically. Private community-based mutual aid associations – organized for economic security within working-class and immigrant neighborhoods throughout the US, Great Britain, and elsewhere – came to be rapidly replaced by formal, for-profit corporations such as banks and insurance companies. Informal, but regular and enduring systems of support among people who mostly knew each other became formal contracts between companies and each of their many thousands of unrelated clients. Community or religious **norms** of protecting and helping those whose needs were greatest were replaced by political policies and systems of aid. As these financial "safety nets" became instituted into legal and political structures, the informal systems that had performed these functions for centuries faded (Durkheim, 1964).

Changes in the economies of scale altered the relations between corporations and government on many levels, altering the democratic process. Industrial leaders, popularly called "the captains of industry" in the US, invested heavily in the campaigns of candidates who would support corporate interests. Media giants, like William Randolph Hearst (1863–1951) and Father Charles E. Caughlin (1891–1979) used their newspapers and radio shows to mobilize people against policies and politicians whom they opposed. Increasingly, political candidates in the industrial democracies had to be "media friendly" in order to win. After 1960, they increasingly had to look good on television as well (Lang and Lang, 1961).

New technologies of production working at a larger scale than ever before, with significant interactions between government and industry, allowed for rapid and widespread changes in patterns of production in many countries at once. Without this alignment of interests and coordination of efforts, the two world wars would probably not have been possible. The twentieth century witnessed previously unthinkable changes in the nature of war, which briefly seemed to promise a war to end all wars. These wars themselves massively boosted productive capacities and technological developments throughout the industrial world.

Partly as an outcome of this expansion of war's reach and ferocity, the victorious industrial democracies initiated supranational and later transnational governance bodies, as well as the organization of entities designed to foster less lethal conflict resolution among nations. Although global trade and international treaties were both old news by this time, the idea of a formal, enduring organization or agency existing "above" the level of sovereign nations was new. The League of Nations, the United Nations, the World Court, and NATO, to name a few, were all created in response to the new realities of worldwide wars and the existence of "weapons of mass destruction." The OECD, mentioned above, defines its role as uniting member-states "for a stronger, cleaner, fairer world economy." This goal would be meaningless without some kind of widely shared idea of a world economy to begin with.

Changing patterns in the organization of labor since industrialization also contributed to the restructuring of the political management of the economies of the affected nations, introducing the conditions that we now describe as "class conflict." Pre-industrial societies certainly did not lack hard-working people of no property and little money. Nor was there a lack of conflict between the wealthy and the poor. But it was with the dramatic shifts in the nature of employment that the rise of the factory essentially created the working class in its modern form (Thompson, 1963; Marx, 1867). Under earlier guild systems, for example, a journeyman would live for a limited number of years as a poorly paid apprentice before becoming his own master and (hopefully) moving up into the merchant class. "But as apprentices were gradually depressed to the status of permanent wage earners, and masters became manufacturers and capitalists, this pattern of social relations came to an end" (Bender, 2007: 9). The newly emerging patterns of conflict between owners and workers, in turn, fostered the creation of organized labor, and the introduction of organized efforts to prevent labor organizing through both legal and illegal means.

As we will see in chapter 2, changes in the nature of class relations gave birth to Marxism, conflict theory, and the idea that excessive **exploitation** of the working class would destabilize industrial society. Exactly what this all led to and how is subject to some debate. But the early twentieth century witnessed the formalization of militant labor federations into non-militant unions, industry-wide concessions to labor throughout the manufacturing sector, increases in wages and salaries, the gradual introduction of health and safety laws, child labor laws, and pensions. Organized associations of the new working class were not only able to fight against changes in industrial relations, but also enter into collective bargaining processes as the legitimate representatives of "workers" as a social group. In myriad complex ways, the rise of organized labor helped foster the creation of the modern "social movement" through which a wide assortment of communities and constituencies could pursue collective claims against states or other targets.

Combinations of all of these factors, particularly the post-World War II expansion of industry, the rise of labor concessions, the professionalization of management, and the increasing differentiation of roles within large corporations essentially created the middle class in its modern form. (The early industrial **bourgeoisie** against whom the **proletariat** struggled in Marx's accounts were a kind of middle class, but a different kind.)

As the middle classes grew in size and importance, the working classes shrunk as a proportion of the population. At the same time, the upper classes – as a class – yielded influence, or at least reorganized, as corporate and political leaders increasingly held power through the management of powerful organizations and institutions, rather than through class location alone. (Don't worry if these notions of "class location" and "the struggle of the proletariat" are unfamiliar to you. Chapter 2 will help.) As the political and economic systems of the industrial nations reorganized around the growing middle class, states invested heavily in new forms of middle-class housing – the suburbs. This required the construction of highways and new practices in development planning, leading in turn to larger national governments and, in the US, a reorganization of the relations between state and federal governments.

Thus the rise of middle-class jobs simultaneously fed the growth of suburbs and the decline of urban areas, thereby creating new forms of segregation. The concurrent separation of living space and living conditions by class and race institutionalized forms of **stratification**, the division of society into layers by socio-economic status.

New forms of class-based segregation and rising inequalities led to considerable changes in the formal agencies and institutions of society, including the legal system (Heydebrand and Seron, 1990), housing (Park, Burgess, McKenzie, and Wirth, 1925), surveillance (Foucault, 1977), and policing (Garland, 1990).

And so on . . .

What organizations do

This brief history of the twentieth century through the lens of organizational analysis suggests there is hardly any facet of modern society that can be properly understood without an understanding of organizational processes. Of course, the same history has been presented in other forms, in which the driving forces come from technology, secularization, or the media. Those histories, though different, are equally valid. Since we are looking at organizations, we will gloss over those other dimensions of social change and instead examine the role of organizations in contemporary society, what they do, and why. These, of course, are the defining questions for this chapter and most of the book.

First, why are formal organizations the dominant form of social action in modern industrial nations? There are very few questions that can be helpfully answered with the phrase "what else could it be?" but this might be one of them. Both governments and corporations pretty much have to be formal organizations, or dense agglomerates of organizations. This is due to several key features shared by states and most of the larger corporations: they are large, and potentially huge; they have a very broad range of responsibilities and functions; they need to be stable and resilient; and they need to somehow unify all of these parts and roles into the form of a relatively coherent **social actor**. In order to accomplish that unified identity, they tend to need some kind of routine power structure, reliable lines of communication, and centralized management of the money. Those are essentially the features for which formal organizations were invented.

This example reveals further characteristics of organizations. In addition to names, purposes, and memberships, we can note that formal organizations have internal structures that define authority relationships and flows of information, and that they have a division of labor and responsibility. In the familiar bureaucratic form, the division of labor within an organization occurs along what we like to call vertical and horizontal lines, meaning that (1) comparable offices at comparable "levels" branch out alongside of one another (horizontal) and (2) offices are divided into a hierarchy of different levels of authority with a top and a bottom (vertical). Authority and lines of communication are usually determined by this structure.

The classic image of this structure is the corporate "org chart," which flows from the owners/leaders at the top, down through specific paths of increasingly specialized responsibility and decreasing authority. An example of an organization chart from an actual government agency is shown in figure 1.1. Apart from the cute, though

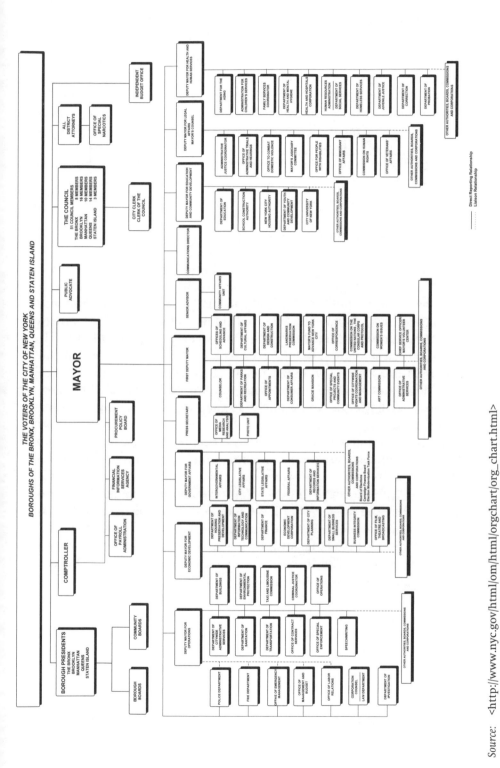

Source: <http://www.nyc.gov/html/om/html/orgchart/org_chart.html>

Figure 1.1 Organization chart for New York City government

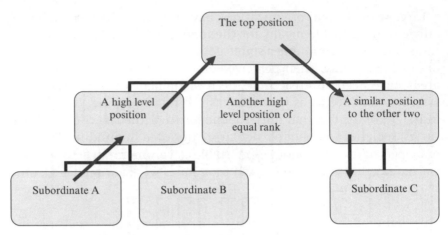

Figure 1.2   Corporate organizational structure

not technically accurate, touch of placing the voters in the top position, this chart clearly indicates that the Mayor's Office is the central position, but that some of the other offices are independent of it. The City Council and the Public Advocate's Office, for example, do not report to the Mayor, while the heads of the many City departments do. And while the City Council does not have to answer to the Mayor, neither are they equal in authority to that position, having no offices under them.

Organization charts also specify the theoretical channels for individual action, such as communication, moving up and down the tree as necessary to find a path from one office to another. This is shown in figure 1.2. I say "theoretical" channels because we don't have to assume that the holder of office A wouldn't just speak directly with the holder of office C. But the formal organization chart shows the lines of decision-making authority and responsibility that govern their interactions. The "correct" or expected way to act in a bureaucratic organization is to "go through channels."

One other thing to notice about organization charts is that they show the structure of relationships among offices, not people. The position of the Mayor of New York City, for example, remains essentially unchanged from administration to administration, while individual mayors come and go. The formal structure of the government or any other large organization is designed to remain consistent and stable without regard for the individuals who comprise it. Likewise, the files and forms and even telephone numbers stay with the offices for years as various office holders come and go. This helps to create "institutional memory," as we observed earlier.

Large-scale, formal organizations have proven to be tremendously efficient and reliable means for the management of highly complex tasks, such as maintaining a stable government or building a national or global economy. Their perceived efficiency and reliability in these areas have been so great that the development of large organized systems often seems as inevitable as the rain in spring. It is easy to lose sight of the fact that until the modern age (the last couple of centuries) societies were not particularly interested in building centrally managed national economies or stable government structures. This isn't to say that governments and economies were not managed; only that they were managed differently.

This chapter has presented the basics of organizational structures and formal rules. We have not yet begun to discuss the human aspects of organizations or organizational action. These "rational" elements of structure and **organizational form** are crucial. But do not let this overview give you the impression that they completely determine the nature of organizations.

In the next chapter, we will explore early organizational theories with an eye on the rise of both **rational systems** of organizing and rational systems for analyzing organizations. Subsequent chapters will build upon these frameworks by identifying the cultural and human elements that such an analysis overlooks.

Key Readings

Aldrich, Howard 2008 *Organizations and Environments*. Stanford, CA: Stanford Business Books.
  A comprehensive examination of the relations between organizations and their environments. Aldrich uses evolutionary models to explain how organizations and organizational populations change, how environments change them, and how they change their environments. A classic work, kept up to date, which gives serious attention to social-change processes from an organizational perspective.
Blau, Peter, and W. Richard Scott 1966 *Formal Organizations: A Comparative Approach*. New York: Routledge & Kegan Paul.
  Thoughtful, carefully presented, and thorough, this book provides several highly useful typologies of types of organizations, compared and contrasted along socially useful dimensions, such as whose interests are served by each. It is an excellent starting point for anyone trying to think about organizational processes in a general sense.
Laumann, Edward O., and David Knoke 1987 *The Organizational State: Social Choice in National Policy Domains*. Wisconsin: University of Wisconsin Press.
  The compelling argument of this book is that (1) organizations are social actors in their own right, not just collections of individual actors; and that (2) organizations as actors are more influential, more powerful, and more thoroughly networked than individuals or groups.

Perrow, Charles 1988 *Complex Organizations: A Critical Essay* (3rd edn). New York: Random House.

This classic review of contemporary organizational theories up through the late 1980s covers most of the historical, social, and intra-organizational bases that you would find in a textbook. But, in this case, the author highlights the notion of power in and throughout each of the developments, ideas, and outcomes of the field, clearly demonstrating that no explanation of any of this can be considered complete if it does not address the workings of power.

Thompson, E. P. 1963 *The Making of the English Working Class*. New York: Pantheon Books.

Marxist interpretation of the division of labor in society. Thompson argues that the stratification of the world into different industrial classes occurred due to a series of choices and actions within the English state, industrial leaders, and workers. Thompson wrote what he considered a detailed "biography" of the emergence of the working class, identifying the key crises and life course events that made them what they are.

Zald, Mayer N., and John McCarthy 1987 *Social Movements in an Organizational Society: Collected Essays*. New Brunswick, NJ: Transaction Publishers.

The first major work to blend organizational theories with social movement theories, significantly changing the way we look at collective action. Zald and McCarthy effectively put an end to the idea that social movements are irrational mass activities, demonstrating instead that they are strategic, purposeful, and organized.

CHAPTER 02

Classic Theories of Organizations

T HE social theorists who studied the consequences of industrialization on European societies laid the foundations for organizational analysis. Living through the simultaneous reorganization of political, social, and industrial relations, the "grand theorists" of the late nineteenth century set themselves the task of explaining the big picture. This required the creation of tools and theories that exceeded the boundaries of economic or political analysis as they were then practiced. Not incidentally, these tools and theories also established the foundations for much of the rest of sociology. In this chapter, however, we will confine ourselves only to the three most influential of the field's founders – Karl Marx, Max Weber, and Emile Durkheim – and only to those aspects of their work that address organizational theory.

In order to understand this earliest organizational work, we need to consider the questions the founders were trying to answer as they undertook this task. Though their approaches were different, these three theorists share a number of important attributes and underlying interests. It would not be unfair to say that they were all driven by one question: what is society? Granted, Durkheim wondered more about how people in a society could share so much collective sensibility when we're all so different, while Marx wondered how the different levels of society could remain in such opposition to each other when we're all part of the same society. Nonetheless, this concept of very large numbers of people across a land sharing some collective identity as members of a society was still being worked out. It should not surprise us that Marx, Weber, and Durkheim all looked to organizations and other associations to help them figure out how people acted collectively. Each of them, in their own way, asked how much individual interest guided us when we joined organizations and worked with others, and how well we recognized our collective interests when we were left to ourselves to think about it. People still wonder about this. Sometimes we refer to it as the problem of structure versus agency.

Each of the three thinkers whose work is examined in this chapter lived and worked at around the turn of the twentieth century during the height of the second industrial revolution. Each remains among the most relevant social thinkers studied today. Collectively, Marx, Weber, and Durkheim raised most of the questions that guide the study of organizations in modern industrial societies. For that reason, I will give more attention to the questions they raised, and a little less to the answers they offered. Since Weber is often referred to as the "father" of organizational sociology, we'll start with him.

Weber – bureaucracy and beyond

Max Weber (1864–1920) bestrides the world of organizational studies like a colossus: his economic writings alone would qualify him as one of the most important theorists of the field, while his political sociology was unparalleled in its day and remains a model of grand theory backed by detailed observations. His analysis of the rationalization of society still reverberates throughout organization theory, while his extensive writings on religion, stratification, urbanism, and research methodology are equally regarded in those sub-disciplines of the field. Furthermore, Weber's talent for synthesizing such a broad range of interests into coherent conceptual frameworks such as the classic *Protestant Ethic and the Spirit of Capitalism* guarantees his place in the canon of classic theory.

Weber was not quite so well regarded during much of his lifetime, and relatively unknown to English-language scholars. There are many reasons for the rise and fall of any scholar's reputation, but here I will discuss the relevance and appeal of this nineteenth- (and early twentieth-) century writer to life in the twenty-first century.

One of the peculiar and somewhat ironic reasons for the present standing of Weber's work is that he has been arguably misread and oversimplified so often. Weber's systematic and thorough analyses of modern organizational, political, and economic systems spurred the development of a host of influential structural theories in American and British sociology, not the least of which may be found in Talcott Parsons's *The Structure of Social Action*. Parsons adopted the founders' questions about the relationship between individual identity and social structure. In his version, social structure is the key and individuals find their places within it according to a variety of factors that I'm going to skip over here. Parsons's work gave rise to the extreme popularity of **structural-functionalism** in mid-twentieth-century sociology. Weber's writings (and Durkheim's even more so) were therefore championed by American structural-functionalists at the height of their own influence. Yet, as structural-functionalism faded in importance alongside the rise of cultural analysis, readers were rewarded to find significant, previously overlooked, cultural models within Weber's structural theories. The less we read Parsons these days, the more we read Weber.

Similarly, while Weber's organizational theory grew out of his economic and political studies, he was far more concerned with such non-economic behavior as volunteerism and values than most later economic sociologists. And so his work has taken on a new significance as the field expands from administrative studies into a more complete **three sector model** (see chapter 7). As we critique and improve upon works that have been inspired by Weber, we keep finding that Weber had anticipated our discoveries.

Finally, it is worth noting that Weber's theoretical "success" has also made it more difficult to teach his work. A hundred years ago, the prediction that capitalism and bureaucracy would combine to create a world defined by efficiency, goal-orientation, and calculability was a bold piece of analysis. These days, living in that world, it's hard to know what Weber was comparing us to. What other kind of world is there?

Rationalization

Weber was a smart and talented young man from a respectable family of upper- middle-class professionals. He entered his professional work at a time when aristocratic rights were fading and new career paths were opening up to men of talent regardless of their social status. He was therefore in a perfect position to observe first hand as traditional forms of legitimate authority in (European) society yielded to newer forms that were based on formal qualifications and training. Studying both contemporary and historical authority, both in and outside of states and governments, including religious authority, Weber perceived a broad pattern of change in how authority operated. Indeed, Weber perceived in this shift a change not only in how people decided what forms of authority were legitimate or not but also in how societies judged the notion of **legitimacy** itself.

In the pre-modern world, magic and mystery were motivating forces. Leaders typically derived their authority from God, not human achievement. (Human achievement demonstrated God's favor, so the two were believed to run together.) The boundaries of the world were unknowable. Truths were more often revealed than discovered. And the quest for a "natural philosophy" of existence was, to a great degree, a theological one. In Weber's term, "enchantment" played a large part in people's search for meaning. In the pre-modern perspective, life was stable and it made sense. People wrote of the "natural order" of the world and society.

With modernity, all of this changed. We use the term "modernity" to describe the newer ways of thinking that evolved alongside the social, technological, political, and religious changes that began (more or less) around the sixteenth century and became dominant by the end of the nineteenth. In this view, the world is changing and changeable, and people are "agents of change." Everything that had once been mysterious and unknowable became measurable and even predictable. Nature came to be seen as a thing that could be overcome or controlled by technology. Newer empirical sciences provided reliable, comprehensible tools for making sense of the world, and often demonstrated the limits to ecclesiastical knowledge. Rational calculation promised to reveal more efficient ways to accomplish tasks, solve problems, or administer a government. Modernity ushered in a whole new world of meaning.

As secular methods displaced religious appeals, the value of rational decision-making itself rose in relation to a perceived decline in the importance of faith. Many familiar accomplishments followed from this shift, from stable international banking systems to engineering feats, to the preference for evidence over supernatural signs in criminal trials, to the rise of the Enlightenment and public debates over the rights of citizens. (Once you admit that the social order of the world is made by people rather than God or nature, you invite a host of questions about how it is made, by whom, and what would be the best way to make it.) Yet along with all of this rethinking came a tremendous focus on calculability and efficiency, effecting a change in feeling that Weber termed (in English translation) "the disenchantment of the world."

Unlike other social scientists of the time who described the shift to scientific thinking as "progress," and who saw the results as a greater "truth," Weber emphasized that the issue was the process of change itself. We did not need to assume that newer ways of looking at the world were better than the old ways. By studying the process of change, we could come to understand what a society valued and why. For example, Weber did note how important it was that rationally calculated approaches to administration allowed for the growth of stable transnational economic systems. But he saw that the greater significance was that modernity had ushered in a period in which the goal of building stable transnational economic systems could seem reasonable all across Europe. People were thinking differently about values, goals, and the means of achieving them. Modern society valued rationality, and rationality encouraged setting clear goals and finding efficient paths toward their achievement.

Forms of legitimate authority

In Weber's day, social rank and power reflected what he termed *traditional authority*. Power was held by those who were born into the ruling class by virtue of their having been born there. These relatively few families of rank were the *aristocracy*, and their position relied on history and custom. People of rank were understood to be superior to people without rank because that was how it was, that's how social rank had ever been determined, and that was what one was taught. Traditional authority did not have to explain or justify itself, and often could not. But it had widespread legitimacy. In other words, aristocracy had been institutionalized; people took traditional authority systems for granted. Thus, as Weber himself experienced first hand as an officer in the Prussian army, the officer corps would be made up of men who held social rank outside of the military, and the soldiers of lesser rank would necessarily come from the lower-status groups. To do otherwise would allow a common man to give orders to one of higher birth, which would upset the traditional order of things. Yet, Weber noted (and he was certainly not the first to see this), birthright alone did not make an officer competent.

In contrast to traditional forms of authority – in government, the military, and in the industrial world – Weber described the increasing appearance of *rational-legal* forms. Such forms were *rational* in the sense that authority had to be justified in terms of some recognized criteria. They were *rational-legal* in the sense that decisions or appointments were expected to follow some procedure or process that was widely recognized as legitimate and backed by written contracts or verifiable rules. Positions had qualifications, and one had to meet those qualifications to occupy that position. The new elite would be those who had proven themselves to be "experts" in their fields. In contrast to such experts, Weber saw many of those who governed or led by birthright as "dilettantes" who were not capable of fulfilling their necessary roles (Weber, 1967 [1925]: 224).

The cornerstone of legitimacy for the more rational procedures was that they applied equally to all. Once the rules or qualifications for some position were defined, anyone who met those qualifications could seek the position. This didn't actually mean that anyone could grow up to be president, but it did mean that birthright alone was less important. One could achieve status through accomplishments in one's life. In this sense, the turn toward rational-legal forms of authority and decision-making opened the doors to such notions as equality before the law, regardless of social class and even democracy in government.

Weber also explored the nature of *charismatic* leaders – individuals whose vision and commitment inspired followers in ways that no rational appeal could. Consider any heroic epics you might have read. The heroes are usually identified in early childhood, or even at birth, as superior to others. They are better, stronger, faster, and born to do great deeds. Similarly, in stories of prophets and mystics, their arrival is anticipated in dreams and heralded by signs from nature. Calves of the wrong color are born on the same day as the prophets and the stars themselves point the way to their cribs. Nature itself – in such stories – announces the birth of a hero. In real life, great charismatic leaders can emerge from anywhere and come to be seen as heroic, larger than life, and endowed with the unique qualities that the moment demands.

Weber did not place any great stock in prophetic dreams. Even so, he lamented the disenchantment of faith in great leaders, as rational-legal forms came to dominate in society. Inevitably, he wrote, authority and responsibility must pass from charismatic leaders to the hands of others, and inspiration must give way to rules. This transition had to be accomplished if the belief system that the leader had established was to live on past the leader himself. An organization was the thing that remained after the great leader had passed. Otherwise, the group, community, or other collective would simply break apart with the loss of its founder.

Religious devotion provided the clearest example of this process for Weber. Neither Jesus nor Buddha, for example, had set up churches. They both taught, and other people followed them out of deference to the authority (or legitimacy, charisma, truthiness) of their personal appeals. But in time, as the teachers passed from the world and the students remained, their followers codified the teachings into rules and practices, organized the study of their lessons into formal institutions, and established authoritative bodies of learned students to judge who was qualified to teach in the name of the founder. "A permanent religious community develops only when the prophet's personal mediation of divine grace becomes the function of a permanent institution," as Weber biographer Reinhard Bendix (1962: 90) expressed it. Churches and temples, however mystical they are in their daily practices, embody the rationalization of the sacred.

Weber thus described two bases for people to act together as communities. In one case, they follow a great leader out of faith in the person. In the other, they follow rules out of faith in the institution. The first sounds authoritarian and the second uninspiring. But Weber was not such a pessimist. To Weber, disenchantment was the cost we had to bear in order to promote the kinds of meritocracy on which ideas like democracy depended. Great leaders had their moments, but we had to get on without them. Bureaucracy, for all of its inhumanity, was an idea whose time had come.

Bureaucracy and the ideal-type

Here we look at what could be called Max Weber's most famous and most misunderstood turn of phrase: writing in *Economy and Society,* he referred to the "superiority" of bureaucracy as resting on its ruthless efficiency. From this, one can easily imagine Weber as an early industrialist, calculating the piece-rates of wares, oblivious to the people involved. But this would be a mistake.

Weber was concerned with authority and power. Perhaps concerned *about* power would be a more accurate description. Rational systems of organizing placed limits on personal power. A bureaucratic government might be less interesting than a charismatic hero, but there was less danger of despotism and arbitrary abuses of power when the rulers had to negotiate with congresses and parliaments in order to get anything done. Whether in government, the military, the church or the workplace, all of those rules and procedures protect people from their leaders.

Weber defined and explained the workings of bureaucracy through his formulation of an **"ideal-type"** model of the bureaucratic form. The ideal-type is an analytic concept introduced by Weber as a method for studying concepts that can take many different forms. It has nothing to do with ideals, referring instead to the description that *most typifies* something. His ideal-typical bureaucracy describes the most thoroughly bureaucratized structure that one can imagine in some environment. An ideal-type is neither good nor bad. For that matter, bureaucracy is neither good nor bad by itself. Recall Weber's underlying questions. He wasn't seeking the formula for a utopian society. His efforts to describe the institutional arrangements that shape our social relations arose from his interest in the social relations, not a fascination with institutions.

Using the ideal-type as a point of comparison, one can compare such divergent organizations as a neighborhood association, a crime family, and the Pentagon, each of which partially resembles the ideal-typical form. Defining the bureaucratic ideal-type allowed Weber to study the effects of bureaucratization across all of society. Due in part to this term, however, his description is commonly misunderstood to be a model of the ideal or perfect bureaucracy, thereby fostering the impression that Weber celebrated the rise of bureaucracy.

Bureaucracy depersonalizes everything, which, by itself, is not a good or a bad thing. But it has certain advantages over absolute and arbitrary power. In a bureaucratic form of organization, roles and responsibilities, power and privilege, are divided among a fixed and identifiable set of offices with a formally defined set of

Table 2.1: Bureaucracy at its most bureaucratic	
Power	Resides in offices, not individuals
Communication and authority structure	Hierarchy, a stable chain of command from the topmost, central position down through the ranks
Division of labor	Specialized, focused, highly differentiated
Forms of action	Driven by rules and formal procedures, all of which are written and available to anyone
Goals	(1) Efficient production of whatever objects, cases, or units are being processed (including people); (2) self-perpetuation
Administration	Separate from ownership; administrators have daily control of the operating details; staff do not report directly to owners

relations among them. Individuals take on both the responsibilities and authorities of the offices when appointed to those roles, but leave them behind when replaced. Authority is thereby temporary and its legitimacy relies on the organization rather than the personnel. The essential characteristics of Weber's ideal-type of bureaucracy are summarized in table 2.1.

The impersonal machinery of bureaucracy is designed to continue operating as the people within it enter and leave. But that should not imply that it does not matter which people are in the office at any moment. Likewise, it is assumed that appointment to a position is based on qualifications in some way that can be demonstrated. But the definitions of those qualifications can be changed throughout the life of the organization in ways that can powerfully reshape it. Weber wrote:

> Bureaucratic administration means fundamentally domination through knowledge. This is the feature of it that makes it specifically rational. This consists on the one hand in technical knowledge which, by itself, is sufficient to ensure it a position of extraordinary power. But, in addition to this, bureaucratic organizations, or the holders of power who make use of them, have the tendency to increase their power still further by the knowledge growing out of experience in the service. . . . It is a product of the striving for power. (1967 [1925]: 225)

For most of the rest of this book, references to large formal organizations will mean organizations that approach Weber's ideal-typical bureaucracy. In our age, bureaucracy has become almost a synonym for formal organization. Even those organizations that deliberately avoid the strict hierarchies that characterize bureaucracies typically will still resemble the ideal-type in other respects, such as the power of offices, rather than people, and the use of formal procedures.

There are exceptions, of course. Military forces are typically organized in an **echelon** system. While members of the military are subdivided by such groupings as regiments, units, or battalions, the concept of echelon, or rank, cuts across all of those. At any given rank, one answers to all those of higher rank, and one has some authority over all those of lower rank. A formal bureaucracy exists, but an organization chart would not fully explain the authority relations around it.

The iron cage

In Weber's work, bureaucracy is the embodiment of rational culture. It organizes people into orderly, inhuman mechanisms of production whose efficiency can be measured and even adjusted. Observing that "No machinery in the world functions so precisely as this apparatus of men and, moreover, so cheaply," Weber saw the rise of this form as inevitable across all forms of social, political, and industrial life. Further, in his comparisons between meritocratic hierarchies and over-paid dilettantes, Weber highlighted the positive characteristics of the bureaucratic form: fairness, consistency, efficiency.

But whatever the advantages of bureaucratic forms in systems of production or task management, Weber also warned us of the underlying costs that came with it on the social and cultural level. "Rational calculation . . . reduces every worker to a cog in this bureaucratic machine and, seeing himself in this light, he will merely ask how to transform himself into a somewhat bigger cog. . . . The passion for bureaucratization drives us to despair" (Weber, 1967 [1925]: liii). Rule of law justifies itself. Without actual values, without wisdom, rules can simply perpetuate more rules. A structure of legitimate authority designed to protect individuals from arbitrary power can transform itself into a power system designed to protect its own power.

The ideology of rationalization was an "iron cage" that we were making for ourselves. The lingering question of Weber's writings on organizational transformations is whether all of this efficiency is really worth the cost. Interestingly, Peter Baehr (2001: 164) has argued that the iron cage is a mistranslation or reinterpretation on the part of the American sociologist Talcott Parsons; that the correct term should be a "shell as hard as steel." The difference is small, but philosophically significant. "A cage deprives one of liberty, but leaves one otherwise unaltered, one's powers still intact even if incapable of full realization. A shell, on the other hand, hints at an organic reconstitution of the being concerned; a shell is part of the organism and cannot be dispensed with." We are not people trapped within a machinery of production; we become part of the machine itself.

Durkheim and the division of labor in society

Emile Durkheim (1858–1917) established the first sociology department in Europe and the first journal of sociology in France. One of the founders of the field, he is sometimes referred to as the first "scientific" sociologist. His efforts to develop a scientific methodology for the social sciences were laid out in *The Rules of Sociological Method* (1895), and are further demonstrated in such classic works as *Suicide: A Study in Sociology* (1897) and *The Elementary Forms of Religious Life* (1912). His unique approach was also reflected in his dissertation research, published in 1893 as *The Division of Labor in Society*. It is this early work that has had the greatest impact on organizational theory.

Durkheim's sociology was particularly concerned with the idea of social solidarity in an increasingly complex world. He observed great changes happening in the social environment: larger populations living together in conditions of higher density, rapid mobility, and relative anonymity. These changes brought about a greater variety of social interactions with more unknowns than in the past, and the fact they were so widespread meant they affected everything, from the growth of cities to the fragmentation of family life. In day-to-day interactions, one was now as likely to be dealing with strangers as familiar members of one's community. In an older, pre-modern community, where everyone knew and depended on everyone else, routine interactions almost automatically led one to feel connected to the social whole; to share the community's **norms**, values, and ways of doing things. In the modern world, traditional norms and expectations would no longer suffice to ensure that people would act for the general benefit instead of personal advantage.

Nonetheless, Durkheim argued, newer social rules and social roles were emerging to manage all of this complexity. And these new roles involved a far greater *division of labor in society*, or social differentiation, than previously known. Instead of small communities in which almost everyone you knew or encountered lived much the way you did, Durkheim observed society entering into a complex world in which even familiar old tasks were broken down into numerous specialty tasks and separated from one another. In the traditional village, for example, many families would farm, and each might bring their produce to market to sell and trade with each other. By the late nineteenth century Durkheim observed that some people would raise the food, others transport it to markets, and others still would sell. Each person in the process only did their small part.

> The savage goes from one occupation to another, according to the circumstances and needs affecting him. The civilized man devotes himself entirely to a task which is always the same, and offering

less variety as it is more greatly restricted. Organization necessarily implies an absolute regularity in habits, for a change cannot take place in an organ's functions without the whole organism being affected by repercussions. (Durkheim, 1964 [1893]: 242)

As in Weber's models, the division of labor included larger bureaucracies in work and government. Durkheim, however, was not particularly focused on work relations. He was interested in the collective identity and the need for some kind of shared consciousness that allowed people to think and act as a community. How, Durkheim asked, are we to continue to function as a society when the social world is broken down into so many disconnected parts? What protects our shared social identity in the face of all of these fragmented individual identities and interests?

Durkheim proposed that social systems could adjust to new conditions much the way organic systems rebalance themselves in response to environmental changes. Complexity, anonymity, and mobility broke down old patterns of social solidarity, but the increasing social differentiation could be more of a natural corrective than a symptom. The division of labor allowed larger, more complex societies to still function as a unit, with each distinct function forming a recognizable part of the whole. To the extent that each person, or group, fulfilled social roles that only made sense from the larger, social perspective, individual actions and pursuits still tied one in to the social identity. Durkheim referred to this outcome as "**organic solidarity**."

Did it work? There was, Durkheim explained, an inherent danger built in to this system. The problem was **anomie**, often translated as "normlessness." This refers to the particularly modern condition of being so circumscribed by small, specialized roles that the connection between one's individual life and the larger social world is not seen or felt. Or worse, anomie could occur when one had some small social role that did not actually mesh with the social whole, creating a sense that one did not belong in the known social world. In his study *On Suicide*, he argued that the dangers of anomie are particularly keen for members of cultural or religious minority groups whose group norms and traditions are already viewed with suspicion (or at best disregarded) by the larger society. The higher suicide rates seen among Protestants in Catholic France could indicate the greater sense of dissociation and isolation among members of that group, for example. Anomic individuals live within society, but feel apart from it.

The more fragmented a social system is, including systems of production, the harder it is to feel a part of it. Thus both bureaucratization and ethnocentrism contribute to anomie. Bureaucratization creates hierarchies in law, work, politics, and even in the family. Bureaucratic systems of action, of work, and of decision-making in general are optimized for the general case or the average need. Special cases cause problems, and so individuals with special needs are seen as problems. Individuals who are not like the general case are then at odds with society.

Ethnocentrism – the belief that one group's norms are right and true, and that other people's norms are wrong – explicitly represents other cultures as deviant. So, in a white, European, Catholic country, everyone else including most foreigners, Jews, and Protestants, not to mention the poor and most women, were abnormal cases. The bureaucratization of social life marginalizes all those who do not fit well with the dominant perspectives. This fragments society. For those who are marginalized, the resultant feeling is a sense of anomie.

The larger social whole needs to be felt, or at some level believed in, to bind its members together. Durkheim used the metaphor of an organic body that remains healthy because its many parts work together, and which becomes unhealthy when they do not. As society became more complex and structurally fragmented, each individual became *more dependent* on the functioning of the whole, and, therefore, more conscious of the needs of society. Feeling those needs, the individual would choose to uphold their social obligations. "Man's characteristic privilege is that the bond he accepts is not physical but moral; that is, social. He is governed not by a material environment brutally imposed on him, but by a conscience superior to his own, the superiority of which he feels" (Durkheim, 1897: 252). One hopes.

Durkheim's concept of organic solidarity was somewhat optimistic and contrary to the popular ideas of several of his contemporaries. The philosopher Adam Smith, for example, had postulated that rational self-interest would provide an incentive for individuals to continuously seek to contribute to society because this would maximize the rewards that they could receive from the social world. Though he never exactly said that greed was good, there is some support for that idea in Smith's model. Highly skilled people press themselves to do their best because they want the greatest rewards, while less skilled workers accept poorly paid, low-status jobs because they need the money in order to live.

Comparably, the English sociologist Herbert Spencer (1820–1903), in his writings on "the social contract," suggested that complex societies were characterized by constant negotiations among people of different levels – or **strata** – based upon what each needed or could provide for the other. This differentiation into economic strata, known as stratification, served society because it created a wide variety of needs and abilities. Spencer viewed society primarily as a collection of individuals, and the contract as the main mechanism through which social cooperation could be assured. Thus laborers who had little to offer beyond their labor power would seek to sell their labor power where it was most useful to others and to society at large, in exchange for which they would be paid. Imbalances and exploitation might exist in some parts of the system, but, overall, the variety of opportunities and forms of work available in a large and complex society would lead to a stable equilibrium of sorts that served society's interests. Although the economies of the present are considerably different from those of the late nineteenth century, Smith's and Spencer's ideas remain powerfully popular. Durkheim's response might be less well known, yet it is a crucial part of the economic debates of its time.

Solidarity forever

Recall that the public debates over the nature of economic theories were largely about the hope for social solidarity in an increasingly complex world. In both Adam Smith's and Herbert Spencer's theories a complex division of labor was seen as more efficient than earlier forms, and this efficiency had the potential to benefit all of society. Durkheim shared Smith's and Spencer's interest in social stability, and derived many of his greatest ideas from their work. He also saw the possibility of a greater social solidarity emerging from social differentiation. But he rejected several of their key assumptions. For one thing, Durkheim did not trust market forces and self-interest to regulate either social or individual well-being. As to the notion that the division of labor produced the greatest amount of happiness, as both Smith and Spencer assumed, "nothing is less evident" (Durkheim, 1893: 234). His notion of anomie reflected, in part, his concern that too much individual interest and competition would lead to social fragmentation and excessive stratification. A system of social organization that served the interests of some against the interests of others would represent, to Durkheim, a failure of social solidarity by fostering competition and contention. This competition would, at the social level, discourage members of a society from thinking about their social roles. "Man is the more vulnerable to self-destruction the more he is detached from any collectivity, that is to say, the more he lives as an egoist" (Durkheim, 1972: 113). At the individual level, a competitive market system would encourage social changes that harmed some people because it rewarded others. Without an underlying moral philosophy, or a powerful normative connection to the well-being of society, Smith's model would lead not to harmony but to social disparities.

Durkheim also criticized Spencer for failing to take power seriously. A contract may bind both parties equally, but if that contract were written entirely by one party and not open to negotiation, then it can hardly be considered an agreement mutually derived or mutually beneficial. Interests matter, but so do values. Durkheim viewed Spencer's social contract as a system that justified harms done by the powerful to the powerless by pretending that market forces were to blame. The underlying social model of "economic man" on which Spencer's contract relied gave the appearance of being value-neutral. But it favored the values of the wealthy and powerful.

In contrast to Spencer, Durkheim emphasized that individuals had social identities and social roles. Reducing those roles to contracts removed the moral and normative dimension and, therefore, eliminated the connection between the individual and the social whole. Spencer's approach left no room for individuals to choose how best to be members of a society. Without that, from Durkheim's perspective, it doesn't even matter whether the organization of work is more efficient or not. To Durkheim, individuals actually pursue social connectedness by joining organizations, particularly social, non-economic ones.

Both Smith's and (to a lesser degree) Spencer's analyses are considered economic theories with moral implications. In contrast, Durkheim does not appear to be particularly engaged with economics at all. His interest in the increasing specialization of function in all realms of social life, including systems of production, is normative. That is, Durkheim's approach relies on the value of having members of a society sharing an interest in the well-being of all and recognizing their collective sensibility. As he explained, "if the division of labor produces solidarity, it is not only because it makes each individual an exchangist, as the economists say; it is because it creates among men an entire system of rights and duties which link them together in a durable way" (1964 [1893]: 406).

Karl Marx and the spirit of capitalism

Karl Marx is widely regarded as a social critic, a political economist, and an enemy of capitalism. We associate his name with "Marxism," though he dissociated himself from that term. For our purposes, it is also useful to think of Marx as a philosopher and a labor historian. Marx's critiques of capitalist systems of production derived in large part from his philosophical analysis of labor relations. While he famously described the material conditions of deprivation and suffering of the exploited working class, the heart of his opposition to capitalism was rooted in the larger question of what kind of society we wished to build for ourselves. Capitalism, he argued, was an economic and social system of every man for himself locked in a perpetual competition against everyone else. If we didn't want to live like that, he concluded, we would need a different system.

In his long career, Karl Marx (1818–83) authored a handful of classic books, including *The German Ideology* (1845), *Das Kapital* (or *Capital*, 1867) and *Critique of Political Economy* (1859). Better known and more often read are his literally hundreds of articles, pamphlets, and essays on philosophy, economics, politics, history, social justice, and the family. (Marx criticized marriage as the legal enslavement of women.) He also left behind a wealth of letters on which scholars have drawn to further probe the complexities of his worldview. He was an academic, a journalist, and an activist. As a founding figure of sociology, his work has directly influenced every generation of political and social scientists since his own time, as well as several revolutions of world-altering significance. In the next few pages, I will summarize this body of work into a few memorable phrases and propositions. His original writings, however, are well worth the time it takes to explore them.

Marx saw economic inequality, or stratification, as the one big truth around which everything else orbited. People in any society could be divided into different classes. Knowing what class you were born into, Marx would be able to tell you most of what you needed to know about your life and your life chances. The lower down you were in class standing, the worse off you were, and the less likely you were to escape your fate.

Marx's fortune-telling was much more than a party trick, of course. For one thing, class location was not absolute. That is, you could move up, or down. Now this promise of what we call class mobility might sound nice, but Marx saw the downside to it. For, if we assume that the lower classes could rise up the ladder, then we must also assume that the upper classes wouldn't want them to. For them, the promise of class mobility is really a threat. After all, for one to rise, another must fall. It isn't hard to imagine, then, that a good deal of the energy and efforts of the dominant groups in society would be spent keeping others down.

For Marx, the stratification of society into different social classes was not an accidental outcome of the division of labor. It was the desired goal of the ruling class. And the notion of certain forms of power having greater social legitimacy because they were based on "fair" procedures might be better understood as a set of techniques designed to make the power of the ruling class appear to be legitimate. For Marx, the history of the world was all about how rulers rule. His work was guided by a few key assumptions. First, that society is characterized by divisions and different socio-economic strata; that these strata include a small elite and a large mass of "common" people; and that the majority of what occurs in a society reflects the competition between the elites and the masses. That is, there is a constant struggle at work in all societies between those who dominate and those who are dominated. Second, that the driving mechanism of all social divisions and competitions is economic inequality. Political divisions exist in order to formalize and propagate economic divisions. Power was not a goal, in Marxian analyses. It was a means for maintaining wealth. So the various social divisions of society, whether pre-modern or modern, exist primarily for the purpose of creating inequalities of wealth and of convincing people that these inequalities are somehow natural.

A third key assumption is that the stakes of economic competition are not simply economic, but encompass all aspects of life. Thus, under industrial capitalism, the defining conflict is between capital and labor, or the bourgeoisie and the proletariat, and the underlying struggle to determine whether the proletariats are just workers serving the bourgeoisie or complete human beings with lives outside of work.

In order to get a better handle on these ideas and their contributions to contemporary organization theory, we need to explore a couple of key concepts: exploitation and **alienation**.

Exploitation

Exploitation is usually pretty straightforward. Relatively powerless people can be overworked, underpaid, and generally abused by those who have power over them. In various popular descriptions, such abuses are aberrations from the "proper" working of an economic system. Yet Marx provided a three-volume demonstration that economic exploitation was pretty much an essential feature of capitalism, without which the system won't work. And the main reason for this is the profit motive.

Recall that the way in which capitalism is supposed to benefit society is that it provides material incentives for people to maximize their creative energies in productivity and the marketplace. By "material incentives," we mean luxury goods, comforts, sexual opportunities, health, and well-being for the wealthy; food and shelter for the poor. Profits primarily come in two forms: return on investment (for capitalists) and wages (for workers). So the incentive system for workers means that you need a job, and you need to work hard to keep your job and increase your pay. And the incentive system for owners means that you need to find ways to produce more of what you make for less investment so that you can sell goods at a higher profit. Unfortunately for workers, once capital has invested in its tools and materials (fixed costs), the only consistent and predictable way to increase profits is to reduce wages. Demanding more work output for the same wage amounts to the same thing.

Several key Marxian conclusions follow from this. First, profit derives from the "surplus value" of a **commodity**, which is the difference between what something costs to produce and what you can get for it. If the exchange value of a commodity is fairly stable, then the best way to improve profits is to reduce production costs. That means paying workers less money for the same work. In Marxian terms, the principal role of a manager is to exploit the workers in order to maximize the profits of production for the owners. This exploitation is not an accidental by-product of tough market competition. It is the definition of capitalism. Therefore, in a functioning capitalist economy, the great mass of people endures a life of constant threat, hardship, and exploitation. In a dysfunctional capitalist economy, it's mostly the same thing, but with more people starving and freezing to death.

Alienation

A second observation addresses one of Marx's most unique contributions to economic analysis: human value. The "value" of a laborer in the larger world equates almost entirely to the exchange value of his labor power. That is his commodity (and it's generally "his" in the writings of Marx and his contemporaries). When the worker sells his labor power, he is selling himself. If he receives nothing in exchange for it, then in the eyes of the world he is worth nothing. This, of course, is how slavery works, and why working a slave to death was often viewed as similar to breaking one of your own tools. If a worker sells 100 percent of his labor power, then all that he is belongs to someone else, even though the worker is paid. The goal of the working class is not to do the least amount of work for the most pay, as F. W. Taylor thought (chapter 3). The trick is to make enough to live on while still retaining enough independence in or out of work to be said to have a life. The production of surplus value, meanwhile, pushes in the opposite direction. The "need" to get as much labor power from a worker for the least exchange value amounts to the pressure to more fully enslave the worker and thereby reduce his worth to virtually nothing.

For Marx, the problem with capitalism is not that the work is hard, the pay low, and the opportunities for improvement are so limited. His point is that we are as much the products of our work as our work is the products of our efforts. Our lives are defined by our actions, and if our actions are simple – e.g., just selling apples in a market – we still derive satisfaction from meeting the goals we bring to the task, such as earning customer loyalty or making enough to take care of our families. But if our identities and efforts are kept separate from any sort of goal or value to be found in the work then we are alienated from our labor. And this is much worse than simply being underpaid. The crime of capitalism is to organize a society around exploitation, thereby defending its ability to crush the humanity of the entire working class. Viewed from this perspective, it's a moral question. Thus, Marx's economic critique begins with the meaning of "value" and includes the meaning of life itself.

Through labor, we produce objects of value. But what is this value, Marx asks. First, of course, there is **use value**. A thing produced has value if others can use it. It also has **exchange value**, which is the measure of what we can get for it. A diamond has greater exchange value than a lump of coal. Therefore the labor of mining for diamonds can be exchanged for far more than the labor of mining for coal, even if the work is comparable in other respects. But, because the work is comparable, and because the laborer does not own the mine, the diamond miner is paid as little as the coal miner, and both are paid as little as a street sweeper. (Streets used to be cleaned by people walking with brooms.) The value of their labor is reduced to the exchange value of what they can get for it. And as long as the work is brute simple, requiring more in sweat than special knowledge, and as long as other workers are hungry enough to do the job for less, the exchange value for labor will tend to be far below the exchange value of the commodities that they produce.

By separating the exchange value of labor power from the value of the things that labor produces, capitalism *alienates* workers from their work. "Owing to the extensive use of machinery and to division of labour, the work of the proletarians has lost all individual character, and consequently, all charm for the workman. He becomes an appendage of the machine, and it is only the most simple, most monotonous and most easily acquired knack, that is required of him" (Marx and Engels, 1848, *The Communist Manifesto*, quoted in Feuer, 1959: 14). The lowest apprentice with the lowest pay could at least point to the master's works and say "a part of me is in there." The hardest working farmer struggling against the most barren land can say "I tamed that turf." But a modern industrial factory worker cannot make any such claims, looking over a parking lot filled with cars, by saying "I tightened a great many of those lug nuts." Admittedly, cars came into the picture many years after Marx's death; but the ideas apply.

Now the interesting part, philosophically speaking: if a laborer is defined by his labor, and the proletariat is typically alienated from the product of their own labor power, then it follows that the working class are alienated from themselves. They are split apart from their own identities. They have only a gaping hole in that part of their existence that most defines them. Further, and more philosophically, this process also robs the bourgeoisie of their humanity.

> The possessing class and the proletarian class represent one and the same human self-alienation. But the former feels satisfied and affirmed in this self-alienation, experiences the alienation as a sign *of its own power*, and possesses in it the *appearance* of a human existence. The latter, however, feels destroyed in this alienation, seeing in it its own impotence and the reality of an inhuman existence. To use Hegel's expression, this class is, within depravity, an *indignation* against this depravity, an indignation necessarily aroused in this class by the contradiction between its human *nature* and its life-situation, which is a blatant, outright and all-embracing denial of that very nature. (Marx, *The Holy Family*, quoted in Jakubowski, 1990: 87)

So the pre-industrial life of a hard-working apprentice dreaming of a better life gives way, under capitalism, to a permanently working laborer who can no longer afford dreams, suffering at the whims of a barely working owner who has forgotten how to dream. All around, it's a bleak picture for individuals. At the social level, of course, it gets worse.

Conclusions

The three theorists whose work we have reviewed shared several key concerns. Each of them observed dramatic social changes occurring as modernity fostered industrialization, shaking up the traditional order of things. Marx saw new forms of wealth and power concentrating at the top of the social order at the tangible expense of everyone else. Durkheim saw the social order breaking down and wondered what would hold us together when the familiar ways of life passed. And Weber saw the arbitrary and often parasitical power of the social elites yielding ground to new systems of authority in which opportunities abounded, but little other purpose could be found.

Their three perspectives are quite different. Yet all three of our founding fathers may be seen to be responding to the same processes, and to each other. In all of their models, industrial growth, increasing concentrations of people, and changes in the nature of political power made the world more complex. This complexity yielded a greater division of labor and encouraged greater specialization. A working person's life became narrower. New social and physical boundaries grew between people, threatening social solidarity. Such changes might well have looked like the end of human community, ushering in a modern world of isolated laborers in which each person was only responsible for themselves, cities looked like factories, and no one felt any responsibility to the larger social world. The collected works of Marx, Weber, and Durkheim are enlightening, but not cheery.

Many of their fears have come to pass, as well as other problems that they could not have anticipated. Others have not. As we turn to the rise of administrative theories in the first half of the twentieth century, it is useful to recognize that early theorists in this area shared their contemporaries' concerns with alienation, anomie, and solidarity, whether they use these terms or not.

Key Readings

Bendix, Reinhard 1962 *Max Weber: An Intellectual Portrait*. New York: Doubleday.
  Coming early in the American discovery of Weber's work, this biography of ideas highlighted Weber's thinking and writings on inequality, authority, and stratification. It is required reading for any serious study of Weberian conflict theory.
Durkheim, Émile 1964 [1893] *The Division of Labor in Society: An Essay on the Organization of Advanced Societies*. Translated by George Simpson. New York: Free Press.
  Examines how and why we have a highly differentiated society, and how that affects the notion of "society." Countering Marx, Durkheim claims that individuality can thrive within active social solidarity. Durkheim's first large study, this work is both highly structural and deeply cultural; one of the great examinations of what it means to be a small part of a big thing.
Durkheim, Émile 1972 *Selected Writings*. Edited by Anthony Giddens. Cambridge: Cambridge University Press.
  The authoritative, comprehensive English translation of Durkheim's writings. Giddens draws upon his study of Durkheim's philosophical background, as well as his political theories, to interpret and present the core ideas and readings from Durkheim's body of work.
Durkheim, Emile 1979 [1897] *Suicide: A Study in Sociology*. Translated by John A. Spaulding and George Simpson. Edited by George Simpson. New York: Free Press.
  A study of the impact of social structures and processes on individuals, *Suicide* also introduced innovative methodologies, using statistical analysis of national-level data to explain patterns of outcomes at what appear to be individual-level phenomena.
Lukes, Steven 1972 *Emile Durkheim: His Life and Work, a Historical and Critical Study*. Stanford, CA: Stanford University Press, 1985.
  An intellectual portrait of Durkheim, very much rooted in the social and historical context of his life. It is highly detailed concerning Durkheim himself, his career, his times, his ideas, and his publications.
Marx, Karl 1967 [1867] *Capital: A Critical Analysis of Capitalist Production*. Vols 1–3, edited by Friedrich Engels. New York: International Publishers.
  This three-volume set is the major text of Marx's critiques of capitalism, containing all of the cases, theories, models, and explanations on which most brief summaries of "Marxism" are based. *Capital* presents the academic basis

for opposition to capitalism, in contrast to the *Manifesto*, which offers the popular argument against it.

Marx, Karl, and Frederick Engels 1998 [1888] *The Communist Manifesto*. London: Verso.

As the name implies, the *Manifesto* is a call to action for the masses. It is the popular counterpart to *Capital*, and the definitive argument for revolutionary change in the "political economy" of the nations of the world.

Tucker, Robert C. 1978 *The Marx-Engels Reader*. New York: W.W. Norton & Co.

A comprehensive spectrum of Marx's thoughts and ideas, from his early education to his major works. This collection captures the philosophical explorations of "young" Marx, the development of his social theories, his political activism, and his interpretations of contemporary developments and social conflicts in his lifetime.

Weber, Max 1930 [1904] The *Protestant Ethic and the Spirit of Capitalism*. Translated by Talcott Parsons. New York: Charles Scribner's Sons.

Responding both to Marx's critique of capitalism and his own examination of American capitalist growth, Weber argued that the individualist, interior moral injunctions of Protestantism had become a secular, social imperative used to justify industriousness and rationality. Thus the cultural domination of a religious philosophy, as seen in the US and Prussia, created a moral context for our devotion to capitalism.

Weber, Max 1958 [1946] *From Max Weber*. Translated and edited by H. H. Gerth and C. Wright Mills. New York: Galaxy.

The definitive English translation of Weber's many pursuits from all stages of his career. For those who are unfamiliar with his work, this is the place to begin.

Weber, Max 1978 [1921] *Economy and Society: An Outline of Interpretive Sociology*. Edited by Guenther Roth and Claus Wittich. Berkeley, CA: University of California Press.

It is difficult to capture all of Weber's wide-ranging sociological explorations of politics, culture, economics, and society in a single book, or even two thick volumes. The English translation of *Economy and Society* accomplishes this as well as one work can.

CHAPTER
03

Management and Administration

I had a temporary job once, working at the warehouse of a national tax accounting firm. Some time in March before all the forms have to be filed, they advertised for extra labor to get everything out in the mail on time. (This was before electronic filing. Actually, this was before personal computers.) The accountants created all of the forms for their thousands of customers and everything was printed at the warehouse. There, one group of minimum-wage employees would pull the different forms off the printers and sort them by form number into dozens of different bins. Then another group would sort each bin according to tax ID number, so that they were ordered from low to high. Finally, I and others like me would go from bin to bin pulling off the 1040s first and looking for every other form in any bin that matched that nine-digit taxpayer ID. We worked quickly and the piles of new forms just seemed to get higher throughout the day. At 11:50, a bell rang and we went to the lunch room with our sandwiches from home. At 12:30, the bell rang again and we were back on the line. We each got two bathroom breaks, one before lunch and one after. While we worked we didn't talk to each other, didn't stretch our backs, didn't stop for a smoke or a coffee. Any unscheduled breaks were met with threats from the supervisor that we would be fired on the spot if we didn't get back to it.

I lasted one week. As soon as I got my first paycheck, I fled. My dignity wouldn't allow me to take any more of that. As I left, I didn't stop to say goodbye to the seven or eight other workers in my team, mostly "retired" women who couldn't afford to stand up for their dignity so easily.

At the time, the only question this incident raised in my mind was "How badly do I need a job?" These days I can only wonder whether there was anything about the work that required it to be so much like a sweatshop. Would it really have slowed things down any if we could have gone to the bathroom without permission? Was it really necessary to keep threatening everyone? Who decided that this was a good idea? And weren't sweatshops supposed to have been a relic of the past, like poorhouses and telegraphs?

How work works

Industry, at the start of the twentieth century, strongly resembled the system of oppressive relations described by Marx. The whole of what we would now call the hierarchy of management was about three steps high: workers answered to foremen who answered to owners. Work was supervised, but not exactly administered.

This changed, quickly. As Rakesh Khurana (2007: 23) summarizes it, "by the early 1920s, managers constituted a sizable and universally recognized occupation group – the 1920 United States occupational census estimated that there were 2,612,525 executive and manager positions in business." There were many technical, legal, and financial reasons for this growth, extensively documented and analyzed by business historian Alfred Chandler, among others. Yet the growth industry behind this change was that of administrative theory, or systems of management. Management "experts" introduced new ways of thinking about the organization of work. The first half of the century witnessed the rise of the idea of the professional manager and the shift in control from both owners and workers to the management middle ground.

The first great wave of administrative theory, under the rubric of what we now refer to as "rational systems," was established by practitioners during the decades before the Great Depression. The next wave, beginning with the Human Relations Movement, dominated the 1930s through the 1950s. This was the first widespread paradigm shift in administrative theory to have been developed and championed from within a university MBA program, and marked a significant shift in the professionalization of management (Khurana, 2007; Hinings and Greenwood, 2002; Stern and Barley, 1996). Though the two systems of thought were quite different in many respects, they shared several key assumptions that were common at that time: that management was a science; that responsibility and decision-making rested with managers; and that management's main subject was not the work but rather the worker. The science of management was the science of control.

Karl Marx, of course, had an explanation for why control was so central to the organization of work. But we can look at it in many ways. The administrative theorists who first took up the questions of workplace management as a science were driven by several straightforward goals and trying to answer several simple questions. The main goal was to produce more work, more quickly, with less investment. Industry was growing, and so were the organizations through which work was managed. The underlying question for this new science was "What is the best way to organize labor?"

And yet, throughout the writings of the people who tried to answer this question, another question lingers: "Why don't workers work harder?" And behind that, in the debates and contrasts as we moved from Fordism to Human Relations, lay the question: "Is society really at all like a machine?"

This chapter will review the last century of ideas about management in industry. As various ideas went in or out of fashion, as proponents moved from observation to experimentation, from systems of complete control to systems of partnership, each new model was driven by that same pursuit to get more work out of the workforce, and justified by the idea that "the machinery of production" would work most efficiently when all the parts were lined up correctly. Parts, in this sense, included the workforce.

Rational systems – Fayol, Ford, Taylor

Think of all of the different issues that go into making a series of decisions about doing something. First, there may be empathetic considerations: how are others going to feel about it? Then there may be personal, psychological considerations: is this the kind of thing that I want to do? There may be moral and ethical considerations: how would I feel about having to justify these actions? Or less moral ones: what can I get out of it? There may be legal considerations: would I do the same thing if I were under police surveillance? Finally, there are rational considerations: is this an efficient and cost-effective way to get what I want?

Toss out the emotional, personal, ethical, and legal worries, and what's left is a rational system. It's a context in which there are goals and actions, in which accomplishing the goals efficiently, predictably, and consistently are highly valued, and in which you don't really talk much about those other outcomes. Rational systems are tightly controlled, limited in scope and purpose, and highly mechanized. Even where the use of actual machinery is limited, the goal of rational organizing is to structure the human system "like a well-oiled machine." A familiar name is applied to the authority relations that best fit this system: bureaucracy.

In early modern industry, one of the greatest sources of unpredictability was the fact that work was controlled by workers, particularly in the skilled crafts. Offices and government were increasingly bureaucratized and rationalized, but the "factory floor" was still an assemblage of craftsmen, each doing their own work. The *rationalization* of production, then, sought to alter the social relations and division of labor in manufacturing in order to make it more mechanical, systematic, and manageable.

One pioneer of administrative theory was Henri Fayol (1841–1925). Fayol championed the professionalization of management as a science. Best remembered for his management "principles," including the use of organizational charts with clear and delimited lines of authority, and "command and control" mechanisms, Fayol spent much of his career advocating the adoption of a consistent and recognized system of tasks, goals, and means for administration. In this, he succeeded. In books such as the one that you are currently reading, Fayol is generally regarded as an early proponent of the rise of a management ideology and therefore partially responsible for everything that's wrong with massive bureaucratic structures. For the most part, though, Fayol had a different vision in mind and probably shouldn't be blamed for too many of the negative aspects of contemporary corporate life.

Fayol's work helped to dramatically increase the power and authority of managers. Yet he also studied and described rational limits on management. He distinguished managerial skills from technical skills, as well as separating administrative spheres of control from technical ones. Workers worked, while managers mostly administered work, which Fayol saw as a distinct profession. He warned of the limits on "span of control," which defined management "capacity" in terms of direct control. Management, according to Fayol, was a matter of direct supervision in which managers should limit the number of subordinates reporting to them. As a rule of thumb, you might say that no manager should have direct control over more people than you could comfortably fit into one decent-sized office all at the same time. To make this work, many companies would have to reorganize their management structure. A "first-line" manager with 21 people under him would become a second-line manager with three first-line managers reporting to him, each supervising seven of the work staff. It is easy to see that the widespread adoption of limited spans of control encouraged an increase in the number of managers within an organization.

Limited spans of control, plus the use of org charts, encouraged tall bureaucratic structures of control that tower over the less differentiated field of workers at the bottom. These tall structures of management greatly increase the distance between owners and workers, placing numerous barriers between the decision-makers and those who carry out the decisions. Today, we can look at the huge gulfs between lower-level workers and upper management as evidence of the inhumanity of work or as a symptom of the disengagement between decisions and their consequences. It is easy to lose sight of the fact that Fayol was actually trying to define management as a social science, and that he was deeply concerned with the issue of social relations between managers and workers. Much of the blame for our selective memory of Fayol probably belongs to Henry Ford.

Ford did not introduce the first factory assembly line, but he made more of it than any of his predecessors. Famous for his technological innovations and cheaper production systems, Ford's great innovations were in the control of the production process. He did not simply organize factories, but also factory towns, factory stores, and factory town newspapers. His factories were physically laid out and otherwise supervised in ways that not only controlled the specific tasks of his workers, but strictly limited the space in which they could move. Beyond the factory floor, Ford opposed what we would call free assembly even during off hours. Workers who gathered together outside of work to talk about work were subject to threats, intimidation, and the loss of their jobs. These efforts were backed by factory rules, absolute authority in the hands of foremen over workers, and, occasionally, violence. For this last part, Ford hired the famous Pinkerton's detective agency to suppress worker organizing and disrupt collective action.

Modern innovations in workplace flexibility and shared responsibility, introduced from the 1970s on, are collectively referred to as "post-Fordism." Fordism itself may be conceived of as the opposite of that – a system of near-complete surveillance and control. While much of this control was directed toward Ford's famous disdain for unions, an undeniable priority was a highly efficient and profitable mass-production system based on standardized outputs. When labor disputes and high turnover rates threatened the steady production of his factory system, Ford raised the worker pay to $5 per day, nearly double the amount many of the workers had been making. Having thus regained the participation of the workers, and eliminated the **piece-rate** pay system in which workers were paid according to the amount of work they accomplished, Ford proceeded to raise the production rate by several hundred percent over the next decade (Meyer, 1981).

The famous five-dollar day was not actually a straight salary. Half the pay was defined as profit sharing and was given out selectively as a reward for what Ford considered proper habits and discipline. The pay scheme formed part of a complex system of rewards and controls designed to mold the kind of workforce that would not only endure Ford's high-speed factory, but also demonstrate their loyalty and submission to management. The "profit-sharing" portion of the pay was awarded following a thorough investigation of each worker's home life and personal habits, undertaken by the company's "sociology department" (Meyer, 1981). A variety of unapproved habits could deprive a worker of half his income, from arriving late at work, to drinking, to organizing workers, to skipping church. Henry Ford thus embodies the comic-book image of the early twentieth-century capitalist exercising awesome authority over the lives of "his" workers, an image that would become less popular during the second half of the century.

But the central figure in the rise of "rational" management systems is that of Frederick Winslow Taylor (1856–1915). Taylor's system of "scientific management" spawned a movement that swept across the United States and, to a lesser degree, Europe, redefining the rules and practices by which labor was supervised.

Taylor, Taylorism, and Taylorization

Taylor began his studies of factory operations in 1881 at the Midvale Steel Company, while working as a chief engineer. Almost obsessively focused on efficiency, he observed the minute details of workers' actions, timing each step on his stopwatch. To Taylor, the semi-organized structure in which each worker managed their own tasks was haphazard and wasteful. He introduced a system of what we would now call "micromanagement," which he termed "scientific management," to optimize labor. He told workers when to stand or sit, how much to carry, how long to rest. By "optimizing" each task, he was able to increase the rates of production in numerous mechanical jobs. Taylor called this system a way of ensuring that no worker was forced to do more than he (*sic*) could do. Critics simply called it "deskilling," since it transferred craft knowledge from the workers to the shop manager. Once day-to-day – or moment-to-moment – operations were in the hands of supervisors rather than workers, skilled laborers could be much more easily replaced by unskilled ones.

The first sentence of Taylor's *Principles of Scientific Management* reads: "The principal object of management should be to secure the maximum prosperity for the employer, coupled with the maximum prosperity for each employé." He promised to introduce a system of administration that would develop the skills and contributions of each worker to his highest state, or "maximum efficiency," for his "natural abilities" (1967: 9). A cornerstone of his system did involve raising the daily wage of workers under his system, although their piece-rate – the amount earned per unit of work completed – declined. As with Ford's system, individual workers could make more money if they agreed to a complete reorganization of their daily tasks, and if the result was more profitable for the company. The short-term results were mutually beneficial to both employer and employee. The long-term results were more ambiguous. As Taylorism shifted job control from the workers to management, it paved the way for numerous abuses and the suppression of labor organizing. Taylor's intentions in this area remain unclear. While he distrusted labor and placed his faith in benevolent management, he was silent on the concept of management that was not so benevolent.

From the start, Taylor was blending three concepts. First, he fully shared Weber's interest in a rational and predictable system of administration. Second, he shared Fayol's enthusiasm for a detailed division of labor in which complex jobs are best handled as a coordinated system of very small tasks. And, third, he explicitly designed his model around the assumption that each person in the system has a relatively fixed "natural" level of ability. Without actually invoking the language of class superiority, Taylor divided the productive world into thinkers and doers. Administration and as much of the decision-making authority as possible belonged in the hands of the educated thinkers, and out of the hands of the laborers whose minds were presumed to be simpler. Similarly, in his examples and explanations, Taylor assumed that the "natural" state of work relations was for the workers to try to avoid work and serve their own interests against the company's. Management existed in order to control that. In contrast, he never appeared to wonder about the interests or intent of management. In his writings, he assumed that management would act rationally and focus almost exclusively on production rates. Rational administration would increase profitability and wages, and everyone would be happier.

Taylor's unexplored faith in the integrity of management partially explains why his system ultimately failed to ameliorate industrial hostilities. It turned out that when management was in charge of both workers' interests and their own, it didn't make the workers happier. The fact alone that production was less reliant on the skills of individual workers allowed management to demand more than just work, to fire people arbitrarily, and even to block fired workers from getting new jobs elsewhere in the same industry.

Taylor's language would strike a contemporary reader as grossly elitist and even contemptuous of the working class. Even so, he appears to have been earnest in his belief that scientific management would be as good for the workers whose jobs were simplified and controlled as it would be for the managers who controlled them. Describing his goal of overturning centuries of craft-based labor in favor of a modern factory system, he promised "an almost equal division of the work and the responsibility between the management and the workmen. The management take over all work for which they are better fitted than the workmen, while in the past almost all of the work and the greater part of the responsibility were thrown upon the men" (p. 37).

Taylor's *Principles* offered concrete advice and step-by-step instructions on how to reorganize a work site. In one famous example, involving the menial task of loading pig-iron, Taylor introduced the figure of Schmidt, a strong, hard-working and not too bright laborer with a family that he can only just manage to support through his job. Schmidt is capable of working harder, and willing to do so if he can get a higher daily take-home pay for it. The description was fictional, representing the kind of negotiation that one needed to go through to introduce Taylor's task-management system. Schmidt's dialogue was written with a mock accent ("Vell, I don't know vat you mean") and with a semblance of confusion and uncertainty. The foreman's responses were bullying and insulting. Taylor comments on his dialogue:

> This seems to be rather rough talk. And indeed it would be if applied to an educated mechanic, or even an intelligent laborer. With a man of the mentally sluggish type of Schmidt it is appropriate and not unkind, since it is effective in fixing his attention on the high wages which he wants and away from what, if it were called to his attention, he would probably consider impossibly hard work. (1967: 46)

Once Schmidt was on board with the new system, Taylor could pick out a second and then a third worker to convert. Taylor emphasized that you cannot just issue new rules and change people's work habits. The change has to happen gradually with the cooperation of carefully chosen workers. By picking the right workers, one or two at a time, and offering them slightly higher wages in exchange for higher labor output, you can raise the average work rate. Once several of them have agreed to be managed in the new system, the rest can be much more easily coerced into conforming. Since the average rate had increased, the rest of the workers can be reclassified as underperforming and, if necessary, fired. Taylor also notes that in his application of this system to the pig-iron handlers at Bethlehem Steel, only one man in eight could actually do what he was asking.

> With most readers great sympathy will be aroused because seven out of eight of these pig-iron handlers were thrown out of a job. This sympathy is entirely wasted, because almost all of them were immediately given other jobs with the Bethlehem Steel Company. And indeed it should be understood that the removal of these men from pig-handling, for which they were unfit, was really a kindness to themselves, because it was the first step toward finding them work for which they were peculiarly fitted. (1967: 64)

In the case of Bethlehem Steel this is quite possibly true. And it need not be considered Taylor's fault if many subsequent companies followed his instructions only to the point of firing large numbers of people without actually finding them other positions. Taylor seems to have assumed that most companies would prefer to fully implement his program.

Taylor's own description of how he came to develop his system is curious and revealing. He begins with his first foreman job in which, having just been promoted from worker to foreman, he deemed himself to be entirely aligned with the interests of management against the interests of the workers. He immediately initiated changes in the production system to compel greater output for the same wages, setting in motion three years of "piece-work war" between himself and the people whose work he oversaw, during which he received numerous threats and constantly expected to be physically attacked.

Taylor understood that the increased work requirements were not in the workers' interests, and he described his life of "one continuous struggle with other men" as a "bitter" form of existence (1967: 52). His innovation was, essentially, to share the benefits of increased production with the workers by giving them a pay increase in exchange for their cooperation. In theory, higher rates of productivity meant higher profits, some of which could be shared with the workers. In many respects, Taylor was trying to give capitalists what they wanted without the abuses that Marx warned of. He appears to have considered his system to be good for all, and honestly wished that workers could better appreciate his intentions. Curiously, Taylor criticized Fordism for deskilling the workers, which remains the standard criticism of Taylorism. It is possible that Taylor simply did not consider his system as applying to skilled work.

Taylor promised that scientific management would bring about a new era of labor peace in America, since the interests of workers and management would coincide. But workers didn't see it that way, and Taylor was occasionally attacked by aggrieved workers until he started hiring bodyguards to accompany him on a job. Factories that tried to implement Taylorism met with considerable resistance from labor, more so than in other factories. Eventually, the system mainly fell out of favor in most countries.

The Taylorization of society?

Is Taylorism over? The actual formula and plan developed by Taylor is no longer promoted as a path to success in industry. Philosophically, however, the hyper-rationalization of everything seems only to have increased. That interpretation, at least, is the heart of such works as George Ritzer's *The McDonaldization of Society* and Alan Bryman's *The Disneyization of Society*. The rationalization of society that Weber described provided the justification for Taylorism in the work world.

These principles have seemingly reached their pinnacle in the fast-food industry, where the roles of the staff, the customers, and even the food are reduced to their simplest, most efficient, and impersonal forms. The combination of our faith in rationalization itself, coupled with the enormous financial success and worldwide acceptance of fast food, has encouraged what Ritzer describes as the dominance of these principles in almost all other aspects of our lives. In stores, airports, schools, and even churches, human activity is replaced by mechanical or computerized processes that offer "efficiency, calculability, predictability and increased control" (Ritzer, 2000).

To this rational model, Bryman adds the influence of a consumer-oriented society. The need to attract and please customers drives changes in the goals we set for our organizations and institutions. It determines the technologies used to measure and evaluate calculability, predictability and control. Surprisingly, it also requires greater control of the consumers themselves as a result of the need to manage the consumer experience.

Consider an example: I like to do a lot of my writing in coffee shops. I know all of the local coffee places around where I live, and I've been in a lot of Starbucks. As is the case for fast food, if you have seen one Starbucks, you have seen them all. They use the same decor, the same furniture, price-boards, music, and signage. In the branch that I'm in now, the manager is currently setting out sale items on a shelf. It is a slow process, because the corporate headquarters distributes instruction books with photographs of exactly how the various shelves should look. With each cup or thermos, she has to check the book to be sure she's placed it in the exact right spot. I have heard the staff here joke to customers that they can't do anything about the cold in here because the thermostat is in Seattle.

There have been many studies of rationalization, McDonaldization and/or Disneyization at all levels of society in recent years. One frequently used case is that of education. An assortment of studies suggests that there has been a steady increase in the use of testing and standardization, among other related techniques, in all levels of education regulation throughout the industrial world over the past several decades. In Scotland, for example, the MacFarlane Report (COSHEP, 1992) recommended reorganizing higher education around "a new emphasis on the auditing of quality and performance in teaching, with concomitant attention to enhancing quality and increasing efficiency" (Hartley, 1995: 413). In Alberta, Canada, a series of Advanced Education and Career Development (AECD) proposals have ushered in a highly comparable system with its own emphasis on performance measures (Barnetson and Cutright, 2000). In Germany and France, as well, an increasing trend toward efficiency, calculability, predictability, and increased control have been noted (Musselin, 2005).

In the United States, the No Child Left Behind Act (NCLB, 2002) mandates "highly qualified" instructors in every classroom without actually defining what that means. One result of this has been a marked increase in attention to a narrow range of formal training as criteria for hiring teachers, coupled with increased use of performance measures once they have begun working. Critics of the NCLB Act describe its mandates as a "political spectacle" intended to force schools to shift their resources from education to measurement, calculability, and accountability (Berliner, 2005). Supporters say that accountability is necessary in order to raise the quality of public education. This rationalization of education implies standard curricula, standardized testing, and the orientation of teaching to measurable goals, such as test scores. For higher education instructors, the pressure to demonstrate quality in the classroom may mean more reliance on student "consumer" evaluations. (Fewer assignments and more cookies, perhaps.) Outside of the classroom, the trend to find numbers that prove our quality leads faculty to count the number of times our research is referred to in other people's journal articles, which is a bit like counting your online friends to prove that your opinions are respected.

Similar concerns about the changes in education policies and accountability are being raised by both grade-school teachers and college professors in multiple nations (Hayes and Wynyard, 2002). Of course, critics of these critics point out that professional teachers have always objected to what they perceive as "outside" interference in their work, and it is unlikely that any shift in education policy has not been accused of "dumbing down" our schools. Is the present rationalization of education different? Since this book isn't about education, I won't try to answer that question. Drawing on the organizational roots of this trend, however, from Weber to Taylor to Bryman, I will offer one small prediction. The risks and benefits from the rationalization of education are likely to be similar to the losses and gains that we have seen occurring in industry. That is, standardization and control restrict the actions of the least effective schools, altering their practices to more closely resemble the typical practices of the field. This could help. At the same time, the same standardization is applied to the best schools, forcing them to become more average. Thus one recent case study of changes in education policy under NCLB found the reforms to be both a success and a failure, depending on which school you looked at, what resources they had to support their changes, and what criteria one uses to define success (McDermott, 2006). Whether this is a good thing or a bad thing for you, as a student, may depend on the kind of school you attend.

Critical reactions against Taylorism

Taylorism, Fordism, and the rationalization of production overall rely on the notion that rational control is efficient. This assumption does not simply explain the harsh factory conditions of the early industrial period. The same argument lies at the heart of virtually all hierarchies throughout our organizational society. The division of authority into chains of command and control is taken for granted within companies, schools, clubs, religious institutions, and basically every organized corner of our lives. This system of authority is presumed to be necessary because we live in large, complex societies, and the act of organizing has become, since Weber's and Taylor's day, the act of forming hierarchies.

What do these hierarchies do for us? Answering that question depends on what we mean by "us." According to Taylor and Ford, the strict division of control was the most efficient form of large-scale organizing there could be. It was "the one best way." Labor historian Richard Edwards points out, however, that this assumption is almost never tested. Even where contrary evidence exists, as in cases of highly efficient worker-managed production facilities, the owners and decision-makers in industry are not usually interested. The reason for this, Edwards suggests, is that efficiency is not the important part. Rather, "hierarchy at work persists because it is *profitable*" (1979: viii; emphasis in original). The strict division of control means that a relatively small number of people get to decide how resources are invested and profits are distributed. Typically, they take most of the profits for themselves.

Unfortunately, there isn't space in this chapter to review the historical argument that Edwards presents. A few key observations will have to do for now. For one thing, we should note that the rise of industrial capitalism fostered the rise of organized resistance to industrial capitalism in every nation and just about every industry. Radical workers' associations fought against owners, leading to long confrontations, strikes, and shutdowns in some of the most oppressive industries such as steel, mining, silk, and railroad construction. Less radical unions demanded the right to collective bargaining, leading to innovative changes in workplace relations, including weekends off and a reduction of the standard workday to only eight hours. Journalists, writers, intellectuals, and some politicians raised concerns about the worst abuses in many factories, leading to the introduction of child labor laws and workplace safety inspections. Generally speaking, the workers were not objecting to improvements in efficiency.

Another crucial point to note is that throughout the industrial world, the majority of governments have used the power of law to support the rise of industrial capitalism and to restrict the workers' opportunities to protest. By doing this, governments mostly were not protecting the efficient organization of mass production for the good of society. They were protecting the rights of owners to define work-place control, compensation, and work conditions. At present, the relationships between government, corporate control, and labor vary considerably throughout the industrial nations.

Edwards's argument is international. Picking up on some of these themes and much of the same historical record, Charles Perrow re-examined the rise of industrial capitalism in the United States. Perrow certainly acknowledges the importance of profit, but he also recog-nizes that these same forces operated differently here from the rest of the world. All industrial nations practice some form of industrial capitalism, but few have been more committed to unfettered industry for so many decades as the US. The difference is political, in Perrow's argument, and the key factor is power. Capitalist organizations grew larger everywhere as capitalism itself grew. In the US case, though, Perrow sees the rapidly growing power of capitalist organizations as organizations, not as industry, driving the changes. Organizations are larger here, and wealth is more highly concentrated in fewer hands. These two facts are not unrelated. One of the accomplishments of the growth of large organizational systems, he argues, is that they change the way wealth accumulates. "We hear that efficient forms prevail over inefficient forms, and so we think that the prevailing organiza-tions must be reflections of this efficiency. True, in general and in a largely tautological sense, but whose efficiency is being realized; for whom is it inefficient?" (Perrow, 2002: 11).

Inequality is central to most critiques of Taylorism and all that followed in its name. Some of the critiques, like Perrow's, are quite general and cover a historical period in which Taylor himself is just one player. Others focus much more on the specific changes in indus-trial capitalism ushered in by Taylor's principles. This brings us back to the question of workers' expertise and the control of labor.

Scientific management did reorganize the technology of produc-tion, and did sometimes increase productive output. But the lasting impact of Taylorism was to shift the balance of power in the work-place, and help to counter the union movement. Taylor's system made workers more expendable, more easily replaceable, and created greater competition among workers for the jobs that remained. This strengthening of management against the interests of workers formed the basis for Harry Braverman's (1974) response, *Labor and Monopoly Capital: The Degradation of Work in the Twentieth Century*.

Braverman brought a Marxist reading to scientific management, focusing attention on who wins and who loses. The explicit goal of this system, all agreed, was to produce more goods for less money. Capitalist theories called this "efficiency." Marxist theorists call this "exploitation." Apart from the obvious problem that it was the workers who were producing more for less, while other people were pocketing the surplus, Braverman and other critics objected to the fact that workers lost control of their own work. His notion of "degradation" in the workplace followed from Marx's "alienation of labor." The work process was not simply taken out of workers' hands. It was redesigned to operate against the interests and needs of workers, and over their objections. Whether the goal was to make productive labor more efficient, as Taylor and his supporters claimed, or to increase management control for its own sake, as Braverman and other critics contend, the result was the same. The human value of a laborer was reduced to the economic value of what he could produce, while the social dimensions of being at work were represented as "distractions" from production. As workers' obligations to employers increased, the reverse decreased. If a worker was injured on the job, or off, and unable to keep up, he would be tossed out and replaced, same as any other mechanical part. The absolute abuse of workers was not a necessary part of production. But this was clearly not a system designed to make people happy with their jobs.

Writing in 1974, Braverman was explicit in stating that the main degradations of Taylorism had not ended with the apparent demise of the movement. The idea that companies "owned" workers' time and attention remained evident; modern versions include the notion that making personal phone calls from work or talking with your co-workers during work hours amounts to "stealing from the company," which is a phrase I have heard in several of my jobs. The transfer of skill from workers to management continued throughout most industries and many professions. The lasting appeal of this shift, Braverman argued, was not that management experts could increase output or plan more accurately. The advantage was that it made all workers replaceable, creating "an army" of potential replacement labor waiting for each job. The combination of managed tasks, even in skilled work, and economic uncertainty would result in a permanent level of job insecurity that could end labor organizing once and for all. Moreover, this shift translated easily from Taylorism into the post-Fordist approaches that followed it.

But, if Taylorism's greatest problems remained in the systems that replaced it, then why did Taylorism come to be replaced? We can trace three parallel developments that undermined the assumptions of scientific management and rational systems generally toward a more "natural" or adaptive model of organizations. The first was the recognition that Taylorism was not able to deliver on all that it had promised. Attacks on the system itself, mostly in print, and on Taylorized factories, mostly involving strikes, worker organizing, and slow-downs, convinced the system's proponents that maximizing efficiency would be a more complex matter. Workers, clearly, had to be considered as distinct from non-human tools.

The second development was that organizations became larger, more diverse, and more complex than anything Taylor had experienced or foreseen. The old factory system, with one owner, one foreman, and a mass of workers, did not even apply well to factories by the early twentieth century. At the turn of the twenty-first century, it is not difficult to find corporations employing over 100,000 people. Fayol's concern to limit management span of control to seven or eight workers is quaint at best in such an environment. The corporate world has simply outgrown the early administrative theorists.

And corporations have grown in other respects as well, moving from "the factory" into global webs with separate control centers for production, distribution, and marketing. Increasingly, owners are leaving the day-to-day management of their corporations to professional managers while they oversee the reach and power of their worldwide corporate empires. These developments have led to the massive growth of management and other professional employees, workers whose job descriptions do not encourage one to compare them to parts of a machine. Taylorism did not help executives to manage managers. New models for organizing have had to address the knowledge and skills of workers who had been hired for those skills.

Finally, a series of innovative studies of behavior within organizations turned up a surprising result: human variability matters.

Organizations as human systems

One of the great watershed events of organizational research was the multi-year series of studies at the Western Electric Company plant in Hawthorne, Illinois. The work began in 1923, though the development of the theory is attributed to the subsequent work conducted under the nominal supervision of Elton Mayo between 1927 and 1932, and written about for decades after. The Hawthorne experiments, conducted by Fritz Roethlisberger and his colleagues, allowed Mayo to first challenge, and then reject, the assumptions and principles of scientific management. It formed the empirical foundation on which the subsequent "human relations" movement in management theory rested, and it introduced key ideas from sociology into the study of management and organization. It replaced "rational systems" thinking with a **"natural systems"** approach (Scott, 2002), which I will describe below. The Hawthorne research and, even more so, its many subsequent analyses and interpretations revolutionized organizational studies by defining work as a social activity and management as a human problem – all of this despite the fact that the Hawthorne data do not actually support the majority of the conclusions that are typically drawn from it.

The Hawthorne research began as an ordinary research project designed to find ways to improve productivity in the manufacturing sector. Following the logic of scientific management, the researchers sought to identify simple environmental variables, such as lighting and other physical conditions which, if scientifically optimized, would yield the most productive work process. Carefully dividing the workers under study into two groups, the control group and the experimental group, the research team began to manipulate the conditions under which the experimental group worked. After nearly three years of work, two findings became apparent. One was that changing the physical conditions had no discernible effect on output, which was a disappointment to the researchers. The other was that during the period of research, productivity improved fairly consistently among the experimental group, even when theory suggested that it should fall off. Improved lighting; productivity went up. Diminished lighting; productivity was still up. This was the baffling part. At this point, Western Electric could have abandoned the project, but they turned instead to Mayo and his team from Harvard.

In a series of experiments, the research team constructed separate spaces for groups of workers in which they could manipulate the work environment. In the "relay assembly test room" experiments, for example, five women were moved to a test space in which a series of manipulations and measurements were made over the course of several years, including the introduction and removal of breaks, shortening, then restoring, the number of work hours in the week, and experimenting with different styles of supervision. These changes yielded results similar to the experiments with the men in the wiring room. As described by project leader Fritz Roethlisberger (1941: xx), "it did not take the experimenters more than two years to find out that they had missed the boat." Rather, "the great *éclaircissement,* the new illumination, that came from the research" was that the experiments had social meaning to the subjects. They were not simply doing their work any more; they were performing for the research team. Roethlisberger explained:

> What I am saying is very simple. If one experiments on a stone, the stone does not know it is being experimented upon . . . But if a human

being is experimented upon, he is likely to know it. Therefore, his attitudes toward the experiment and toward the experimenters become very important factors in determining his responses to the situation. (1941: xx)

As was the case with scientific management, the conclusions here provide a curious mix of notions that have been so thoroughly integrated into contemporary analysis that it's hard now to imagine them as anything but obvious, along with notions that have been so subject to criticism in the intervening years that we might hesitate to believe they were once taken seriously. But, yes, a team of top specialists in industrial relations spent almost five years in a single plant in order to discover that conducting experiments on people affects the way in which people behave. This was the main contribution of the famous "Hawthorne effect." Developing this point further, they concluded that the primary reason for this effect was that workers crave a sense of group solidarity, which they lacked in their normal factory jobs. The interest that the researchers paid to them as people, with the implied sense that the company cared about their work conditions, was the main force bolstering their morale and driving them to work harder. Even so, as William H. Whyte (1957: 38–9) wrote, "In the literature of human relations the Hawthorne experiment is customarily regarded as a discovery." Yet Elton Mayo "had come to quite similar conclusions many years before, and for him the Hawthorne experiment did not reveal so much as confirm."

Recent scholarship has indicated that many of the results claimed by the Hawthorne team, including Mayo and Roethlisberger, rely on a highly selective, possibly even misleading, use of the data. In some cases, the data contradict specific claims, such as the assertion that the workers in the experimental rooms were happier than other workers, or that nothing in the experiment was coercive (Bramel and Friend, 1981). Using very Taylor-like language, for example, the researchers indicated that a couple of the women initially in the relay assembly tests "left" and were replaced. This sounds neutral enough, except that the workers who left were the ones who were least happy, cooperative, and successful in the experiment. The ones who remained were the ones who responded in the manner that the researchers preferred. This small detail undermines almost any conclusions that they could draw from the experiment.

If the Hawthorne experiments had actually been the foundation for the human relations school, then it probably would not have gotten very far. Instead, the experiments and their popular analyses led industry away from the mechanical view of workers because they came at a time when industry was ready to abandon that view.

Human relations in industry

In reality, the notion of the workplace as a social system had already emerged as a question along with the movement of sociology into small group studies and social psychology. Thorstein Veblen's *Theories of the Leisure Class* (1934), Charles Cooley's "looking glass self" (*Human Nature and the Social Order*, 1922), Vilfredo Pareto's *Mind and Society: A Treatise in General Sociology* (English translation, 1935), and George Herbert Mead's *Mind, Self and Society* (1934) were all in popular circulation during the same period as Mayo's *The Human Problems of an Industrial Civilization* (1933) and *The Social Problems of an Industrial Civilization* (1939). The human relations school thus formalized numerous sociological insights for industrial use. A great many of these insights are still applied. Chief among them is that the social context of work really does matter. Whether it matters in exactly the way Mayo specified is less important.

Proponents of human relations began with a small number of key assumptions: that workers and other participants can be made to share in the goals and interests of the organization; that tasks can be defined or presented so that participants will want to do them; that human beings, unlike machine parts, have their own goals and needs; and that social relations are the key element in the process. They introduced the notion that incentives do not have to be monetary and that sanctions do not have to be coercive. A small bonus, or even a simple award, can give recognition to individual efforts, and corporate recognition reinforces the sense that the worker is part of a social group. An underlying assumption of this approach was that happy workers would be more productive, so that attention to social dimensions of the work environment would pay for themselves in increased profits. This proposition was a substantial departure from the scientific management assumption, shared by Marxists, that worker–management relations would always be competitive, if not hostile.

Another insight of this approach was that it helps to listen to workers' input, or even to ask for it. As part of their experimental research, the Hawthorne investigators conducted interviews with workers throughout the studies. One unanticipated result was that workers liked to be interviewed. Intended to help the researchers measure the effects of their experimental changes, the interviews also provided the workers with a clear and consistent opportunity to provide feedback on what they thought about the work environment. They offered advice to the researchers, and seemed to believe that the experts wanted their advice. This led the research team to re-evaluate the role of feedback in worker–management relations.

Worker feedback, and the assumption that one should ask for it, has been integrated into contemporary work settings in a number of ways. Many workplaces have suggestion boxes. The same principles are applied to non-work organizations as well. Service companies routinely ask customers to follow every transaction with a brief satisfaction survey. College classes almost invariably poll students on their experiences, as we noted earlier. Hospitals have patient advocates visiting patients at the end of their stays. Feedback is built into all kinds of organized settings, and its usefulness is fairly taken for granted, if untested.

Speaking with workers, or usually just listening to them, was one technique that human relations theorists suggested would improve workers' commitment to their jobs and to their management. Related to this were efforts to diversify job tasks, improve training, and offer clear career paths. In effect, the idea was to undo most of the major organizational changes accomplished by Taylorism and Fordism. Whereas Taylor had assumed that workers would be happy to perform dull repetitive tasks if they could make more money, the human relations proponents claimed that the opposite was true. A worker, they claimed, will give up money, and union activism, if the work was somehow meaningful. Although they rarely mentioned Karl Marx, it appears that the human relations approach was at least partially designed to serve as the antidote to alienation in the workplace.

At the same time, the human relations approach was not a reversal of Taylorism at all. In many respects, it appears to have been an attempt to correct the limitations of the earlier system in order to achieve the same goals (O'Connor, 1999). Strong-arm, individualist approaches to social control had not worked out. The human relations approach introduced a soft approach based on the study of psychology. Rather than crush unions and threaten workers, Mayo taught that one could counsel troubled workers and offer them the support of the company and its leadership. Let them find their fulfillment as members of the company team, and they would have no more need to organize against its interests.

Most significantly, the human relations approach challenged the assumption that workers and managers had to be in competition. Granted, the corporate vision that all were encouraged to share in was essentially the managers' vision. But managers would not have to fight for workers' compliance if they could find other ways to make cooperation worthwhile.

We will look at some of these efforts to elicit cooperation in greater detail in chapter 4. For the moment, I only wish to reiterate a few points about the rational movement in industrial management. First, the massive growth in industry heralded the rise of management as a profession. The old rational systems of direct and detailed supervision of each worker became obsolete as the ranks and reach of management swelled. The profession of management needed more science than Taylor's scientific management approach offered. They needed systems of thought about work and workers, about leadership and control, and about planning. They needed elite business schools and specialized leadership training. The human relations movement in industry drew upon sociology, psychology, and philosophy to offer a complex image of the inner life of "the working man." No longer seen as an extension of the machinery, workers were now to be viewed as a complex problem to be carefully managed. Even so, the underlying goals of this new philosophy remained the same as the goals of Taylorism: spend less, produce more, and resist unions.

Contemporary human resources departments carry on much of the human relations tradition. Among the effects of the human relations school on American industry were the introduction of ergonomic principles in workplace design, free counseling for workers who want it, and even interior design for productive environments. There are specialized decorating principles designed to foster a comfortable, calm, and productive office. "Industrial art" is a field of work in which artists (or people with some art training) produce decorative works that are compatible with the interior design motifs recommended by industrial psychologists. This is art that is intended to hang in corporate settings, and pretty much nowhere else.

Do teal walls and casual Fridays really increase productivity? Perhaps, to the extent that it makes an office look less like a prison. Cement walls and industrial lighting, strict business uniforms, time clocks, and other rational forms of work regimentation can contribute to work stress and make employees feel like cattle. A little relaxation makes it easier to spend all of that time at work. Do human relations in the workplace reduce unionism? Again, the answer is maybe. But the assumption that there should be a relationship between work environment and employee cooperation has carried over from early human relations models into decades of subsequent research and theory.

The collective effect of all of those works define what organization theorist Richard Scott calls the *natural systems* approach to organizations. This perspective recognizes that organizations have informal structures and unofficial systems of relations that coexist with the formal models. Human factors such as status, power, and symbolic communication – in a word, culture – operate as powerfully in a formal organization as they do outside of it.

By the 1960s, the human relations approach to administration began to fade in importance, even though many of their insights and recommendations still guide actual practices today. In place of human relations programs to increase satisfaction, sociologists undertook full-scale ethnographies. By the 1980s, the big new thing in management was the quest to measure and mobilize something called "organizational culture." We will take up this quest in the following chapter.

Key Readings

Braverman, Harry 1974 *Labor and Monopoly Capital: The Degradation of Work in the Twentieth Century*. New York: Monthly Review Press.
  A late twentieth-century – but still relevant – Marxist challenge to contemporary notions of work, progress, and industrial capitalism. Carefully and explicitly defining work around the labor of the working class, Braverman demonstrates that advances in skills, knowledge, and pay at the upper reaches of the industrial world are accompanied by, and rely on, deskilling in the middle and lower end of the occupational ladder.
Edwards, Richard C. 1979 *Contested Terrain: The Transformation of the Workplace in the Twentieth Century*. New York: Basic Books.
  A historical argument about the nature of workplace control. Edwards argues that the visible authority of managers gave way, mid-twentieth century, to the use of bureaucracy as a means for control in large organizations. Rules and rule-mindedness limit workers' options and opportunities, thereby determining outcomes without anyone seeming to give orders. His review of industrial trends incorporates critiques of modern capitalism and the interests and claims of organized unions.
Fayol, Henri 1949 *General and Industrial Management*. Translated by Constance Storrs. London: Pitman and Sons, Ltd.
  Fayol's concise attempt to re-create the profession of management. The book contains the "14 principles" of management as a practice, for which it became famous, as well as a lengthy discussion on how to teach management science.
Roethlisberger, Fritz J., and W. Dickson 1964 [1939] *Management and the Worker: An Account of a Research Program Conducted by the Western Electric Company, Hawthorne Works, Chicago*. Cambridge, MA: Harvard University Press.
  First published in 1939, this is the great explanation and complete presentation of the "Hawthorne effect" and the studies on which it was based. Controversial now, it was revolutionary in its own time for its claims concerning the social environment of the factory and how that could be organized for greater productivity.
Taylor, Frederick Winslow 1911 [1967] *The Principles of Scientific Management*. New York: W. W. Norton & Co.
  Taylor's manifesto, along with examples of how to Taylorize a workplace. Described in detail in the chapter.

CHAPTER 04

Culture in Organizations

I<small>N</small> the film *The Right Stuff,* a group of highly talented, tough, and supremely confident men moved the science of flight forward into the space age by ignoring their agency's priorities and setting the highest possible standards of achievement for themselves. The organization was a limitation, but human drive was irrepressible. In contrast, the film *Apollo 13* showed how a well-trained, professional group backed by a supremely competent technical staff could pull off a nearly miraculous save in the face of a disaster. These people had the right stuff, too, but the organization held them together. The *Apollo* astronauts lived because they all relied on each other.

Films are necessarily simplifications, so we can assume that the reality behind these stories was much more complicated. But each of the films relies on, and even celebrates, the idea that in "his" soul, a professional is someone who invests everything he's got in the job at hand. He digs in, goes the extra mile, and you can fill in your own favorite sports metaphor here. These daring, hardcore professionals seem like a different race of people from the work-avoiding, penny-counting workers of early industrial studies. How did we get from the simple-minded workhorses of the 1920s to the heroic standard bearers of the 1960s? It was a long path. But one of the most crucial steps along the way was the discovery of "commitment." Whether one was committed to an organization, a mission, a nation, or to one's own potential, motivation came to be seen as something that drives you from within, rather than something that was imposed on you from outside.

The discovery of commitment had a short and fascinating life course. When industrial studies were focused on the lower-level wage workers, they found it frustrating that the workers did not give more to the companies. Henry Ford, for example, complained that most people don't want to work as he had worked. He viewed industry as held back by "men who want to be carried on the shoulders of others." Yet, as we saw in the last chapter, when attention shifted to managers and the middle levels of the corporate world, administrative theorists became more concerned with winning the hearts and minds of employees than with regimenting their bodies. By 1957, William H. Whyte was writing of the legions of junior managers who so over-identified with their jobs that they "have left home, spiritually as well as physically, to take the vows of organization life" (p. 3).

This chapter will explore the development of ideas about how people relate to their jobs and organizations. Most of the present exploration continues to focus on industry. I will begin with the pursuit of workers' "commitment" to organizations, which will lead us to the study of "organizational cultures." In chapter 5, I will consider both individual motivations and organizational cultures in relation to dysfunctions and disasters. Chapter 7 will pick up the question of culture and commitment again in the context of voluntary participation in non-profit and charitable organizations.

Culture is a slippery concept, used in many different ways by many different people. So far in this book we have talked about social norms, shared values, and shared beliefs. These are all parts of culture. In order to explain ideas like commitment, then, we need to think about the values that guide our commitments and the beliefs that inspire them. As we noted at the end of the last chapter, rational systems thinkers like Ford and Taylor did not concern themselves much with workers' values, unless they perceived these values as a threat to productivity. So the introduction of cultural ideas into the study of organizations reveals a shift in thinking about the human beings within the systems. This is one of the reasons that the new approach to industrial studies became known as the human relations movement.

The human relations movement in administration took off from Mayo's and others' writings about the social side of organizations. The mostly management school-based theorists urged managers to think of an organization as a social structure, and they sought to analyze formal organizations as small, tightly structured societies. Borrowing extensively from the rest of the social sciences, this human relations school suggested that, like societies, organizations have their own norms, ethical codes, and values.

Richard Scott (2002) uses the term "natural systems" to describe the approaches to organizational studies that focus on social relations and personal motivations. Natural systems models view individuals within organizations as social actors with a variety of interests and priorities, who are therefore pursuing multiple goals, only some of which coincide with the organization's goals. In contrast with the rational systems approaches, theorists in this area of work recognize that individual interests are not simply about getting the most pay for the least work or maximizing their benefits while minimizing their costs. In fact, it is often the case that people who are hired to accomplish an organizational goal become personally committed to achieving it. Sometimes what they want is to get the job done.

To a large degree, the material of this chapter is simply the next step in the development of industrial relations. Fundamentally, however, it also raises the question of what it means to be a member of an organization. What do organizations owe to their participants, and what do participants owe in return? Who is the organization for? The introduction of cultural concerns into the study of organizations opens the door to issues of social meaning, value, and the place of collective action in society at large.

What workers want

Elton Mayo summarized the key elements of "the human problems of an industrial civilization," beginning with the day-to-day issues of worker fatigue, task monotony, and poor morale, leading to ongoing failures of the social order of an organization. The underlying causes and potential solutions, he argued, could be found in the nature of administration. More to the point, Taylorist management philosophies and practices set an organization on a path toward moral collapse, while a healthier system of human relations could reverse the process. Mayo didn't adopt the Marxist notion of alienation. But his concerns with how people feel about performing dull and meaningless work under conditions of constant surveillance and outside control raises some of the same concerns.

Mayo's ideas, and the human relations movement in general, often contradict those of Taylor's scientific management. These contradictions, however, are more about practice than principles. In many respects, human relations approaches were attempting to correct and complete the Taylorist project. One can introduce a human relations language to consider the legacy of Taylorism. From this perspective, it seems that Taylor encountered more resistance than anticipated because workers did not always pursue individual gain against the interests of the group. Many, in fact, preferred to act on behalf of their work groups or craft, often joining unions along the way. And unions opposed scientific management steadfastly. A guiding assumption of the human relations model, then, was that workers wanted and needed to define themselves in terms of their social group. The key to productivity, therefore, was to help them to define the company as their group, instead of the union, which human relations pioneers Roethlisberger and Dickson (1939: 553) referred to as "techniques for

securing cooperation." Cooperation, then, became the central component of the human relations approach.

Mayo claimed that repetitive tasks, pointless labor, and habitual
obedience created morale problems in the workplace, and few could
disagree. The Hawthorne studies showed that "the locus of industrial
maladjustment is somewhere in the relationship between *person –
work – company policy*, rather than in any individual or individuals"
(1960: 112). Invoking Durkheim's notion of anomie and bolstering his
studies with references to ethnographies of working-class neighborhoods, Mayo argued that the cultural norms of an industrial society
could work in both positive and negative ways. In the best cases,
people connect to society through their work and their work-related
identities. They take on visible roles in the social system that reflect
well on their communities. Professional pride in such roles are often
promoted, as in New York City where the police and fire departments
are commonly referred to as "New York's Finest" and "New York's
Bravest," respectively. This personal identification with the purposes
of the organization fosters cooperation and even commitment.

The anomie part comes in where the industrial norms work against
the lived experience of workers. Anyone who has ever worked in
retail, for example, with the security cameras focused on the workers
rather than the customers, can understand what it is like to be seen
and treated as a threat or a problem just for showing up to work.
Industrial practices that view workers as inherently suspicious, Mayo
indicated, teach workers, and the entire working class, not to trust
businesses or other large formal institutions. Not only would this
process make it difficult to manage the workers, but – and this is
the driving motivation behind his work – it would create a moral
failure for workplace relations that could spill over into all relations
with formal organizations and institutions. New rules and harsher
work production quotas could not just be imposed upon the workers
without furthering their experience of disconnection from the organizational world, resulting in a sense of isolation, competition, and
demoralization. This did not foster cooperation.

Mayo pinned his hopes on a professionally trained "administrative
elite" who could view complex industrial organizations as part of a
functioning society. These leaders would inspire collaboration on the
part of the workforce with the higher purposes of the organization.
It is worth noting that much of Mayo's writing on this topic occurred
during the Depression, and the subject of his comparisons was less
often Taylor and Fayol and more often the Soviet Union. Mayo was
advocating a compassionate capitalism. Industry must thrive, but
workers must also benefit. Still, while industry thrived on profits,
workers were apparently suffering from a lack of attention to their

non-material needs. Wages mattered, he admitted, but bonuses were better because they promoted a sense of belonging. Bonuses, however, had to be tied to job performance and not habits and personality as Ford's system had done. Mayo wanted managers to earn workers' commitment to the organization, not force their obedience.

A contemporary and colleague of Mayo's, Chester Barnard, likewise championed the human approach to industrial management. What Mayo termed collaboration, Barnard describes as "cooperation among men that is conscious, deliberate, purposeful" (1938: 4). His model of leadership also included giving attention to worker goals and desires. But a good deal of the job involved finding and providing the kinds of incentives that would not simply reward good work, but restore workers' faith that their contracts represented a moral arrangement as well as an economic one. Proper administration, then, was not about how to make a worker work. It was about inducing workers to choose to contribute fully. Even more than Mayo had, Barnard saw his proposals as consequential for relations beyond the work world.

Barnard presented his thesis almost as though Taylor and Fayol were irrelevant historical anomalies. Those figures of rational thinking had defined workers as an extension of the machinery of production, specifically the most difficult part of the machinery. For them, organizations were all about achieving goals, and the people in them were simply resources to be put to use. Barnard brushed that aside. The technology is not important, he wrote. An organization is a collection of people whose efforts are coordinated. Organizations, in his view, organized values. Though the point could be lost in Barnard's dry prose, this was a radical breakthrough for administrative theory.

Further, with polite nods to Durkheim, Weber, and others, Barnard (1938: 68–9) casually notes that organizations are not defined by their structures at all, but by the actions that go on within them. And since people actually belong to many organizations, and also spend time away from all organizations, even the most integrated and cooperative person will have multiple loyalties and potentially conflicting commitments. The primary concern of the executive, then, is with "the survival of cooperation" within the organization (1938: 7).

The shift in focus from control to cooperation was important for the organization of firms and the experiences of those who worked in them. But what is this cooperation based on? The first assumption of this approach is that people have social needs, that they prefer to be a part of something collective, and that they enjoy committing their loyalties to a group. Such commitments are not based on rational calculation but on non-rational needs, on finding meaning in one's actions. In the language of cultural studies, organizations create meaning. Participation in an organization can be seen as more or less meaningful, depending on how well the mission and philosophy of the organization is defined and presented.

Such commitment is familiar in settings outside of work. Evangelists stand on street corners in all weather, or go door to door, representing their churches. Political advocates leave their paid jobs to work on behalf of causes to which they are dedicated. Athletes train themselves nearly to death on occasion, and too many writers, artists, and poets to count have lived under conditions of hardship and uncertainty in order to create their work. With artists, spiritualists, and some professionals, we speak of having a calling to the task. (That is the real meaning of the word "vocation," though we tend to use it as a synonym for "job.") It is uncommon to approach a job as a calling, to feel compelled from within to do your work. Nor did Barnard expect to create a sense of religious zeal in the hearts of every factory worker. He merely observed that most systems of workplace control and surveillance worked against the possibility of ever identifying with the job, or the organization, to any useful degree at all. By concentrating on members' commitments, Barnard was trying to create a workplace where people could feel a sense of personal attachment.

Barnard's writings on cooperation had included some amount of manipulation. Given the observation, for example, that workers appreciate the *feeling* of being taken seriously when a company installs a suggestion box, it was not a far step for the corporate world to adopt the practice of collecting suggestions without actually reading them. After all, Barnard had not said anything about implementing the suggestions. It remains an open question, then, to what extent industrial leaders used Barnard's approach to earn the trust and cooperation of their workforce, and to what extent they used it to manipulate people into doing what they were told. This ambiguity is not just a historical artifact. Even as Barnard was publishing his prescriptions, readers were divided.

The apotheosis of this ambiguity was offered by Philip Selznick, most notably in his classic study *TVA and the Grassroots*. In this extensive case study of a huge public works project, Selznick followed the development of a new form of organizational administration from its inception through multiple incarnations to the qualified success that it became in time. The TVA (Tennessee Valley Authority) was a unique organization, and the project impacted a wide and diverse population of **stakeholders**. Established in 1933, it was at that time the largest hydroelectric/flood control project ever attempted. The TVA declared upfront its commitment to working with organized labor, to hiring black workers, and to paying all workers fair wages (Neuse, 1983). The events that Selznick studied were shaped by politics and economics at the federal, state, and local levels, as well as by community organizing, conflicting ideologies, and incompatible goals. Amazingly, the long-term impact of this singular study can actually be summarized in a single word: *co-optation*.

The TVA and the hearts of men

Selznick took Barnard's concept of cooperation and ran with it. But then, to an even larger degree, the TVA had done the same thing. With the TVA, Selznick had a case study in which project administrators sought to extend the idea of cooperation to its limit. Rather than merely accept worker input, in the hopes that it would create a more contented workforce, the TVA sought to democratize and decentralize the whole decision-making process, incorporating not only organizational participants, but Valley residents and a number of voluntary associations. In theory, if all of the stakeholders were involved in all of the planning stages, then they would be inherently committed to the same goals and outcomes as the authority itself. The TVA wanted more than cooperation. The administration of the TVA sought to "absorb" elements of the views and values of the organization's participants and to reflect those values in the organization's operations and decisions.

Selznick credits Barnard with having demonstrated the need to ensure the willing cooperation of organizational participants at all levels. The failure of Taylorism, he thought, was that people "resist depersonalization" and prefer to "participate as *wholes*" (Selznick, 1949: 26). With TVA, Selznick discerned an effort to put this idea into practice.

By elevating some workers into higher-status decision processes, trading favors, spending money, and providing opportunities for prestige and influence, the TVA was able to create new interests for some of the people and groups whose cooperation they most needed. For personal reasons, then, as well as collective needs, these stakeholders had something of their own to lose if TVA did not succeed. The authority co-opted the attention and priorities of those with whom it had to negotiate, which made the negotiations much easier. The accomplishment of the TVA was largely political. Project administrators built coalitions of support with the different interest groups within and outside of the agency. In a classic Chester Barnard kind of move, they convinced the different groups of people involved that what they wanted to do was probably about the best option available. They secured cooperation without requiring that everyone agree with them about everything or even that everyone had to do what they said. They convinced people to go along with them anyway.

This approach was far more complex and sophisticated than it might seem at first glance. To accomplish this, the TVA violated several of the defining characteristics of formal organizations. They blurred the boundaries between those inside the organization and those outside. They broke the chain of command to require participants high up on the ladder to seek consent from participants below. They allowed workers to work through informal channels of communication and authority to find their own solutions, rather than forcing them to follow the chain of command. And they defined the goals of the organization in terms that depended on the goals of the participants, rather than forcing the usual sharp distinction between them. And it worked, for the most part. The "grassroots administration" was not always literally respected. Nonetheless, in Selznick's assessment, it served as a "morally sustaining idea" that the legitimacy of the leadership of the TVA derived from the participation of the other stakeholders.

Selznick was clear that he was not interested in describing a better way to manipulate workers. "The significance of cooptation for organizational analysis is not simply that there is a change in or a broadening of leadership . . . but also that *this change is consequential for the character and role of the organization*" (1948: 35; emphasis in original). The organization adapts. It responds to external interests and becomes a different kind of organization according to the needs of its participants and others in the community.

Selznick thus raised a new question about the social purpose of organizations. The TVA project was not a firm; it was a public works investment, the goal of which was to serve the Tennessee Valley and beyond. It was intended to provide both electricity and good jobs. Hence, when Selznick looked at the "character" of the organization, he was asking how well the organization served those who depended on it. He worked with the radical notion that the organization had obligations to its employees and its community. Barnard and others had asked what workers' goals were, and when did they conflict with the goals of the organization. Selznick asked what workers' goals were and how well could the organization serve them.

There are many ways to describe the impact of Selznick's TVA analysis on organizational studies. Certainly, the concept of co-optation has become an essential part of the field as a result. The study of social relations in formal organizations moved beyond the human relations perspective to incorporate this perspective. And once Selznick had raised the issue of the social impact of organizations on the communities in which they are situated, it was more difficult for future analysts to overlook it. From my perspective, however, his key accomplishment was to reconnect organizational studies to sociological theory. Selznick's work drew upon the guiding questions that we saw in chapter 2: what kind of society are we building and what kinds of organizations serve its needs? Selznick thereby laid the groundwork for the American social theorist/organizational analyst of the mid-twentieth century, Robert King Merton.

What workers feel

Over several decades of writing, Merton drew attention to the unanticipated impact of everything on everything else. Specifically, Merton was concerned with the fact that we regularly act thinking only of the consequences we wanted, as though those were the only consequences that mattered. We can't ever know all of the likely results of our actions. Nonetheless, we tend to act as though that wasn't a problem (Merton, 1936). More generally, sociologists (and others) lacked any sort of well-developed theory of unintended consequences, focusing instead on expected outcomes. Merton criticized economic models of "rational man," for example, for implying on the one hand that a rational actor could actually calculate the real results of his [sic] actions prior to making a decision while, on the other hand, assuming that a social actor could be counted on to narrowly pursue his own interests without concern for the larger social impact of his actions.

Drawing on both Marx and Weber, Merton examined the impact of bureaucracy on the lives of working people in industrial societies. The rules and structures of bureaucracy, he noted, condition us to do particular tasks rapidly, efficiently, and without thought. This is the intended consequence while at work, which makes us efficient at our jobs. An unintended by-product is that this high level of skill and training leaves us mostly unfit to do anything else. We minimize our own skill set and limit our adaptability by repetitively practicing those tasks that our jobs require of us. Rational systems, it seems, have irrational consequences.

This "incapacity" did not just apply to pig-iron handlers. Merton had no difficulty demonstrating its effect in a modern office. Nor was it much of a stretch for him to connect the actions of the office, or the many thousands of such offices, to a worldview, a way of living and thinking, and, ultimately, to a way of feeling.

> For reasons which we have already noted, the bureaucratic structure exerts a constant pressure upon the official to be "methodical, prudent, disciplined." If the bureaucracy is to operate successfully, it must attain a high degree of reliability of behavior, an unusual degree of conformity with prescribed patterns of action. Hence, the fundamental importance of discipline which may be as highly developed in

a religious or economic bureaucracy as in the army. Discipline can be effective only if the ideal patterns are buttressed by strong sentiments which entail devotion to one's duties, a keen sense of the limitation of one's authority and competence, and methodological performance of routine activities. The efficacy of social structure depends ultimately upon infusing group participants with appropriate attitudes and sentiments. (Merton 1968 [1957]: 252)

Committing ourselves to our jobs, as the human relations theorists wanted, requires us to develop an "appropriate" set of values and attachments that are consistent with the needs of the organization. But, contrary to the fears and stratagems of that school of thought, over-conformity could be as great a problem as under-conformity. Indeed, Merton suggested, working in a bureaucracy was itself the most effective training for thinking like a bureaucrat. The greater the pressure that is on the worker to perform his or her task with the desired discipline and speed, the deeper the conditioning may run. This makes us more rigid in our thinking when we need to be flexible, and more attuned to following the rules than to achieving our deeper purposes.

One does not often hear that being highly practiced at something is a limitation. The problem can be better expressed as a thought experiment. Imagine any given bureaucratic organization. Now suppose that there are workers there who occasionally prefer to go outside of the regular system of rules and procedures. Such actions would be viewed with suspicion, and might be thought to introduce inconsistencies and inefficiencies. These workers would not do well in the bureaucracy because they do not embody the principles of reliability and consistency. Now imagine that you are a successful employee in such a tightly functioning office, and you become responsible for processing some case or other that was a bit unusual. You could deal with it effectively, with a little innovation and flexibility. Or you could process it in the usual way, which you know wouldn't be as good. Which do you do? If you are committed to the larger mission of the organization, you innovate. But if you are well trained and fully engaged with the values of the organization, you keep quiet about that and just do your job. Hence, "over-conformity" to the system creates its own inefficiencies and failures. Bureaucracy defeats itself by creating a class of bureaucrats whose main problem is that they are committed to their work. This insight is unlikely to amaze anyone who has ever worked within a cubicle, but it had quite an impact when it was first put into words.

Once people started looking at it, bureaucracy was easily shown to be irrational on many levels, contrary to Weber's analysis and all that had followed it. Alvin Gouldner (1954), for example, demonstrated that strict rules, regular procedures, and a clear chain of command yielded a complex system of negotiations through which workers and supervisors manipulated one another. A manager or foreman could try to elicit greater cooperation from his or her workers by selectively ignoring certain rules that the workers didn't like. This made the supervisor and the workers co-conspirators against the company, engendering personal loyalty by undermining the system. As well, the company might pressure the workers to conspire in the avoidance of health or safety rules that slowed production down or added costs, though this created the risk that people would get hurt or that a disgruntled worker would report them. Similarly, workers could slow things down or create inefficiencies by choosing to follow every rule on the books. Given the vast number of checks, reviews, and meetings that any moderate-sized bureaucracy might "require" for any kind of task, a literal interpretation of the whole package would bring most workplaces to a standstill. This tactic has been used as a threat during contract negotiations. Further, supervisors used rules as an excuse, claiming that they shared the workers' preferences about some issue or another, but that they were bound by the rule. Rules can, of course, be selectively invoked as punishments, threats, or deliberate acts of discrimination. And, since workers routinely violate one rule or another practically every day, the occasional documentation of them could be used to justify firing or demoting any workers who create problems for their supervisors. Ultimately, a highly bureaucratized organization is able to function with just as much arbitrary behavior, unpredictability, and personal interest as any aristocracy.

Bureaucracy as a culture

The image of the over-conforming, white-shirted office worker became a staple of both academic and popular works of the 1950s and early 1960s, including films, plays, and novels. William H. Whyte's *The Organization Man* (1956) contrasted the "generation of bureaucrats" with "the well-rounded man" who had a life outside of work. C. Wright Mills's *White Collar: The American Middle Classes* found the new bureaucratic person to be "more often pitiable than tragic" (1956: xii). Erving Goffman's *The Presentation of Self in Everyday Life* (1959) described the professional demeanor of a corporate employee as a "performance" rooted in the local norms and expectations of the work environment. It seemed that years of management efforts to mold and constrain the lives and qualities of workers had also molded and constrained the lives and qualities of managers. We were all good workers; but our values, desires, and imaginations had diminished.

The critique of bureaucratic life was more often psychological, symbolic, or philosophical rather than organizational. One could argue that it was, in fact, Durkheimian. The major critics of the period raised concerns about the big social issues. What sort of people were we? What did we value? Bureaucratic offices and factories might be rational ways to accomplish our industrial goals, but was that the best organizing principle for our lives? Given the fact that rational systems of organizing relied on clearly defined lines of authority and obedience, then part of our training for the industrial world involved learning to obey. Such a training, according to this critique, began in our schools where children were organized into little work groups and encouraged to discipline themselves in preparation for their eventual contributions to the social order.

Erving Goffman (1959, 1971) emphasized the symbolic dimensions of life in a highly organized world. One familiar aspect of his analysis is that employees must do more than simply take work-related instructions from their supervisors. They must constantly reinforce their willingness to be led, to demonstrate their deference to their superiors. Office life wasn't just about work. It was about who sat closer to the windows and who got on the elevators ahead of whom else. Executives had to act like leaders, whether they were leading or not. Receptionists had to look receptive. In short, Goffman argued, the social order of the workplace had to be clearly communicated and reinforced constantly through language, acts, and ritualistic behaviors.

Earlier, I had introduced working definitions for organizations and institutions and briefly considered the relationship between the two. In order to study culture within organizations, it helps to expand upon those definitions a bit. This will help to introduce the "new institutional" perspective on organizational analysis which provides the framework for understanding the culture of organizations.

If an organization is a named and identifiable group with structures, practices, goals, and members, then we can now ask, what is organized by this entity? That is, what makes an organization more than just a group? An organization has goals. Therefore the structure of relations and functions within it *organize* the tasks necessary to pursue these goals. Activities are organized. An organization is also a structured system of interactions, both formal and informal, some of which are fairly stable and some of which change more rapidly. So social relations and human interactions are organized.

Familiar patterns of organized activities and social relations carry with them values, normative expectations, and the appearance of naturalness. That is, the more we organize aspects of our lives around consistent and recognizable ideas, the more those ideas become taken for granted and even take on a life of their own. This process by which an idea, that was once seen as one option among many, comes to be seen as the way in which the world works is called **institutionaliza- tion**. And the conceptual models that describe how this happens in and through organizations are known collectively as institutional theory. Selznick's analysis of how the informal and formal proce- dures at TVA merged to form a new set of practices, for example, is a classic work of institutional theory. In that case, novel ideas about project planning and plant operations moved, over time, from being strangely unfamiliar to just being "how things are done here."

Once particular ideas become institutionalized within the world of formal organizations, they take on a life of their own beyond any given setting. A small business, for example, may have a customer service desk in which one employee of limited authority attempts to deal with customers' problems and questions. An international conglomerate may have a customer service center with scores of employees doing the same thing via phone banks. Likewise a govern- ment agency might set up a service bureau to serve much the same function for their clients. The nature and limitations of customer support in a modern industrial bureaucracy are familiar to most of us, so that we can imagine what they do and how they do it without needing to know anything about what products the small busi- ness sells, what industry the conglomerate is in, or what services the government agency performs. "Customer service" represents an institutionalized – familiar, taken-for-granted, and mostly inflexible – area of organized life.

Goffman (1961) introduced the term "total institution" to define places where some institution completely defines the life of those within it. Prisons and mental institutions are clear examples, along with military units, cloisters and abbeys, and some boarding schools. The institutions are total in the sense that all aspects of the inmates' lives are determined by them. Inmates eat, sleep, or socialize when, where, and with whom the institution tells them. Total institutions have strict hierarchies with an absolute barrier between the staff, who give instructions, and the inmates, who take instructions. Goffman's study of the inner workings of asylums is a fascinating fieldwork study that offers many contributions to the study of organizations. Among them is the observation that all formally organized systems share characteristics with total institutions. In a sense, all of the organizations that we have looked at so far are institutional, to a degree. The total institution defines just how highly institutionalized an institution can be.

Consider the simple question of "appropriate behavior." Out in the free world, individuals act, dress, and speak as they wish, within some generally understood limits. One of the most important "entrance rituals" for a new inmate, then, is the "unlearning" of many of these forms of expression. The inmate's clothing is taken away and replaced by some kind of uniform. In most cases, this extends to cutting their hair, taking away any make-up or jewelry, and basically teaching them to look, act, and speak like the rest of the inmates. As an experiment, you might try visiting different workplaces – a fast-food restaurant, a bank, or a high-end clothing retailer. Watch the staff for a bit; listen to them speak with each other or with customers. How alike are they, and how much individual expression are they allowed? This will give you a sense of how thoroughly the social life of this place has been institutionalized. You might look at yourself as well, at work or at school, and ask how much your appearance or language has changed since you came into that setting. But don't panic. If you have changed to blend in, this doesn't necessarily mean that you are being forced or pressured to do something artificial. You might just be very skilled at reading the local codes and symbols, and at adapting them to your own needs. These are social skills that we learn through our time at work and in school.

Highly institutionalized features of life or behavior pass beyond question or discussion. "Social knowledge once institutionalized exists as a fact, as part of objective reality," Lynne Zucker explained. Whatever decisions or concerns once existed about this knowledge, it has ceased to be a question and has become instead an answer. "For highly institutionalized acts, it is sufficient for one person simply to tell another that this is how things are done" (Zucker 1977: 726). Similarly, a group or organization may present itself as special by comparing itself to the others in its field and claiming, "We do things differently here."

Rules and procedures, whatever their original purpose, also become institutionalized within organizations. To the extent that everyone in some setting agrees on, or at least recognizes this local knowledge, the easier it is to organize everyone's cooperation. More than just familiar patterns of behavior, the recognized and repeated ways of doing things take on lives of their own, to the point where it would be difficult to justify doing something else. They become mythic, as John Meyer and Brian Rowan described it. "Institutionalized products, services, techniques, policies, and programs function as powerful myths, and many organizations adopt them ceremonially" (1977: 340). Bureaucratic forms and procedures are just one example of a model that has been institutionalized throughout the organizational world. There are non-bureaucratic forms and practices as well that may have equal power. Just as the British Prime Minister must ceremonially ask the Queen for the right to serve, CEOs must report annually to shareholders. Both of these ceremonies have some use, but the enactment of them is mostly scripted in advance, and only one outcome would be acceptable to the participants. The Queen is no more likely to say no than the CEO is to say that he or she has done a lousy job. Still, it would not seem right, or legitimate, to skip the process.

Even where a better, faster, cheaper, or more efficient technique exists, these mythic methods and means come to define the culture of an organization and must be adhered to. Neither rational considerations nor interpersonal strategies can explain the decision-making process where legitimacy is at stake. Institutionalized practices embody that which is considered legitimate in an organizational culture.

The practices that achieve this taken-for-granted status are not arbitrary. Meyer and Rowan describe the many benefits of a standardized toolkit for organizers. Firms can be created more quickly and new functions introduced within existing organizations if they are created along easily recognizable forms. More importantly, since certainty and predictability are often valued more than efficiency, institutionalized procedures may be valued most for their familiarity. This also means, however, that certain forms of organizing will be adopted because they are institutionalized, without much concern for their specific qualities. Meyer and Rowan observe:

> Ceremonial activity is significant in relation to categorical rules, not in its concrete effects. A sick worker must be treated by a doctor using accepted medical procedures; whether the worker is treated effectively is less important. A bus company must service required routes whether or not there are many passengers. A university must maintain appropriate departments independently of the departments' enrollments. Activity, that is, has ritual significance: it maintains appearances and validates an organization. (1977: 355)

As individuals within organizations, we must think of how our actions *appear* to others, sometimes even more than the actual intended consequences of our acts. Decision-makers may be punished for making a good decision by questionable means, just as they are protected from punishment when using institutionalized means, even if the results are poor. In order for your actions to seem legitimate, you must go through the expected steps. In a sense, you have to demonstrate conformity.

In one test of this idea, Martha Feldman and James March studied "information gathering" as a ceremony of mythic quality in the decision-making process. Information is useful, of course, but their work focused on the necessity of being seen to gather information. Among their findings, they concluded that:

> (1) Much of the information that is gathered and communicated by individuals and organizations has little decision relevance. (2) Much of the information that is used to justify a decision is collected and interpreted after the decision has been made, or substantially made. (3) Much of the information gathered in response to requests for information is not considered in the making of decisions for which it was requested. (1981: 174)

Nonetheless, it would be quite challenging to justify important decisions if one did not make a show of collecting data first. Thus, while information gathering is clearly a justifiable act in a rational sense, much of it is done for ceremonial purposes, to show that one is doing the proper thing.

Everett Hughes anticipated these results in his discussion of how the division of labor at work is distinguished from the division of responsibility:

> David Riesman . . . tells of the wonderful briefs which young lawyers draw up for presentation to lower court judges who can scarcely read them, much less judge the law that is in them. The ritual of looking up all the past cases, and the art of arguing out all possibilities are gone through, even when the lawyer knows that the decision will be made upon a much simpler – perhaps also a much sounder-basis. What is more: the ritual and the art are respected, and the men who perform them with brilliance and finesse are admired. The simple client may be dazzled, but at some point he is also likely to think that he is being done by the whole guild of lawyers, including his own, the opposing counsel, and the court. In a sense, the art and cult of the law are being maintained at his expense. The legal profession believes, in some measure, in the cult of the law. (1951: 324)

Organizational cultures at work

Cultural theorists have come to define organizations as both systems of meaning and sites where meaning is produced. Thus an organization may be said to cultivate a particular kind of culture. That is, as the organization comes to institutionalize particular ways of doing things, participants in that organization will "learn" the value of doing those things. Further, as those participants who embrace the preferred practices tend to be rewarded more readily than those who don't, one also learns the value of just going along with the flow. Alternatively, some kinds of culture might shape an organization despite its leaders' efforts and intent to do otherwise. A high-risk culture might permeate certain organizations, for example, despite the organization's efforts to discourage risk-taking. Factors that arise both from within and from beyond an organization change the culture of an organization, which alters its practices and priorities. For example, as many of the "old guard" of an organization retire or are promoted, and many new people come in, the culture of the organization may shift with the change in personnel. At the same time, a strong sense of cultural persistence within an organization may create a powerful buffer against change, even when change is needed. That is, when people retire or leave more slowly, and the new people coming in are trained in the familiar ways of doing things, then it may become difficult for members of an organization to imagine better ways of doing things.

The culture of an organization interacts with the world outside. As Frank Dobbin observed, the larger culture within which modern industry developed tends to be rational and calculative, and very much in line with bureaucratic thinking even in situations where this would not seem to be the most useful orientation. Both the proliferation of bureaucratic cultures and values within organizations and the distrust accorded to other organizational forms can therefore be treated as reflections of the culture. Nonetheless, organizational cultures are distinct from one another across different segments of society and sectors of organizing. There is a great deal about an organization's culture that is cultivated from within. And many activities and ceremonies may become markers of legitimacy that have little to do with bureaucratic norms. Just as IBM cultivated a culture of cautious planning, for example, Microsoft cultivated a culture of not being IBM. Where IBMers became noted for blue suits with white shirts, Microsoft managers during that company's rise in the 1980s famously wore sneakers to work.

In some notable cases, an organizational culture can be remarkably out of alignment with the wider culture. Chapter 5 will consider some of these cases, including highly masculine work environments that encourage gender discrimination, and "high-risk" cultures that implicitly encourage finance managers to get around accountability and regulation. More often, a "local culture," or a unique sub-culture, can develop within a workplace or other organization, defined in terms of shared experiences that are unfamiliar beyond the one group. Over time, the sub-cultural properties of the group reinforce one another through language and behaviors that are infused with meaning that others cannot see.

Organizational studies traditionally looked at the "normal" characteristics of organizations without much attention to the ways in which deviant cases or unique sub-cultures can develop inside them. This has changed in the past few decades. Sociologists have begun to incorporate cultural studies and anthropological research into the study of organizations, revealing complex and deeply rooted organizational cultures. As Gary Alan Fine has noted, "The cultural forms that characterize an organization fall into numerous traditional genres: slang or jargon, jokes, ideology, sagas and histories, rituals and ceremonies, and stories" (1984: 243). Corporate culture certainly has its own variation on conventional language, as do high-tech cultures, sports cultures, and media cultures. Think of jocks, geeks, punks, and gear-heads, and you will begin to get a sense of how people with shared interests and experiences come to be seen as a separate culture with its own language, **rituals**, and possibly hairstyles.

A large bureaucracy may develop a culture of conformity, for example, if it is widely perceived that rules are valued more highly than outcomes. Alternatively, some group within that bureaucracy may cultivate a culture of innovation, either because it is expected of them or because they have found a way to get away with it. To put that in a different language, participants in an organization negotiate acceptable and expected ways of doing things, justifications for those ways, and acceptable variations on them. If a sub-group within a larger structure had some reason to be different, they might be able to convince others that these differences are consistent with the shared goals of the organization. Certain workers might negotiate a more relaxed dress code, flexible hours, or a penchant for risk-taking if their interactions with others are not disturbed by such deviance.

A brief personal story comes to mind. A couple of decades ago, I worked for one of the world's largest computer firms. One evening, the night before a holiday, I had completed my work day and gone home for dinner, when I decided to go back to work to finish my current project before the long weekend. Dressed in blue jeans and a T-shirt, I returned to work to put in three or four hours of unpaid overtime. The following Monday, when I arrived at work at my scheduled time of 8:06 a.m., people were already talking about how I had been seen speaking with a high-level manager while wearing a T-shirt. The fact that I was doing work in my spare time meant nothing compared to the *faux pas* of dressing as though I didn't take my job seriously. To my mind, this was not a results-oriented work culture. Compliance with the behavioral norms of the corporation had become more important than getting things done.

Culture shift

The field of cultural studies is something of a sub-culture of its own, with its own language and values. One of the ideas that we can take from this field is that of multiple "logics," referring to the variety of ways of planning and pursuing goals that are available to us simultaneously in any setting. Sometimes these logics can contradict each other, which mostly leaves us free to choose. For example, if I want to borrow money, I might reflect on how credit is the engine of a working economy. On the other hand, if you want to borrow money from me, I might recall Shakespeare's advice to be "neither a borrower nor a lender." Both logics are sound.

Ann Swidler (1986) has written of such logics as our cultural "tool kits," containing different languages, values, associations, and meaning systems that we draw upon selectively or habitually as a situation requires. Applying this notion to formal organizational settings, organizational theorists Roger Friedland and Robert Alford investigate "institutional logics" – ways of thinking that are learned through observation and which seem more like simple reality than a set of choices or preferences. Friedland and Alford observe that members of such organizations typically share many of the cultural assumptions imported from the wider society, as well as their unique experiences within the organization. But the experiences of the organization are interpreted through the filter of the culture at large. "The central institutions of the contemporary capitalist West – capitalist market, bureaucratic state, democracy, nuclear family, and Christian religion – shape individual preferences and organizational interests as well as the repertoire of behaviors by which they may attain them. These institutions are potentially contradictory and hence make multiple logics available to individuals and organizations" (1991: 232).

The capitalist institutional logic is a powerful one in industrial nations, particularly in the United States which has never had a strong labor party. This cultural context places a very high value on employment, defines citizens primarily by their occupations, and supports the authority of management over workers in most conditions. Workers are therefore prepared to accept a limited amount of personal control over their work day and to accommodate disagreements with their supervisors. It is part of what we're paid for. Even so, an abrupt change in work practices may be perceived by workers, or volunteers in other circumstances, as a violation of the taken-for-granted ways in which things are done. This can create a sense of shock and deep unease, or worse.

Suppose, for example, you worked for a company that proclaimed it never laid workers off, even in hard times. This is a strong statement of commitment to the employees. It might lead you to feel more committed to them in return. Now imagine that one day the company announced that it was laying off a large mass of people. Clearly, their boast about past commitments was not a promise about future behavior. On the surface of things, you might start worrying about your own job security. But deeper down, your whole sense of identity as a member of that company will have been upended. The sudden and unexpected change could well feel like a betrayal of the *person–work –company policy* relationship.

This sort of violation can significantly transform a workplace from a culture of cooperation to one of opposition. And, as Rick Fantasia (1988) demonstrates, a workplace culture of opposition to management can become a culture of worker solidarity, collectively risking jobs and incomes in the face of management practices that they can no longer accommodate. Strikes, slowdowns, and just general bad feeling can easily follow.

A cultural shift can also occur when an organization gives explicit attention to the unquestioned assumptions of its relationship with staff, participants, or employees as the case may be. Daniel Zwerdling (1984) extensively studied the movement toward workplace democracy that flourished somewhat in the industrial nations during the 1970s. Such "experiments" were, above all else, attempts to revolutionize the entire concept of a workplace culture. Drawing on the experiences of the TVA and other cases of participatory management, the workplace democracy movement sought to "humanize" the work world, to break the sharp distinction between work and "life." Democratically managed workplaces were about more than changes in authority structures. They created innovative policies to accommodate people's non-work obligations, reduce job stress, and create a new feeling towards participation.

One of Zwerdling's more dramatic case studies was that of IGP, a privately owned insurance company that switched overnight to worker co-ownership. Remarkably, this massive reorganization did not emerge from worker demands or out of any gradual changes in the nature of the organization. In fact, up to that point the company had been a fairly traditional small business with a hierarchical chain of command. On his own initiative, the president of the company simply announced that the workers would own half the company from that day forward. Initially, employees were confused and suspicious of the move. In time, however, workers did become active in leadership, voted themselves more benefits, relaxed the surveillance and control mechanisms, and formed self-guided work teams. The work teams took over the hiring and firing responsibilities for their areas, and when the board of directors attempted to reintroduce a traditional hierarchy in 1977, the board was voted out (Zwerdling 1984: 117–18). The culture of the organization had changed.

In sum, culture in the largest sense shapes the culture of organizations. Also, an organization's culture can depart from the norms of the culture at large. And, as elements of organizational cultures become institutionalized across multiple industries, the culture at large is shaped by cultural forces that emerge from these industries. You can see elements of this as business jargon or technical jargon work their way into popular culture.

Dress for success

European and North American popular culture raised the alarm about faceless bureaucrats from the late 1950s on. The late 1960s witnessed the rise of a youth counterculture that dressed in traditional workman's clothes – blue jeans – and rejected "the establishment" norms. The seventies gave rise to workplace democracy movements, *Small is Beautiful* movements and a back-to-the-land/organic farming movement. A casual observer might have thought that bureaucratic corporate culture had run its course. This, of course, was not the case.

From 1930 through 1980, at least 30 success manuals achieved long runs as *New York Times* best-sellers (Biggart, 1983). The year 1980 alone saw three popular powerhouses: *How You Can Become Financially Independent by Investing in Real Estate*; *Crisis Investing*; and *The Sky's the Limit*. And 1980 was also the year that Ronald Reagan was elected President in the US, one year after Margaret Thatcher had been elected Prime Minister of the UK, ushering in a powerful "conservative realignment" in both nations. Countercultural movements notwithstanding, Americans were still reading *How to Win Friends and Influence People*, the highly influential success manual from the 1930s.

Nicole Woolsey Biggart examined the advice and imagery of these 30 books, charting the rise and fall of four dominant themes across those turbulent decades. Although several books from the 1970s actually advised readers to seek happiness outside of work, they were over-matched by "entrepreneurial schemes" and "manipulation manuals." As Biggart summarized the trends, "these four themes directly reflect the socially approved work opportunities defined by an advanced industrial system; they show no evidence of protest against what Marxist scholars have described as an alienated work life." As for the millions of readers who kept these books on the best-seller lists, "workers apply to themselves the techniques and routines of modern organizational activity; that is, they 'self-manage'" (1983: 299).

Professional journals, seminars, and job-training programs also help teach people how to make themselves more desirable as employees. Stories about competent professionals whose careers were undermined by their casual dress or informal manner are routinely offered as cautionary tales – not as a caution against arbitrary systems of judgment but as a warning against neglecting care for one's appearance (Smith, 1998). Much of this work takes off from Goffman's writings about the ways in which we "present ourselves" in different settings. "Similarly," Goffman observed, "executives often project an air of competency and general grasp of the situation, blinding themselves and others to the fact that they hold their jobs partly because they look like executives, not because they can work like executives" (1959: 47).

While US workers were studying techniques for molding themselves into committed strivers for advancement, corporations were hiring armies of consultants to teach them the best techniques to capitalize on this trend. Managers explicitly sought to "engineer" their companies' cultures, as Gideon Kunda documented. In Kunda's study of a successful high-tech firm, ambitious professionals made public displays of commitment, working themselves to the point of burnout, competitively depriving themselves of sleep, and pushing their groups to meet impossible deadlines. Management encouraged such competitive overwork, organizing a two-day indoctrination seminar to teach the culture to new hires, and bolstering the message with periodic team-building events and related ceremonies of community. Interestingly, Kunda found that employees viewed the seminars as manipulative and distrusted most of the assurances about community. But in their actions and their words they strove to demonstrate their commitment to "the culture." It was, first of all, the only clear path to promotion. But also it was just the way things were done there. Artificial, unhealthy, and controlling, that was the culture they had chosen to join.

In Kunda's case study, a particular kind of culture was deliberately cultivated to serve identifiable and familiar goals: produce more stuff for the same cost. Two notes of caution should be added here. First, while various participants can seek to alter the culture of an organization, it is not something that can just be assigned. Culture happens in the constant interactions and re-combinations of people's ideas, values, goals, and beliefs. This leads to the second caution. We need to look at organizational goals and organizational cultures separately.

Conclusions

Out in the larger world, we know that culture is not a monolithic entity. There are sub-cultures and countercultures and local cultures. You might occasionally read about a gun culture or a dance culture, the military culture or the car culture. Organizations are part of this cultural landscape and they cultivate their own local norms, customs, and ways of doing things. In the case of the high-tech firm studied by Kunda, they called it "the culture." Often, however, the differences between the culture of an organization and the culture in which that organization operates will be small, unnamed, and mostly unnoticed. In a society driven by belief in a work ethic, organizational cultures will tend to demand signs of commitment to one's job. In a society in which peace and reconciliation are paramount, organizations will downplay the impact of their internal hierarchy and stress other values, such as open communication.

What makes organizational culture unique in many of the studies that we've reviewed is that the organizational context filters out much of the diversity of social life. The world inside the organization is smaller, more homogeneous, more directed, and more rule-bound. In such conditions, questionable beliefs, common assumptions, and familiar perspectives reinforce one another, and may amplify. If those shared ideas include a belief in the value of competition, the organizational life may be highly competitive. If cooperation is valued, then competitive behavior is likely to be viewed with much greater disdain within the organization than outside it. And if a small number of people don't quite share those assumptions, things might get rough for them. The following chapter will have more to say about that.

Key Readings

Barnard, Chester I. 1938 *The Functions of the Executive*. Cambridge, MA: Harvard University Press.
   Barnard's theories on organizations laid the foundations for much of the human relations movement that followed. While centered on the tasks of management and administration, the book covers far more ground than the word "functions" would imply. This is Barnard's definitive work on why and how organization theory needed to change from its rational-theory perspective to something more human.
Gouldner, Alvin W. 1954 *Patterns of Industrial Bureaucracy*. Glencoe, IL: Free Press.
   Gouldner demonstrates that the social organization of a workplace exists in a constant state of negotiation among different interests, job levels, professions, and other groupings. Whatever we might think about the consistency, or even the "iron cage" of rules and procedures, the messy reality shows that rules and structures are tools that can serve a wide variety of goals.
Lipsky, Michael 1980 *Street-Level Bureaucracy*. New York: Russell Sage Foundation.
   Lipsky distinguishes between policy decisions that are made in agencies, on the one hand, and actions that people actually take, on the other. He notes that the discretion to follow, bend, or interpret rules is essential to the jobs of service workers who face the clients and have the responsibility to get things done. Whatever else may be wrong with our social services policies and programs, he shows, we are unlikely to ever see improvements if we continue to think abstractly about rules and systems.
Mayo, Elton 1960 [1933] *The Human Problems of an Industrial Civilization*. New York: Viking Press.
   Mayo's presentation of the Hawthorne experiments, from which he derives most of the human relations approach to organizing. A slender book that

spans a world of change, this text demonstrates his keen interpretive abilities at work on an ambiguous set of data.

Merton, Robert K. 1936 "The Unanticipated Consequences of Purposive Social Action." *American Sociological Review*, 1(6): 894–904.

Another powerful blow against the assumption that industry was driven by rational choices. Merton demonstrates that actions have longer-term consequences than we like to imagine, that outcomes rarely occur as planned, and our attempts to treat outcomes as the results of a rational plan are typically made up after the fact.

Meyer, John W., and Brian Rowan 1977 "Institutionalized Organizations: Formal Structure as Myth and Ceremony." *The American Journal of Sociology*, 83(2): 340–63.

This deceptively simple article turned a spotlight on the ways in which we perform "rational" actions for reasons that have little to do with rationality. Myth and ceremony confer legitimacy in a formal organization, and legitimacy is often more essential than efficiency, predictability, or accuracy.

Selznick, Philip 1949 *TVA and the Grassroots: A Study in the Sociology of Formal Organization*. Berkeley, CA: University of California Press.

Selznick's famous case study of the Tennessee Valley Authority demonstrated that the "character" of the organization was shaped by the merging of interests and ideas from the multiple stakeholders in the project. This organizational character, in turn, influenced the values of the participants, all of which had as much if not more influence over the organizational outcomes than did the formal structures and mission.

Swidler, Ann 1986 "Culture in Action: Symbols and Strategies." *American Sociological Review*, 51: 273–86.

A seminal article in the study of culture and in the integration of culture into the study of other things. Swidler shows that culture is not just "out there" to be discovered. Rather, it is fluid and open to interpretation and even strategic uses. In this article, she re-envisions culture as a toolkit from which we selectively pick our tools.

Zucker, Lynne G. 1977 "The Role of Institutionalization in Cultural Persistence." *American Sociological Review*, 42 (October): 726–43.

A pioneering study of how organizational forms and procedures take on a life of their own, and how people come to have faith in them regardless of their practical values. Institutionalization emerges as a dynamic process, less a reaction to the environment and more a series of discoveries, negotiations, and impressions.

CHAPTER
05

Organizational Dysfunctions

W E have seen that organizations are not rational machines, gliding smoothly through predictable and regular operations. Many of the mechanisms of organizational control that are designed to increase rationality also introduce irrationalities. Systems that are designed as though the human beings within them are mere extensions of the machinery run into the reality that people have their own goals and interests, many of which conflict with those of the organization. Employees, volunteers, owners, managers, and investors all vary in their abilities, integrity, and commitment. No amount of coercive control or cooperative communication has ever been able to line up all the human parts to serve only the organization and nothing more. Things just don't always work the way the organization wants them to.

The reverse relationship may also hold. Sometimes, despite the skill and seriousness of the people involved, organizations create failures. We have seen that organizations develop and propagate local cultures that encourage or discourage risks at inopportune times, justify unnecessary actions, suppress unwanted data, and pressure participants to repeat procedures that no longer produce the desired outcomes. All of these irrationalities, chaotic features, and unpredictable interactions among incompatible trends have effects in the world beyond the organizations in which they occur.

This chapter reviews several of the built-in problems with our large organized systems. There are many ways in which problems are built in. In general, however, the risk of problems, failures, crises, and disasters is both always present and always apart from the "normal" functioning of our large systems. We often prefer to think of organizational failures as having been caused by outside factors that are beyond our control. But dysfunction and the potential for greater dysfunction exist alongside positive functioning. Even when our technologies, agencies, and personnel are all doing what they are supposed to, there is a "dark side" to organized systems.

For purposes of discussion, we can characterize these built-in problems as everyday dysfunctions, built-in failures, and disasters. This chapter will show that each of these problems stems in part from familiar organizational characteristics. To some extent, each of them is also the result of expecting too much of our organizations, or possibly just believing in them more than we ought to.

Everyday dysfunction

C. Wright Mills once offered a useful guideline on the difference between an individual problem and a social issue:

> When, in a city of 100,000, only one is unemployed, that is his personal trouble, and for its relief we properly look to the character of the individual, his skills and his immediate opportunities. But when in a nation of 50 million employees, 15 million people are unemployed, that is an issue, and we may not hope to find its solution within the range of opportunities open to any one individual. (Mills, 1959: 9)

We can apply that standard to organizational settings. If, within any given organization, one manager discriminates against certain employees, or one service worker refuses to help certain types of clients, then the problem is with those people and the solution probably involves removing them from those positions. If, on the other hand, such things occur thousands of times each day throughout the millions of organizations and agencies of the industrial world, then the problem is built into the system of organizing.

How do individual prejudices and other limitations become organizational characteristics? That's a difficult question. But the previous chapter's discussion of culture sets up one useful way to answer it.

Within any given society, the priorities and prejudices of the dominant culture partially shape the nature of the organizations that operate there. If environmental consciousness became popular in a society, it would also become more highly valued within organizations. If hard times led to greater economic fears and competition throughout the wider culture then, all else being equal, competitiveness would likely come to be perceived as an organizational asset as well. Individual characteristics that are most admired in the culture will be admired and rewarded in organizations, a phenomenon known as in-group privilege. Groups of people who face prejudice and stigmas in society will confront similar problems in jobs, schools, social agencies, and other organizational settings. This is called out-group antipathy.

Organizations, however, are also distinct from the larger society. An organization, with its own rules, boundaries, and habits, may overturn, reverse, or exaggerate conventional prejudices. How an organization reflects or modifies the cultural impulses of the world around it is a matter of the culture of the organization. Organizational cultures reflect the types of people who make up the organization, the needs and goals of the organization, and the ways in which things get done there, resulting in "local" preferences and tendencies. Professionals in a high-technology field, for example, share specialized training and value up-to-date knowledge more in their work than most of the rest of us do in ours. Both athletic ability and diplomatic abilities are valued in much of the world, but only one of them carries any serious weight on a football team.

Like most organizations, teams bring together people who share important qualities to do things that emphasize or rely on those shared qualities. Athletes act together in physical competition, engineers act together in problem-solving, and actors in performance. This means that members of organizations start off as more similar to one another than the general population through self-selection, and they exaggerate their similarities through collective action. Their shared limitations, prejudices, or preferences need not always become amplified, but there is an ever present danger that all shared perspectives, with all their problems, can run wild. For this reason, one may find far less tolerance for differences and open-mindedness in general within some organizational settings than out in the rest of the world. And as the members of an organization or industry continue to have more regular contact with people in this setting than out of it, reinforcing one another's values and assumptions, these shared tendencies can come to seem like simple truths. This is sometimes called an "echo chamber effect."

Thus people who are fairly similar in background and outlook tend to cluster together in organizations. Once there, they exchange ideas that are more likely to support their initial preferences and less likely to challenge them. They also face shared challenges and problems, and exchange shared ideas about the nature of these problems and how to solve them. Over time, a shared culture with its own norms and values grows within the setting, shaped by individuals, but amplified by the interactions within that setting.

Returning to the first example, above, individual prejudices can cause any number of problems, including discriminatory practices. This is a fairly well-understood phenomenon with recognizable costs. When an individual fails to recognize or reward the talent or needs of an employee, a customer, or an applicant, the organization both suffers and causes harm. Promising students are turned away from good schools, to the detriment of both the student and the school. Talented employees whose efforts are not acknowledged may stop trying. So the first level of harm is that people's careers and opportunities are blocked. These are harms within organizations that have recognizable impact on people outside of them.

One may accurately claim that such dysfunctions are the result of individual actions, not organizational procedures. Following Mills, however, we need to note that the potentially arbitrary power of some people over others is built into our organizational systems. In fact, that is one of the main things that are organized. The same administrative and managerial offices that have the power to evaluate applicants, optimize efficiency, and alter the rules and procedures of an organization can use this power fairly or unfairly at any time. The formal division of authority within most organizations limits the ability of other participants to intervene or correct such problems.

Not surprisingly, power can be abused. Hierarchical power structures allow bosses to become bullies (Leck and Galperin, 2006) and co-workers to act as aggressive mobs (Westhues, 2002). As is the case with discrimination, the formal **authority structure** of organizations leaves entire strata of participants vulnerable to the preferences of others. Both the vulnerability and the abuse of it can become institutionalized within particular organizations, industries, or sectors. Yet, due in part to our prejudices against the less rational dimensions of organizations, people often have trouble seeing the relationship between cultural inequalities and behavior in organizations. That is, part of our training in rational approaches to organizing is to believe that our organizations are rational. We don't have a well-developed language for seeing culture, class, or inequality as they operate within formal settings.

Some of these prejudices and problems are due more to the ordinary practices of everyday life than to any particular abuse. Consider what it means to dress for success. For men, this isn't too hard. Business suits are fairly common in many professions, and a shirt and tie will do for a lot of other jobs. For women, though, this can get tricky. A woman who wears a suit may not be perceived as a competent professional but rather as a woman who dresses like a man. A woman who prefers women's fashion can always be dismissed as "too feminine," which somehow implies that she is not serious about her work (Smith, 1998). And while some women can find a middle ground with a woman's pants-suit or other sexless fashion, that can invite scorn in its own way. It often seems that looking successful means more than simply having a good suit.

When attitudes or behaviors become normal in some setting, when ideas or perspectives are taken for granted there, even if they would seem odd elsewhere, it becomes very difficult to identify the source of the problem. If you have ever felt that you were discriminated against in some organization, you might have found it strangely difficult to get others in the same setting to understand your feelings. It's often much easier to show that some unwanted outcome has occurred than it is to identify its cause. As Barbara Reskin concisely noted:

> studies have shown that levels of inequality in work organizations are affected by organizational demography, organizational leadership, the degree to which personnel practices are formalized, recruitment methods, external pressure, and the availability of slack resources. But we failed to grasp their most important message: Inequality at work does not just happen; it occurs through the acts and the failures to act by the people who run and work for organizations. (2000: 707)

One landmark study of the effects of gender-based inequalities within organizations was Rosabeth Moss Kanter's (1977) *Men and Women of the Corporation*. Kanter examined the distribution of jobs and job-types among men and women within a large firm. That many women were shunted into dead-end career tracks or that many men were handpicked for fast-track assignments by the upper management was probably not a great surprise. That people are deeply affected by their work experiences, such that prior success feeds confidence and self-esteem while blocked opportunities and negative events generate self-doubt probably needed to be explained, though it was unlikely to be controversial. The particular contribution of this book, however, came from Kanter's demonstration that numbers may matter more than particular prejudices. Many of the negative conditions faced by gender or ethnic minorities in organizations are caused by, or exacerbated by, the fact that they are in the minority *in their jobs*.

Kanter found that when women made up less than 10 or 15 percent of a work environment, they acquire a *token* status in which they are perceived as women first, organizational participants second. The larger group, the *dominants*, are highly aware of the tokens, but see them primarily as tokens of their group rather than as people with individual qualities. A woman in such a situation who achieves some success is likely to be credited as accomplished "for a woman." Similarly, any woman's failure is likely to be perceived among the majority group as a demonstration of women's failures. Among members of the dominant group, on the other hand, individuals are judged or credited based on their individual accomplishments. Dominants also showed a strong tendency to apply conventional prejudices to members of the token group even when the observed reality did not conform to those beliefs. In one telling example, the men in a mostly male department described the relationship between two women as "catty," a common term used against women, whereas the women in question appeared to be friends whose relationship was supportive and positive. Somehow, a few men who only occasionally interacted with the women had created a fictional version of what was going on in the office, based primarily on gender.

By focusing on the numbers, Kanter was able to argue that the problem had more to do with the token group's minority status than with specific gender prejudices. In circumstances where the presence of women was comparable to the presence of men, the men had a much greater tendency to view the women as individuals, and a lesser likelihood of resorting to hostile or discriminatory language. Of course, the familiar prejudices were still there, if less visible. The men hadn't become enlightened about gender. They were simply more likely to perceive the women at their level as managers first, and women second, rather than the other way around.

Similarly, Kanter found that when it came to promotions, a male-dominant upper management tended to view women candidates as "different" and therefore unknown, strongly favoring candidates who resembled the group that was already there. Yet, when more women were involved in management to begin with, women candidates were more likely to be judged based on their records rather than as token representatives of their group. In that case, the upper-management men were more likely to support the women applicants. The situation conforms strongly to the idea, described in chapter 4, that groups and organizations develop local cultures with norms, values, and prejudices that are informed by the world outside, yet distinct from it.

A considerable body of research attests to the continuing power of token status on gender and ethnic minorities throughout the industrial world. Token "successful blacks" in a white environment, or "successful women" in a male environment, are expected to assimilate to the perspectives of the dominants, and may be "revealed" or "discredited" (to use Goffman's terms) if they actually bring in a different point of view or set of values (Moahloli, 1997). At present, one can still hear terms such as "woman doctor" or "male nurse" to refer to doctors and nurses who are not conforming to gender stereotypes. The language doesn't actually suggest that the job of a male nurse is different from that of a "nurse." It only suggests that something odd is involved.

For members of minority groups, there are many costs to being labeled as odd or perceived as a token. Affirmative action policies, for example, seek out qualified minority applicants and in some cases assist them in applying for competitive positions. The assumption is that there are qualified people in both dominant and minority groups, but that the minority groups have less access under normal circumstances. Members of dominant groups, on the other hand, sometimes describe these policies as tokenism or assume that the applicants are necessarily less qualified. Some opponents of affirmative action claim that those hired through affirmative-action recruiting are taking away jobs that are supposed to go to members of the dominant group. In such an atmosphere, successful minority candidates have reported feeling that they could never afford to make a single mistake for fear that this one event would be used as "proof" that minorities as a whole are less able than dominants (Carter, 1992).

Corporate culture in the industrial world is typically a male culture, and some portion of this culture is aligned against the interest of women within it. A masculine culture often not only enacts certain forms of behavior that are perceived as gender-specific, but may actively promote these behaviors and their underlying attitudes as an affirmation of masculinity. The television show *Mad Men*, for example, depicts a 1960s corporate culture in which male executives routinely hire secretaries for their looks, and spend their days casually making sexually suggestive comments at them. Contemporary research finds that such overt sexual harassment is less common these days, though it still occurs. Even so, women face many career barriers as women, many of them related to the popular assumption that women would rather stay home with their kids than earn a living in the workforce (Stone, 2007).

In all of these cases, outright hostility is less common than casual behaviors – everything from sexist jokes to making business decisions in bars after hours to bragging about one's sex life while at work. For men, going along with these casual expectations can serve as a demonstration of collegiality. For women, going along or not can be a career-defining test. Sexual harassment cases are particularly problematic in this context, because men who practice or simply witness such harassment may not perceive or acknowledge that anything has actually happened. Men who stare at, comment on, or make suggestive comments about women in the workplace may describe their behavior as a form of play in which other men are their audience or co-participants, while the women involved are not seen as participants, and, therefore, not perceived as having been affected by the game (Quinn, 2002). The women rarely describe such events the same way. They experience a work environment that is "hostile" to women.

Judith Lorber and Patricia Yancey Martin (2007) note that leadership positions are not simply more often filled by men, but actually occupied by men who embody recognizable markers of masculinity. For example, taller men have considerable advantages over shorter ones, independent of their accomplishments and abilities. Equating masculinity with leadership sets invisible social barriers that cannot easily be breached by creating rules against discrimination. And, of course, defining male characteristics as inherently superior to female ones creates tremendous advantages for men even where the attributes, such as physical strength, have little or nothing to do with the work, as in management (Lorber and Martin, 2007: 232).

At the social level, if particular groups routinely face discrimination, harassment, or social stigmas, then those groups will suffer a cascade of troubles. In the US, for example, discrimination against African Americans in education has been practiced in one form or another since the days of slavery. During the slave years, only whites were allowed to go to school, and many states had laws preventing anyone from teaching a black student. For over a century after the abolition of slavery, there were legal and institutional barriers against equal education. African Americans were more likely to be taught in inferior schools with below average resources. The most successful ones were still often denied a place in most colleges and universities. This pattern of discrimination was supported by shared assumptions, values, and practices in schools, school boards, courts, colleges, city councils, and beyond. And, not surprisingly, a conventional reason offered for racial discrimination in hiring was that African Americans were "not as educated" as whites.

Discriminatory actions do not require hostility or hatred on the part of those committing the acts. Often indifference or carelessness is enough when the behavioral patterns are routine within a culture and supported by a set of beliefs. In the language of organizational theory, discrimination may be institutionalized, taken for granted, and accepted as reality. Individual acts of discrimination are often visible and in violation of known rules. But institutional biases are not seen as acts, and are therefore not seen at all.

Dysfunctional norms

We have seen that formal organizations rely on informal patterns of social relations. The present discussion has shown that informal relations can cause harm, both through deliberate abuse of power and through a lack of attention to the nature of local norms and practices. This observation recalls Weber's antipathy to unchecked power, and reminds us of why he saw advantages to bureaucratic forms of organizing. If you actually follow the rules of a strict bureaucracy, then you have a meritocracy. Playing favorites, promoting people you like, and creating unequal career paths are all violations of those rules.

Such cases reveal how ethical or professional norms can be skewed, or can be avoided. A further everyday threat to the proper functioning of an organization comes from the routine situation in which the norms are unclear or full of contradictions. These are circumstances that Robert Jackall has termed *moral mazes*.

Jackall describes the moral and practical world in which managers operate. He recognizes that this world is part of our own, and yet that it has its own rules. The structure of the work world shapes the priorities of those in it. As Jackall explains, "the hierarchical authority structure that is the linchpin of bureaucracy dominates the way managers think about their world and about themselves" (1988: 17). Management is described as a form of leadership, and managers in Jackall's study judge themselves on their ability to take charge of a situation. Yet few things are as dangerous for a manager as being held responsible for a bad decision.

Jackall's study examines the effects of the organizational structure on individual managers' ways of thinking. Corporate managers work under conditions of constant uncertainty, ambiguity, and flexibility. They have responsibility, yet fear blame. Management, therefore, becomes a political game. Managers, fearful of standing out and attracting blame, constantly look to each other to discern norms and expectations, to hint at standards and to infer consensus. More importantly, they look to each other to know what transgressions are tolerated or encouraged, and which are punished or discouraged. Many of the stories in Jackall's book involve "sucking up," and the term "C.Y.A." occurs frequently.

Jackall describes the world of corporate management as inherently corrupt. This is not due to a widespread intent to commit crimes, but rather because this world is morally ambiguous and highly focused on end results. There are stories of personal graft, greed, and abuse, of course, along the lines of payoffs from suppliers and kickbacks from customers. But there are also accounts of honest mid-level managers who discovered corporate secrets, such as improperly buried toxic waste and routine safety violations. Many of these stories ended with the manager being transferred somewhere or having his or her job redefined so that they were no longer involved with this issue or able to learn of its resolution. The clear implication was that the skeletons had been deliberately hidden back in the closet. Politics overshadows competence in the life of a corporate manager.

The managers in Jackall's study are not necessarily bad managers. The point is that corporate norms both discourage and encourage unethical behavior. Large, formal organizational systems prohibit and require rule violations. Oversight procedures that we establish to ensure that money and other resources are not misappropriated may be deliberately used to prevent legitimate work from happening, possibly in order to protect a political agenda. "Streamlining" those same oversight procedures in the name of efficiency creates visible exposures through which people can steal from or manipulate the programs that are supposed to be protected. The same practices that are designed to reward people for their accomplishments create incentives for some to steal credit for the accomplishments of others and generally add a competitive dimension to a shared task. We use the term "office politics" to describe the many ways in which co-workers can undermine each other, interfere with each other's work, and generally seek personal benefit at the expense of the organization's purpose. Organizations also engage in politics, controlling the flow of information across their borders, and presenting themselves to the world in opportunistic ways. And all of this manipulation and competition occurs within a structure that is built upon the idea of fostering coordination among its members.

Other than those who feel they have been punished for it, managers do not like to discuss politics. Recent interview and survey data among British managers show that political behavior is normal, expected, and often perceived as necessary (Buchanan, 2008). Yet, when researchers attempted to describe organizational behavior as "political," their informants were offended. Viewed from the outside, all of this political maneuvering, shifting blame, hiding bad news, and lying to superiors might seem unethical or worse. Yet it is possible that such activities are so normal to the world of corporate management that managers themselves only see it as doing their jobs.

The overall result is a set of institutionalized practices that avoid risk and aim for mediocrity. "In a world where criteria depend entirely on the interpretive judgments of shifting groups in an ever-changing social structure, where everyone's eyes are fixed on each other and on the market exigencies, the construction of notions of quality become highly political since individual fates depend on the outcome" (Jackall, 1988: 197). A purely rational examination of organizational behavior would assume that organizations efficiently process materials and information to create goods and services, and that managers exist in order to keep everything moving smoothly. In contrast, a close look at the world of management reveals that crisp and efficient processing might be too much to expect of a modern bureaucracy. Rather, we should assume that work at this level of organizations is geared toward a fairly safe kind of mediocrity. Individual managers can rarely afford to risk the kind of unusual behavior it takes to be the best at what they do. The external pressures from supervisors and co-workers demand conformity to the routine.

Bastard organizations

In a wide assortment of writings over several decades, Everett Hughes made a practice of distinguishing between those aspects of the social world that people believe ought to be there – ones that we like to study – and those that most of us prefer not to think much about. For any legitimate business or service, he noted, there are alternative organizations providing the same services in a less legitimate fashion. Each time we pass a law or formalize a procedure defining the correct and acceptable way of doing something, we create a business opportunity for those who are able to do those things differently:

> Kangaroo courts in prison and armies and the Tong courts of the earlier Chinatowns meted out the justice of a particular group that did not accept or trust established justice. The popular justice of the frontier and the lynchings that continued in several Southern states until the 1920's were bastard institutions, not formally legitimate but highly conventional and supported by popular opinion. (Hughes, 1971: 99)

Further, the definition of a legitimate institution as legitimate implicitly defines other ways of doing things as illegitimate. Defining marriage as the acceptable and preferred institution for sexual relations, he noted, also defines other relations as deviant. "Now marriage is always defined not merely as an enduring relation between a man and a woman, but as between a man of a certain class, religion, ethnic character, age, income, kin relations, and a woman with appropriate, although not always identical traits" (p. 100).

Hughes's point has taken on new salience in political debates on marriage. Historically, in religiously defined states, a marriage between a member of the dominant religious group and a spouse of another religion could not be performed unless the spouse converted. If that didn't happen, then the state would not have to recognize the marriage, and the couple could be considered criminals for believing themselves to be married. Marriages across racial categories have been criminalized in many places at many times. Our contemporary version of this concerns "gay marriage." Homosexual couples are routinely denied the legal benefits that accompany marriage, from tax advantages to inheritance, to the visitation rights in hospitals. Legally, for the most part, they don't count as "family." And while some states have attempted to address this by creating a legal designation for gay marriage or alternative domestic partnerships, others have sought to alter the legal definition of marriage to specify that only heterosexual relationships count. To paraphrase a bumper sticker that I have seen, heterosexual couples have in-laws while homosexual couples are outlaws. The formal definition of the institution creates new categories of deviance and illegality.

Of course, as Hughes pointed out, the same criteria define all of those who have any form of sexual relations outside of marriage as deviant, if not always criminal. Under anti-sodomy laws, which are still on the books in many states in the US, the law also specifies how and where married couples are to have sex when they have it. A surprisingly large number of common practices, which I will not list, are actually against the law.

Built-in failures

Acting with the best of intentions and following all the rules, one can still cause all kinds of harms. So concludes Diane Vaughan whose study of accidents, disasters, and smaller failures has led her to theorize what she calls "the dark side of organizations." People make mistakes. Absent mistakes, they may still show poor judgment. Exercising judgment, they may choose to act against the rules and expectations of their organizations. Even when individuals have good intentions, most organizations have built-in incentive systems that encourage members to hide their mistakes and withhold necessary information from others. Such dysfunctions "can be understood as routine nonconformity: a predictable and recurring product of all socially organized systems" (1999: 274).

The crucial suggestion that Vaughan's work raises is that organizational dysfunctions arise from commonplace activities. Organizations produce both desired and undesired results through the same operations and procedures. We cannot honestly assign credit for the benefits while waving off the harms as something that isn't supposed to happen. Effective administrators pressure their organizations to work more efficiently by allocating less time and money than a task is likely to need. Staff may respond by working harder or putting in extra hours, but they are also likely to skimp on safety procedures and testing. As Gouldner (1954) had noted, this sort of thing is often the desired and expected result, with supervisors making a show of turning a blind eye to the "unauthorized" violations on the part of their workers.

Cutting corners and rationing services is a daily activity in the social services. This is particularly true for economic welfare agencies, whose obligations increase during periods of economic decline, reducing their resources just as they need them most. In such conditions, those staff most responsible for providing aid and services become those most responsible for delaying or denying them (Lipsky, 1980). Such workers are often trapped in a complex and self-contradictory web of needs, rules, and priorities. Lacking the authority to deliver on the promises they would like to make, they have just enough discretion to arbitrarily say "no" to clients. Front-line staff may be trained professionals, but they are still at the bottom layer of a tall hierarchy of rules. Under some circumstances, when the resources are present and the clients' characteristics match the typical or desired ones, then the staff can meet people's needs, allocate resources, and solve problems. Under other circumstances, when the money has run out or someone's case requires extra work, or their paperwork isn't right, it's the job of the staff to deny people what they need. In effect, their jobs require them to find ways to get out of doing their jobs.

Even our efforts to reduce organizational deviance create new opportunities for more of the same. Financial audits limit the opportunities for one to embezzle funds, unless the auditor is part of the scheme. In that case, one has a co-conspirator perfectly positioned to hide the crime. Similarly, we give to law enforcement officials the job of controlling street crime, which requires the criminal justice system to take the word of an enforcement officer over that of other citizens as a matter of course. The criminal justice system itself, then, is well organized to hide the criminal actions of any officer that chooses to commit them. Smaller abuses and dysfunctions are also built into the system of power and discretion. Lipsky, for example, notes that police also have the discretion to arrest some suspects and warn off others. The proper functioning of the system requires that they have this flexibility in any given individual situation. Yet one result of this is a broad and consistent pattern of suspects from the dominant cultural groups benefiting from this, while minority suspects are disadvantaged. As Frank Miller asked, "Who watches the watchmen?"

Vaughan observes that the field of organizational studies has not yet incorporated the study of mistakes, failures, and unintended consequences. By the same token, the field of criminology is weak in the area of crimes committed within the criminal justice system, and medical studies rarely treat malpractice as a normal part of a practice. We study our subjects as though the deviant cases are always surprising and distinct from the organized activities that we "really" plan or study. More generally, our culture has a strong tendency to visualize the best possible outcomes of most things, and shun the negative cases. Karen Cerulo (2006) calls this "**positive asymmetry**," and identifies numerous mechanisms through which the practice is taught and reinforced. We are socialized to anticipate the good, she shows, and our ceremonies and rituals create shared celebrations of success and accomplishment. When the worst occurs, however, we often find ourselves alone and unprepared, not even having the words to describe our situations. In some cases, such as the long-standing, but recently overturned, policy on the part of the US military to disallow media photographs of coffins and funerals of the war dead, there is a rationale and an explanation for highlighting the positive and hiding the negative. More often, we're unaware of how and why we do such things.

Two of the many results of this unwarranted optimism appear daily in formal organizations. First, there is a conspicuous under-planning for errors and failures. And, second, workers seem emotionally disinclined to consider that their work conditions might be overly stressful, dangerous, or exploitive. Cerulo relates this asymmetry to contemporary American culture, and contrasts the US case with much of the rest of the industrial world. Economic pressures force people all over the world to work long, hard hours at stressful jobs, but the US is unique for not mandating vacations as part of work contracts. And even where vacations are offered, Americans frequently choose not to take them. Yet work-related stresses contribute significantly to a host of health problems, from insomnia to heart attacks. "So blind are Americans to the worst-case scenarios of work that we may be working ourselves to death" (2006: 46).

The processes by which we organize our various pursuits have many self-defeating elements built into them. Max Weber's student, Roberto Michels, famously applied this conundrum to political parties and the organization of democracy. The democratic ideal in a large society absolutely requires organization, he wrote. Many people shouting at once while others are silent is not a democracy. There must be an organized system that gives voice to all and carries those voices to some place where they can impact on actions. Inevitably, he claimed, these same organizational systems must also undermine everything that democracy represents. He called this dilemma "the iron law of oligarchy" (Michels, 1962 [1915]).

Why such strong language? Michels was not claiming that organization created the potential for the abuse of power. He saw the consolidation of power into the hands of a small elite as the *inevitable* outcome of organizing itself. And the path from working for equality to contributing to subjugation takes fewer than twelve steps.

First, complex organizations require a division of labor, which creates a power center. Second, the reward and incentive systems provide privileges to those in power that are withheld from others. Third, one has to seek office, which means that those who want power will be over-represented in elections and more likely to end up with some degree of control. Most people, Michels suggested, can only barely commit enough energy to join a union, political party, or committee. Few have enough ambition to actually want to run one. But this gives advantages to those with personal ambition, which isn't always the best thing for democracy. Fourth, holding positions of power gives one the ability to consolidate power, to manipulate the organization for one's own purposes, and thereby to hold off challengers. Naturally, some leaders will always put the needs of the organization ahead of their own interests. But that just makes them more vulnerable to the challenges of those who want their jobs. In time, people who view leadership in an organization as a route to personal privilege are more likely than others to gain power and to do what they can to keep or expand it. The group as a whole may be fiercely committed to democratic principles, but the routine functions of the organization facilitate and even encourage their demise. "Who says organization, says oligarchy" (Michels, 1962: 365).

Michels's analysis offended me when I first encountered it. I had been involved in community organizing, and even held leadership positions in small settings. My colleagues and I were not exactly the Soviet Politburo of the Stalinist era, which of course was Michels's era as well. In retrospect, and with deeper reading, I realized that Michels was not claiming that organizers were hypocrites who gave empty lip service to democratic principles. He was arguing that principles were not enough. The act of organizing carries its own logic and its own imperatives. An organization is an authority structure. With authority comes inequality, no matter how much "voice" its members have.

To some degree, Michels undermined his own assertions that oligarchy was an inevitable "law" of social organizing. His analysis was a warning, not a critique. Armed with self-knowledge, organizers and participants could take steps to counter the oligarchic tendencies of their creations. Organizations are "living forms of social life. As such they react with the utmost energy against any attempt to analyze their structure or their nature." We don't want to look at our weaknesses, as Cerulo observed. We want to believe in our systems. Michels's argument was against blind faith and in favor of hard work. "Democracy is a treasure which no one will ever discover by deliberate search. But in continuing our search, in laboring indefatigably to discover the undiscoverable, we shall perform a work which will have fertile results in the democratic sense" (Michels, 1962: 366, 368).

Disasters

Mary Shelley's *Frankenstein*, subtitled *The Modern Prometheus*, is a classic cautionary tale for the modern age. If it needed a moral, we might choose "just because you *can* make something, doesn't mean that you should." This is especially true when you discover a way to use technology to manage hugely dangerous systems that are too complex for their human designers to control. Yet we do these things anyway.

Every once in a while, a nuclear reactor approaches critical failure, known as a meltdown. Assuming the critical condition is brought under control eventually, without the uncontrollable release of radioactive materials, there is a pretty good chance that no one will be hurt or killed as a result of the incident. Is it accurate, then, to say that nuclear power is safer than driving? Or would that be another example of positive asymmetry?

The question behind the question is which better defines dangerousness: the most likely scenario or the worst-case scenario. The more likely harm would come from driving, which is associated with about 50,000 deaths per year in the United States alone. The worst-case scenario would be the meltdown which could, hypothetically, cause that many deaths in a single day. Driving deaths, however, are part of the normal operation of the car and highway system, which makes this an "acceptable risk." The normal operation of nuclear plants, on the other hand, should not result in any deaths at all. But a nuclear failure could be a disaster of incalculable proportions. So, from a risk-management perspective, a small failure at a nuclear plant is a greater risk because of its potential to become a disaster.

We can define a crisis as a critical threat that is out of control, leading to an unknown potential for harm. A recent analysis of the subject noted:

> A common belief is that some set of factors "causes" a crisis. It would be more precise to speak of escalatory processes that undermine a system's capacity to cope with disturbance. The agents of disturbance may come from anywhere – ranging from earthquakes to human errors – but the cause of the crisis lies in the inability of a system to deal with the disturbance. (Boin, t'Hart, Stern and Sundelius, 2005: 3)

One could almost say that a crisis requires organization.

In many crisis situations, the hazards are not immediately recognized. When the full extent of the problem is identified we demand to know why those responsible were not more on top of it. One can easily suspect that officials choose to downplay the extent of the risk in order to avoid blame. But while there is some short-term incentive to act this way, it also seems likely that the people with specific roles and responsibilities must have had difficulty even *conceiving* of the extent of the failure.

Sociologist Lee Clarke (1989) gives the example of a massive leak of toxic chemicals that occurred in the State Office Building in Binghamton, New York, in 1981. The chemicals, including dioxin, posed a life-threatening risk to all who came in contact with them. Yet, immediately following the spill, an untrained, under-prepared and mostly unprotected team of janitors were sent in to clean up as though it were a normal chemical spill. What could they have been thinking?

In part, Clarke suggests that the people in charge were too thoroughly conditioned to visualize their roles in terms of normal conditions. The decision-makers normally had the job of keeping the buildings, and hence the government offices, functioning. Closing a major state building was a visceral failure to them in ways that a dioxin leak was not. So, in response to a potential crisis, their training taught them to ask "How quickly can I get this building back to work?" The spill was a potential crisis; the poor response to it increased the potential harm.

Crises are usually triggered by unexpected incidents, including such predictable failures as a power outage or the eventual physical collapse of a poorly maintained deep-sea oil-drilling platform. But it is not the incidents themselves that make the crisis. It is the failure of the organizational system's response to the incident that leads to the chaos, loss of control, and mounting damage that characterize a crisis. And while unexpected and uncontrollable incidents will always be with us – more so now than ever, in fact – we still have much to learn about how to prepare for and respond to critical trigger events.

Complex systems, whether technological or otherwise, are comprised of multiple organizations and agencies with a variety of interactions and exchanges. Systems' theory pioneer Herbert Simon defined complex systems as those involving many parts and a greater number of interactions. I prefer Charles Perrow's more concise definition of systems as "organizations and the organization of organizations" (1984: 3). The organization of the organizations may be fairly simple or highly complex. Often it is complex, meaning that the interactions among them are not always routine and predictable, and that the number of organizations involved may not be consistent or even known in advance.

Within any organizational system, Perrow noted, accidents are inevitable. Because we know this, organizations and agencies routinely measure everything that's happening around any places where a dangerous failure is likely to occur, so that when a predictable failure occurs, that information will immediately feed into a carefully designed and practiced recovery system. These recovery systems are designed for specific, predictable failures, and they operate quickly to deal with them. They are not designed to be flexible or creative. They get their information and they act.

Such accidents occur pretty much every day. A sensor fails here; a mistake is made there. Something breaks elsewhere. But as long as the human operators know what to do when they get a failure reading from a sensor, and as long as the sensors work at the moment when the containment shield leaks, and so on, each failure can be corrected. Another way of saying this is that we would be fine if each of these possible failures were not deeply embedded in complex technological, organizational systems with rapid interactions among the parts.

But they are. And it happens that a part can break at the same time that the detection system guarding against that is out of order. Such highly unlikely combinations of failures result in two problems at once: a failure occurs and the wrong information about the failure is transmitted. This combination is likely to lead to a rapid, but incorrect, response from a response team that is highly trained to deal with the kind of thing that they *think* is happening. The response team is responding properly to the given information but their actions only make things worse. From here on, anything can happen. Consider the following event description from Perrow:

> In 1978 a worker changing a light bulb in a control panel at the Rancho Secco 1 [nuclear] reactor in Clay Station, California, dropped the bulb. It created a short circuit in some sensors and controls. . . . the loss of some sensors meant the operators could not determine the condition of the plant, and there was a rapid cooling of the core. . . . The colder, internal walls tried to shrink but the hotter, external ones would not allow shrinkage. This put strong internal stresses on the core. (1984: 44–5)

The plant in question was relatively new and the core held until the operators got the system back under control. Perrow quotes a Nuclear Regulatory Commission spokesman, however, as saying that in an older facility that same event would likely have triggered an uncontrollable meltdown. No amount of safety planning can ever ensure that nothing will be accidentally dropped in the wrong place, that no sensors will ever fail, or that no operators will ever misinterpret a signal. Perrow's point is that none of these errors alone is beyond control, and so they don't appear to have disastrous consequences. Yet they do. It is the unpredictable combination of several unusual events that spontaneously creates situations for which we have no plan and little clear information. Perrow calls these "normal accidents" – significant and unpredictable problems that arise from normal occurrences. A major failure can be a disaster. But a major failure that is ongoing, urgent, and misunderstood is a crisis.

Lee Clarke (1989: 2) observed that organizations and organizational systems "played a central role as agents of harm and rescue, and also as victims" in almost all of the large-scale crises of recent decades. We can easily identify central organizations and agencies in the well-known cases at Three Mile Island, Bhopal, India, the Exxon Valdez spill, and the World Trade Center attack, as well as in less recognized events, such as the toxic leak in the State Office Building in Binghamton, New York, and the chemical plant explosion in Flixborough, England, in 1974. Even so, the official reports and analyses of these crises and many more tend to focus on the twin poles of human error for causes and technology for solutions. You may recall that after the Exxon Valdez oil spill in Prince William Sound, Alaska, in 1989, public discussions focused attention on the culpability of the ship's captain, Joseph Hazelwood, with little or no questions about why a tanker with millions of gallons (tens of millions of liters) of oil was allowed to travel through such a fragile and unique ecosystem. Similarly, after hijackers successfully commandeered several US planes at once on September 11, 2001, the security screening job was completely reorganized under federal control, though none of the weapons carried on board by the hijackers were prohibited at that time. The screeners had not failed in their job. But the system had failed and someone, somewhere along the line, had to take the blame.

Imagining a technological failure, we upgrade to a more complex technology. Blaming human error, we get new people. If we're lucky, the underlying system of dependencies and interactions remains about the same. Of course, having new technology with less experienced operators could acutely increase the risk for the next failure. Recalling Meyer and Rowan's work on myths and symbols, however, we understand that it is necessary for an organization to take bold action after a failure, whether the action is related to the failure or not. You have to be able to show that you are responding to the crisis.

Could we do better? Perrow suggests that it is the combination of complexity and "tight-coupling" that turns failures into disasters. Loosely coupled systems have parts or processes that work in sequence, but without tight synchronization. A storm alert, for example, leads to a broadcast warning in response to which people may change their plans for the day. A tightly coupled system has parts and processes that are bound together in a more immediate fashion. An assembly line, for example, brings a part underneath a measuring arm. In response to the movement of the line, the measuring arm immediately drops down and performs a measurement. Its results instantly determine whether the part is sent up for assembly or down for repair. Tight coupling allows rapid and efficient processing as long as everything is where it should be. But there is no opportunity for second-guessing and contemplation when something goes wrong.

One lesson, then, is that we should be a lot more cautious about ever building systems that (a) are too complex to understand; (b) require tight coupling among the parts; and (c) can kill us. Individual car engines can have tight coupling and complex parts. That is necessary for cars, and not too dangerous. High-speed highway systems, on the other hand, need to have some slack in the system so that we can react safely when something goes wrong.

Vaughan (1999: 294) suggests that disasters frequently occur in much the same way, and for the same reasons, that everyday errors and minor misconduct occur. "Conflicting goals, performance pressures, deadlines, escalating commitment, reward systems that reinforce productivity and undermine safety, and decline of resource slack" ensure that complex systems will not always function as planned. Hostile work environments don't help either. Failures of various sizes are normal and inevitable, so we should at least plan for them.

Failures and human errors in response to failures can also occur when the people involved have too much experience. Freed from too much uncertainty, professionals may enter into a state of too much certainty under conditions where there is not enough information to make a decision (Hughes, 1951). They act with confidence, which is generally a necessary skill in hazardous work. Echoing Hughes, however, Perrow suggested that "an expert is a person who can solve a problem faster or better than others but who runs a higher risk than others of posing the wrong problem" (1984: 322).

Key Readings

Cerulo, Karen A. 2006 *Never Saw it Coming: Cultural Challenges to Envisioning the Worst*. Chicago, IL: University of Chicago Press.
    Cerulo shows a very consistent pattern of American culture, seeing things the way we think they ought to be, and failing to see where they might go wrong. Although this book was written before the housing/banking crash of 2008, its claim that Americans have difficulties with anticipating bad outcomes helps explain this and other disasters.
Gallant, Mary J., and Jay E. Cross 1993 "Wayward Puritans in the Ivory Tower: Collective Aspects of Gender Discrimination in Academia." *The Sociological Quarterly*, 34(2) (May): 237–56.
    Using the case of academic work, where one might think there would be more awareness of gender discrimination and fewer actual incidents, the authors draw out the many subtle ways in which gendered prejudices shape perceptions, define "sides," and ultimately serve to discredit those who get caught up in the dynamics of accusations and counter-claims.
Hughes, Everett C. 1951 "Mistakes at Work." *The Canadian Journal of Economics and Political Science*, 17(3): 320–7.
    A complex and yet humorous exercise in logic, in which Hughes shows that getting things wrong is inevitable and even necessary in most professions, but that the acts of making mistakes and of declaring something a mistake are strangely disconnected.
Jackall, Robert 1988 *Moral Mazes: The World of Corporate Managers*. New York: Oxford University Press.
    Described in detail in the chapter, this ethnographic study of the life of managers reveals the messy complexity of leadership in the face of incomplete data, divided loyalties, fear, self-interest, and an abiding sense of uncertainty.
Vaughan, Diane 1999 "The Dark Side of Organizations: Mistake, Misconduct, and Disaster." *Annual Review of Sociology*, 25: 271–305.
    Vaughan explains how a variety of problems become routinized within complex systems. Drawing together literatures and studies from several fields, Vaughan shows how organizations routinely translate uncertainty and contradictions into "facts," and how "disordered knowledge" is created, protected, and disseminated, resulting in breakdowns and even fatalities.

Organizations and Environments

U P to this point, we have been examining organizational internals. We have considered what organizations do and how to manage one. We have looked at the rapid rise of formal organizations in modern industrial society. And, to a lesser degree, we have considered the impact of these organizations on other spheres of life. All of this is fine, as far as it goes. To truly understand organizations, however, we have to start looking at them in their real-world settings.

This chapter examines the environments in which organizations operate. Taking the environment into account opens up considerable new vistas for analysis and goes a long way toward completing the picture we have drawn so far. By placing organizations in a context of interactions and self-definitions, we can start to understand organizational identities as the culmination of a series of decisions having mostly to do with how organizations relate to each other. Below, I will present a general language and framework for studying relations among organizations. This is followed by a close look at three of the major paradigms under which organizational environments are studied. From there, we will be able to consider questions of how organizations get to be the way they are and to look at some of the key attributes by which we define organizations as similar or not.

Definitions and assumptions

Sometimes it's surprising how easily we can generalize from a handful of cases to a whole field of work. It might seem fair enough that if you've worked at one fast food restaurant anywhere in the world, then you wouldn't feel out of place at any other. But should this work for banks, software firms, or environmental groups? If you have had organizing experience in a social movement in favor of fair wages or against toxic waste dumping in your home town, are you that much better prepared to go to another city, or another country, and help organize a social movement in favor of women's rights in the workplace? Up to a point, the answer is yes, and that point is the extent to which social movement organizations (or banks, or teams, or restaurants) tend to resemble one another in both structures and actions. As we will see below, organizations of any given type frequently lean toward adopting the organizational forms, practices, and public images of other organizations of that type. They define themselves, or present themselves, in terms of what others have done before them. The choice to adopt an organizational identity based on what others do isn't always necessary, and it doesn't always result in the best outcomes. But there are reasons for it.

Our review earlier of the adoption of bureaucratic forms throughout the world of formal organizations might have suggested that organizations take on similar structures because those structures are efficient or successful. Certainly a very large number of analysts and experts have thought that this was the main reason. The last few chapters, however, have shown that such rational considerations do not consistently determine how organizations work. There are also habits, rituals, and best guesses involved. We've also seen that bureaucratic forms aren't always as rational or efficient as they are made out to be. In order to explain why an organization, or a population of organizations, would take on defining characteristics that don't seem to serve them well, we have to look at them from a greater distance. To a very large degree, organizations are driven more by what is happening outside of their borders than by whatever it is they do within them. We refer to organizational models that focus primarily on externals as **open systems** approaches.

Open systems may be distinguished – as you might expect – from closed systems. A closed system is one that is driven and justified primarily by what happens within it, as in the case of the early rational systems models. Analysts and theorists of those models devoted much of their attention to efficiency in production. These works, as we saw in chapters 2 and 3, followed from dominant social theories of the early twentieth century, with their overriding concerns for predictability, social control, and task management. Efficiency experts and administrative theorists, as well as policymakers and corporate owners, relied on rational analyses of costs and benefits to design and justify their organizational systems. The cold, rational calculation demonstrated the legitimacy of each new stage of industrial development. (That's one of the reasons that we call them "rational systems.") In workplaces that can be said to have a shop floor, most of the organization consisted simply of the offices surrounding the shop floor. Most of these organizations were not terribly large by modern standards, and could be ruled from a single office.

The human relations movement exemplified the turn away from

this principle of organizing. The organizations did not change dramatically during this period, but the values and benefits that people attributed to organizations entered an entirely new phase. Organizations were described as social worlds that gave a structure to the social relations among the people within them. The "natural systems" approaches placed a high value on organizational settings that worked with individuals' "natural" tendencies and desires, rather than fighting against them. Formal organizations grew, with many more levels of management and new forms of specialized "white collar" work. For the most part, however, organizations were viewed in terms of whatever they produced.

The next big shift in thinking introduced the notion of organizations as "open systems" (Scott, 2002). The key insight of this approach is that organizations do not exist in isolation. Like people, organizations occupy specific locations within a social structure. They grow, shrink, act, and are acted upon by a world of things outside their own borders, and much of what an organization is depends on those things. Therefore, we cannot hope to understand organizations unless we can take their environments into account. Open-systems approaches to organizational studies look at how environments affect organizations and how organizations seek to affect their environments.

Organizations are part of our social worlds. As individuals, we pass in and out of organizations continuously. Our social environments are structured by these encounters. What, then, makes up the environment of the organizations? We people are in it, of course. But the majority of things that surround organizations in a regular way are more organizations. So one guiding assumption is that the routine interactions and exchanges among organizations primarily define the environment in which any individual organization operates.

There are many ways to view and measure an organizational environment. Most of the resources that an organization needs come from outside its borders, requiring organizations to establish connections within some area of activity to get those resources. These resources include tangible materials, products and services, of course. Wood and metal are tangible resources. Computers are necessary products that come from an organization's environment, and so technical support becomes a necessary service. Organizations also need intangible assets such as information, expertise, and channels of access to key social actors. The notion of "access" is itself a resource that is based on connections outside of an organization. Organizational participants, whether they are clients, customers, staff, volunteers, or respondents, must also connect to the organization from somewhere else. An organization's place in its "social" world largely determines where those people and other resources come from.

Increasingly, information is becoming the most important outside resource that an organization has to pursue. Consider "K Street," the relatively small strip of Washington, DC, where the major lobbying groups reside. Here, a few dozen firms dominate the relations between the largest industries in the United States and the government offices that fund them, regulate them, and protect them. (Of course, within and around those firms there are tens of thousands of individual registered lobbyists.) Despite the constant presence of large sums of cash, most of the business of lobbying simply comes down to the exchange of information: who wants what, or a glimpse into the legislative near-future. As of the turn of the twenty-first century, K Street has acquired the name "the fourth branch of government," placing it on a par with the legislative, executive, and judicial branches. Knowledge, it seems, really is power.

What else do organizations get out of having a good social location? The inter-organizational environment brings a great deal into an organization's reach. Organizations may need access to media, or to courts of law, or to political decision-makers. We can therefore think of the environment in which an organization operates as being full of potential. The degree to which any given organization must or is able to take advantage of that potential is a characteristic of that organization which distinguishes it from other organizations. A well-connected organization has access to resources that a less-connected one lacks. Having cash on hand is a useful thing for an organization, but often that is less valuable than having good credit. An organization is both empowered and limited by the nature of its environment.

Consider one example: the environment for what we in the US call a "private" school, meaning a school that is privately owned and operated. It has competitors, including public schools. It has potential students, teachers, and staff, for whom it must compete. This competition involves interactions that the school can mostly control, deciding how much to invest in its salaries and resources, and how much to put into its programs, buildings, advertising, and so forth. A school has a physical location, which places it in a local community within a school district. All of this may be thought of as the local space of its everyday activities. Moving further out, the fortunes and actions of the school will also depend heavily on the education policies of the state and various other governmental authorities, the economy, housing and other determinants of living quality around it, transportation and parking options, land values and property taxes, and, perhaps most importantly, the reputation of the school's graduates among competitive colleges, if it's a college prep school. The school's former students are also resources that connect the school to whatever businesses and institutions they end up in. If those connections can be exploited, then the school has access to additional forms of support through those alumni. All of these resources, activities, groups, communities, institutions, and agencies make up the environment in which any given school organization operates.

We can formalize this a bit, directing our attention to other organizations and institutions that have some degree of permanence in the social world of whatever organization we are looking at. The environment is the source for all of an organization's outside resources, its exchange partners, and its competition. What else is part of the environment? For schools, the individual teachers who are looking for jobs are not part of the environment, but the college education programs that graduate an increasing or decreasing pool of applicants are. Forget the weather, but include the regulatory environment. Looking a little further out, we can include information about the political and economic environment. Legal institutions and policies concerning taxes shape the environment in which schools work.

For organizational leaders, relations with the organizations in their environment provide one essential benefit and bring one great threat. The benefit is access to resources, as we've seen. The threat is change. Things outside of the organization are things that cannot be fully controlled or planned for. The management of organizational relations therefore can be understood as a balance between the desire to bring in more things of value and the need to reduce uncertainty. Knowing that, we now need to look at how organizations deal with their environments.

The institutional level

You might have noticed that organizational environments played a variety of roles in the classic theoretical works that we reviewed in chapter 2. This is so primarily because those theorists and their contemporaries were looking at organizations within their larger visions of social change and social stability in modern times, not as a specialized sub-discipline. Marx, Weber, and Durkheim, as well as Pareto, Simmel, Veblen, Spencer, and other social theorists of that period, examined organizational processes as a symptom of the increasing influence of business over social status, or as a reflection of a society's cohesion, or as a means for the concentration of wealth and power, all of which placed the organizations they studied within wide webs of political, economic, and social institutions. As sociology professionalized and administrative studies grew, the study of organizations was somewhat separated from the study of politics, economics, and culture. Studies in policy, public administration, or economic sociology attended to specific environmental effects. But few modern sociologists attempted a comprehensive model of relations between organizations and their environments prior to James Thompson's (1967) *Organizations in Action*.

Thompson posited that organizational activity could be meaningfully broken into three concentric levels, each of which operates according to different goals and procedures. Actually, Thompson borrowed the typology of the three levels from Talcott Parsons (1960), but with Thompson's own extension into theories of organizational systems. The technical level is where the productive work gets done. This level corresponds to the shop floor in factory studies. The primary relationships here are between workers and their immediate supervisors. Most of the studies that we have reviewed under the rational systems paradigm have focused on the technical level of an organization, with the possible exception of Fayol's administrative theory. This is because the technical level, as Thompson describes it, is the most rational part of the organization.

The nature of the technical level varies according to the kind of organization. The technical level of a car company is in the factory. The technical level of a school is found in the classroom. The technical level of a news organization is the part where the news is gathered and written up. If you were hired to sit in an office sorting faxes, or if you have ever volunteered to sign people up to clean a local beach, you were working at the technical level of the organization.

Above the technical level may be found the managerial level. As the name implies, this level corresponds to the administration of the organization as an organization, including the division of responsibility and authority, and the supervision of staff. Most of the work described under the natural systems paradigm goes on here. In a news organization, the managers hire reporters, decide how much money goes to research, and, well, organize and manage the organization. Imagine yourself back at that job receiving and sorting faxes. The people who hired you to do this are probably the same people who decided how large a staff was required for all of the different operations of the organization. They decided how much to invest in software and how much in security. The focus of their work is the organization as an organization. That's the managerial level. For the most part, the managerial level tends to be peopled with salaried staff workers, not owners. This is the level where natural systems ideas apply best. Though Thompson did not discuss it, this is also the level where most of the not-quite-so-rational bases for action have been described.

At the top, Thompson described the institutional level. This is where the owners and their agents, freed from the traditional tasks of day-to-day management, look to the long-range survival and growth of their organizations. The institutional level looks outward, attending to an organization's place in its environment. From this vantage point, profits and losses, growth and decline, and other measures of effectiveness may have less to do with optimizing the technical pursuit of tasks and more to do with managing the effects of changes in the proximate and regulatory environments. This level corresponds with the "open systems" perspective on organizations. To adopt Erving Goffman's language, this is the level at which an organization "presents itself" to the world. Actions and decisions at the institutional level rely on the open systems view of the organization.

The institutional level of a news organization is the level that manages the image of the organization, sells time or space to advertisers, and defines the organization's larger mission. The motto of the *New York Times*, for example, is "all the news that's fit to print." That's a very big mandate and a very big claim to live up to, but it concisely captures the paper's intended social role as the "paper of record" in the United States. In contrast, the *Birmingham Post* promises "local news, Birmingham business, guide, politics, and more" (<www.birminghampost.net>). That's a different kind of paper. It's at the institutional level that the *identity* of the organization is defined.

Studies of organizational environments have grown tremendously since Thompson defined his typology, yielding several powerful analytic paradigms and numerous methodological breakthroughs. Three big approaches shape much of the work in this area today. *Network analysis* provides the language and analytic tools to make sense of the connections among organizations, defining a physical structure for the environment in which these relations occur. *Ecological models*, primarily including resource-dependency and density-dependency models provide a general logic for the rise and fall and overall distribution of different types of organizations in relation to the environmental conditions. And neo-institutional theories of relations within **organizational fields** provide a more broadly cultural approach to relations between organizations and their environments.

Relations among organizations

Network analysis

A network is a structure. It is composed of items and connections among those items. Familiar networks include the Internet, which is made up of computers and the communications links among them, and social networks, which are made up of people and their relationships. A more recent form is the "online social network" which is made up of links between individuals' Internet pages. These links are sometimes called "friends with," to suggest that they represent relations among the people involved, though often they only represent a kind of co-sponsorship among web pages. You might also know the trivia game *Six Degrees of Kevin Bacon*, which is made up of actors connected by films that they have appeared in. The world of films includes many people, many arts, and many ways of describing them. In the six degrees game, one constructs a network of actors linked by the relationship "has appeared with."

Visually, a network is often represented as a web of points and lines. The points are referred to as "nodes" in most network analyses, and the lines are "links." A highly connected node has many links. A set of nodes with many links among them is referred to as "densely connected." The same network with the same nodes but many fewer links is "sparsely connected." In online social networking, a person with a large number of "friends" who don't know each other would be at the heart of a large, sparse network. A different person with a similar number of friends, most of whom are also friends with each other, would be part of a large, dense network. Figure 6.1 shows several network structures.

In organizational analysis, you will see the terms ION, IOL, and IOR from time to time. The first is the shorthand for inter-organizational networks. The second is inter-organizational linkages, although the term **inter-organizational relations** (IOR) is much more commonly used. With our jargon now established, we are ready to look at the nature of IORs in an ION. We can start with two basic questions: what sort of relations link organizations? And why do organizations form networks? As before, most of the common approaches to answering these questions focus on managing environmental uncertainty and acquiring resources (Galaskiewicz, 1985; Stark and Vedres, 2006). Organizations form IORs in order to get or exchange resources, and to have a hand in what's going on around them.

One of the primary kinds of links between organizations is an exchange relationship. Suppliers send materials to producers, for example, in exchange for cash. Over time, if some producers tend to make regular purchases from the same suppliers, then those firms have an exchange relationship. Having this relationship, they may come to depend on one another more, or to work out some special parameters for their exchanges, such as discounts or profit-sharing plans. They may enter into long-term stable exchange relations that reduce uncertainty about the future.

Consider the price of oil. As a consumer, I use oil when I buy gas for my car, and when I buy heating oil for my house. The price of gasoline changes frequently, and from day to day I can only hope that there

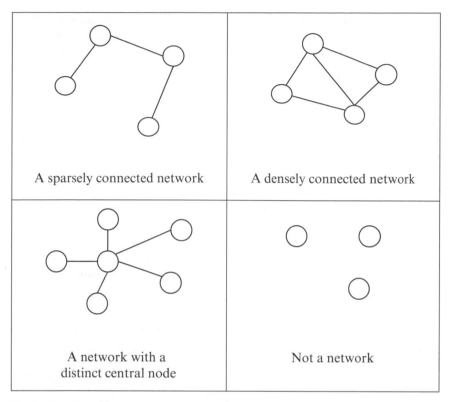

A sparsely connected network | A densely connected network

A network with a distinct central node | Not a network

Figure 6.1   Network structures

won't be a scary new jump in prices. Looking at my gas costs over the last few weeks I might estimate what it will cost me to drive in the next few weeks. But my estimates could be way off if things change, and this could affect my entire household budget. On the other hand, some heating oil companies offer the opportunity to sign a longer-term contract that "locks in" the fuel price of the moment. If the price of oil goes up, my bills stay the same and I win. If it goes down, my bills also stay the same, and I lose. I may choose not to bet against the market, but the contract offers me a way to eliminate some of the uncertainty that comes from fluctuating prices.

For businesses, a regular exchange relationship – that is, a contract – means that supplier organizations can count on having certain customers, and the customer organizations can count on getting their supplies.

Being part of a network implies much more than just having links to others. To better understand the importance of networks, we need to think about some of the things that networks aren't. For one thing, a network is not a hierarchy. A hierarchy exists within a formal organization and creates a system of authority and an expected path for the flow of information. A network is more like a body with no head. Links occur from one place to another, but there does not have to be any point of control or coordination. For a large number of organizations with regular exchanges within some field of work, whatever coordination or planning they do usually has to be achieved without rules or authority. At home, any given corporation might be the very model of a strict bureaucracy. But when interacting with its peers in the marketplace of ideas, the organization just has to work out its place and its relationships. More to the point, organizational leaders at the institutional level have to keep an eye on their environments, weigh each exchange of information, and remain sensitive to shifts in the prevailing winds. Even the most highly bureaucratized organization must find some other way of sharing power, distributing authority, and managing decisions when acting in concert with other groups with which they share some interests (Lune, 2007). Network analysis thus bridges the gap between bureaucratic organizational forms and alternative forms.

Of course nobody wants a free-for-all. Organizations have many techniques for bringing stability and predictability to their networks. For example, without clear authority to guide their interactions, organizations may greatly value tradition and consistency. Sometimes organizations may avoid useful changes in their practices in order to make things simpler for their exchange partners, and therefore to maintain good relations. By the same token, organizations seek to identify the more reliable of their past exchange partners when entering into new arrangements.

Legitimacy is a key resource in inter-organizational relations. Organizations participate in networks of relations, in part, to build their reputations and to demonstrate that they are "connected." In a similar fashion, organizational actors (the people who make the decisions for the organization) are much more likely to enter into a new exchange with an organization that is already in their network (Gulati and Gargiulo, 1999; Stark and Vedres, 2006). In a sense, a network creates a small world of shared meaning and values. Participants grant one another more legitimacy or credibility than they do to outsiders. At the same time, they look to each other for ideas. Organizational innovations, for example, do not simply propagate through some sector of society because they are useful. They spread quickly within inter-organizational networks where some members are early adopters, and slowly through others (Davis and Greve, 1997). In a sense, then, a network may resemble a community of familiar faces even in the midst of a huge and seemingly impersonal marketplace.

Numerous theorists have attempted to explain and predict which environmental conditions favor which kinds of exchanges among organizations, and why (Chandler, 1962; Fligstein, 1985; Ouchi, 1980; Williamson, 1981). A complete treatment of these questions is beyond the scope of this book. For the present chapter, it is enough to know that (1) organizations seek to gain control over environmental uncertainty by routinizing exchange relations with other organizations, or by purchasing those other organizations; (2) that one of the largest areas of concern for organizations is maintaining a regular supply of material resources; and (3) that unplanned or uncontrolled environmental changes can threaten the survival of an organization. Organizations operate within networks of inter-organizational relations through which resources and information are exchanged on a regular basis and in a mostly stable and predictable manner. Understanding an inter-organizational network therefore is an essential step toward an understanding of the organizations within it.

One can use network analysis to ask what the structure of interactions around an organization looks like. This is useful because it can tell us what resources are available at any time, what paths exist for the distribution of products, and how complex the system of relations can be. But one can infer much more from the analysis of an inter-organizational network. Certain networks of organizations in a given field may form a power block (Gulati and Gargiulo, 1999). Seeing the strategic advantages behind these alliances, we can indirectly measure elements of the participating organizations' goals and priorities. Furthermore, since network linkages are mostly voluntary, an organization's network explicitly tells us what sort of resources that organization wants. And by examining the other organizations that could potentially provide those resources, but which are not in the network, we find clues to an organization's "values." For example, a restaurant chain may choose to purchase its coffee from the largest distributor in their areas, or the cheapest, or the one with the best environmental record. Or it could encourage each branch to find its own local distributor in order to support the "local" economy in each of its markets.

One well-known inter-organizational network is the "iron triangle" in defense contracting. In this case, the routinization of inter-organizational relations within the defense industry have created conditions in which the workings of the network may be more important than "outside" defense goals in determining planning, investing, and contracting. The circulation of money, people, and information within the network creates a closed world unseen by most outsiders. Network analysis can give us a glimpse into this world.

Different branches of government have routine relations with particular industries, as is the case for defense departments and the defense industry. Governments purchase goods from industry, and, within any given domain of expertise, both parties value the same backgrounds and knowledge. But, in time, the relations between the state and the industry can become dense and closed off from others, leading to a private world of multiple exchanges. In the case of the US defense industry, for example, Gordon Adams (1981) has documented an "iron triangle" of mutual dependencies through which Congressional committees, the Pentagon, and defense contractors come to rely on one another for information, support, funding, legitimacy, and personnel. Individuals may enter this triangle at any point, appointed to the Pentagon one year, serving in Congress at a later time, and eventually working for the industry lobbying Congress and the Pentagon. Such movement of individuals would only reflect a personal network in operation if it were an unusual occurrence. In this case, Adams demonstrates, it is the normal way of doing business within this tight professionally defined inter-organizational network.

The iron triangle is partly a matter of convenience in which individuals and an industry take advantage of the connections and specialized knowledge that one can acquire through work in a field. That would constitute a manifest function, in Merton's terms. The latent function, then, is to build a closed system of power and privilege in which "outsides" have little chance of observing or questioning, let alone overturning, the goals and priorities of the insiders. In simple terms, the people who design weapons have much more influence over a government's military procurement decisions than do, for example, diplomats and the intelligence community. Close ties between industry and the defense department mean that the organizations that make defense systems may see the Pentagon's "wish list" before government officials do, and may suggest additions or changes. Close ties between the defense department and legislators often lead to generous funding opportunities for military plans that are subject to little oversight or justification, other than vague references to the interests of national security. Thus, the wish lists easily become plans. And close ties between industry and government mean that the organizations that should be competing to meet the requirements of a new round of contracts can often tell legislators what priorities they would like to see reflected in the procurement budgets before those budgets are written. Few outsiders have any say in any of this, or even the ability to closely observe the process. Yet the density and closed nature of the network creates this power structure and alerts us to its influence.

Ecological models

Studies of organizational environments change the focus of our attention from individual organizations to *populations* of organizations. The concept of an organizational population draws heavily on the biology of evolution. Populations of organizations, like species and sub-species of flora and fauna, are groups of organizations that resemble one another in form, consume the same or similar resources, and operate within a shared niche. For example, most producers and sellers of herbal teas within any given nation draw on the same sources for herbs, distribute through the same network of grocery stores and natural foods markets, and target the same consumers. A niche is therefore a local and delimited environment for the organizations within it. As described by Darwin, a resource-rich niche can support large and varied populations. A sparse or hostile niche can only support small numbers of very specialized life forms. In organizational theory, a niche is a "diverse array of environmental properties, including tastes of consumers, potential employees, availability of various kinds of input (e.g., human and financial capital), and legal and regulatory regimes" (Hannan, Carroll, and Pólos, 2003: 314). The niche represents the environment in which an organization struggles for survival. For any given environmental niche, with its own resources, restrictions, and regulations, certain organizational forms will "fit" well and multiply, while organizations whose forms are less appropriate for the niche will fade.

The process of evolution provides a popular metaphor for development and change in many fields. Often such metaphorical discussions misrepresent the concept, however, so they should be approached carefully. To understand evolutionary models of organizational development, it is useful to recall a couple of points from basic biology. One is that neither Darwin nor other natural scientists working with his model wrote about the survival of the "most fit" organizations. Evolution favors the "best fit," which is to say the life forms that work best with the current environmental conditions. When environments change, the forms that used to have the best fit with the environment will no longer fit so well, while other forms better suited to the new environmental changes will do much better. This is "natural selection." The entities that are best suited for the current conditions will thrive, while others may disappear entirely.

Related to this, evolution means change and adaptation at the population level. It does not imply progress or improvement. And it does not refer to individuals. People, as individuals, don't evolve. The species has evolved across generations through natural selection, a process by which those characteristics that best fit the environment were propagated more effectively than other characteristics. In time, the surviving population tends to take on the forms that best match the environmental conditions. Organizational populations also change their forms in this way, though not exactly in the same manner as life forms.

Form over function

Many organizational theorists have written about organizational forms, from Weber on. I have used the term throughout this book. Now that we have the ecological metaphor and its notion of life forms, it is useful to provide a more formal definition of the concept. An organization's form refers to its basic structure, operating principles, and self-definition. The structure can vary along a spectrum from highly bureaucratic to highly decentralized, with formal and fixed lines of authority and communication, or flexible and informal ones. Operating principles indicate how things get done, including the question of how specialized the tasks are, how flexible the decision-making is, and how carefully controlled people or actions might be. An organization's operation also includes the movement of resources – what it needs and what it produces. All of this will relate to an organization's purpose and mission, including such basic considerations as whether it promises shareholder profits, service to a community, social change, building things up, or tearing things down.

Successful organizational forms are reproduced throughout the niches that support them. We can recognize and understand an organization fairly quickly by identifying its form. Consider as an example changes over time in the preferred organizational forms used by for-profit corporations. The early forms were typically what we would now consider small companies, usually housed within some limited space in a single city or town. They were likely to buy their supplies locally, make whatever it was they made out of them, and sell their products in the cities and towns within driving distance of their production sites.

As corporations grew larger, and as the technologies of transportation and communication improved, firms spread out more. A typical manufacturing operation could buy supplies from much further away, ship them to manufacturing sites in many different places, assemble the finished products somewhere else, and sell them anywhere. This shift turned small companies into national corporations, and national companies into global corporate giants. Studies of this corporate expansion introduced a new organizational form known as the M-form, for multidivisional firm.

Changing technologies of communication, mobility, and production, along with the globalization of markets and the massive growth of marketing, all combined to alter the organizational environment in which goods were produced and distributed. This environmental change led to changes in the distributions of the organizational forms that dominated industry. Through much of the latter half of the twentieth century, the most visible change was the diversification of firms, from discreet entities to multiple independent divisions united under a corporate umbrella. Of course, the biggest change in corporate forms in the last decade of that period was the reverse, as large diverse corporations sold off their more recently acquired divisions. Looked at from the perspective of populations of organizations, this reversal suggests that the environment had changed further. Among individual corporations, a more popular explanation was some variation on the idea of "concentrating on the organization's core competencies." Interestingly, the growth of the multidivisional form meant more centralized control over the environment surrounding the core division, as manufacturers bought up their suppliers or started their own distribution divisions. In turn, the break-up of large multidivisional firms meant that these same firms now relied more on their networks for the materials and services on which they depended.

If the M-form is an adaptation to changing environmental conditions, then it follows that firms that adopted this form would have been more successful than those that did not (Williamson, 1970). A more subtle analysis would note, however, that the growing belief that the M-form was superior also qualifies as a change in the environment. Some firms may have adopted new forms because other firms did so, though this doesn't seem to be the main force driving the change (Mahajan, Sharma, and Bettis, 1988).

A typical M-form firm is likely to have several divisions, each of which is fairly bureaucratized with strong control from the top, while each of the components is more loosely connected to a "head office" that directs their goals without direct oversight of their daily activities. The purpose of each component is defined by the head office, which coordinates among the parts and also engages in strategic planning. This form is suited to the needs of global business in a diverse market.

Organizations in other niches will be better served by different forms. A small, owner-operated business is likely to have a short hierarchy with little differentiation among staff, all of whom report to the owner. The structures can be less formal because the owner has control and can make changes spontaneously. But the control over operations may be greater than in a larger organization because the owner is present. A social or sports club might have no hierarchy at all, with decisions made by consensus or majority vote. The purpose of the organization, in this case, is to pool the resources of its members to allow its members and supporters to do whatever sports or activities they came together around. It exists in a leisure activity niche, not a competitive market niche. If there are no profits to be divided, and the organization is defined around the interests of its community, it might more easily accommodate a collective approach to authority rather than attempting to build a hierarchy.

Ecology models view organizational niches as supportive of specific kinds of organizations only. The properties of this environmental niche will favor or impede different kinds of structures and actions, and therefore partially determine the organizational forms that are found there. Concurrently, the combination of organizations, organizational forms, and the competitive or symbiotic resource needs of those organizations give shape to the environmental niches in which they operate (Hannan, Carroll, and Pólos, 2003). In this, the organizational ecology approach breaks with biological ecology models. In evolutionary biology, the environment determines the distribution of life forms. In organizational analysis, the organizations and their environments influence one another. Of course, human beings, as a species, actively alter our environments as well, which suggests that we may no longer be following a biological evolutionary model either. But that's a question for some other book.

Density dependence

Population studies are frequently more mathematical than most of the rest of the field. Analysts do not simply treat the evolutionary language as a set of metaphors for describing the "fitness" of different organizational forms. They have constructed population models in which the rise and fall of different organizational forms may be predicted and explained. One of the crucial features on which their predictions rely is the density of a given form in some niche. By density, organizational theorists mean the number of organizations of a particular form competing within a defined environmental niche. In the early days of local broadcast television, for example, even the major cities had fewer than 10 stations, many of which shut down overnight. This fairly sparse population was all that the environment could support. In today's television world, in which the average US household has more TVs than people, it is possible to receive over 100 stations from just about anywhere in the industrial world. This change is possible only because the stations no longer have to worry about local broadcast capacity. The audience is worldwide, and each station can find its specialized audience niche out there somewhere.

"Population ecologists want to understand the dynamics of organizational diversity, *how social changes affect the mix of organizations in society*" (Hannan and Freeman, 1986: 52; emphasis in original). The rise and fall of organizational populations, from a density dependence approach, is a function of both the amount of competition within the niche among organizations of a given form, and the perceived legitimacy of the form itself (Carroll and Hannan, 1989). The competition part is relatively straightforward and reasonably familiar. In the early period of adoption of a particular form, organizations face little competition from others in their niche. As long as the density of organizations trying to survive in a given niche is below that niche's **carrying capacity**, then all may thrive. But the success and growth of the form will itself increase the likelihood that others will adopt it, increasing the density of comparable organizations, and hence the competition for survival. Eventually, the number of organizations may exceed the environment's ability to support them all, and survival will become more difficult. The rate at which new organizations are established will decrease, as the rate of organizational failures increases. Think of any street corner you know with a successful shoe store on it. That is a niche in which more than one such business can grow. Now imagine two, three, or four more shoe stores right around it. Eventually the competition will drive some of them out of business. The population will have become too dense for the carrying capacity of the niche.

The role of legitimacy is less well understood, and may be more significant to the survival of organizational forms. Recall that organizations depend on their network links to receive inputs, such as material resources and information, and to distribute goods and services. Organizations, pursuing the goal of managing and reducing uncertainty, seek out routine relations with stable exchange partners. Among other things, this means that familiar organizations with familiar organizational forms can attract exchange partners, in part due to that familiarity. Organizations that are "different" somehow introduce uncertainties. Nobody wants that. Even organizations that adopt new organizational forms designed to be more stable and profitable in some niche will suffer from the stigma of strangeness. Strangeness is a disadvantage for an organization with a known identity and purpose. It can be lethal to a new organization with no established network.

The effects of a familiar appearance and a durable reputation combine to give legitimacy to the conventional organizational forms of any niche. Forms that are so familiar as to be expected and even taken for granted are said to be institutionalized. In much of the corporate and political world, bureaucracy is the institutionalized form, and any other form would be viewed with suspicion simply for being different. In this way, organizations of a particular form define what it means to be part of their particular population by rejecting other organizational forms as foreign and dangerous. "The events that institutionalize a boundary around an organizational population often simultaneously codify the features of the form. Both institutionalization and the accompanying codification strengthen boundaries around forms" (Hannan and Freeman, 1986: 62).

New organizational forms arise in response to changing environments or excessive density of known forms within a niche. These new forms may solve problems that plagued the familiar forms, and some existing organizations may adopt the new forms strategically. But suffering from the "liability of newness" (Hannan and Freeman, 1977; Stinchcombe, 1965), these innovations may not take root. However well the form serves the organizations that adopt it, the rest of the environment may still reject it, leading to the demise of the form. For those that endure, legitimacy increases as everyone gets used to them. Once accepted, the new form is likely to be recognized for what it offers to the environment, at which time its population may well increase rapidly. In time, if the new form is highly successful, the population of organizations adopting it will be facing excess density concerns of their own.

The selection process inherent in an ecological model partially explains the rates of organizational founding and failures. This is the structural part of the model. There is an *agency* part as well, in which the relevant social actors make choices. In the case of the founding of new organizations, the relevant actors are the entrepreneurs who create them. Whether these entrepreneurs fully embrace the density model or not, we can well expect that they will prefer to enter into niches that are not too crowded when they are defining the forms and needs of their organizations. Joel Baum and Jitendra Singh (1994) tested this idea with data on the foundings and closings of daycare centers in Toronto. They discovered evidence that day-care entrepreneurs kept an eye on the resource capacities, density, and success and failure rates of similar organizations in different niches. Once the toddler niche had been filled to capacity, for example, a newcomer to the field would have to target an older or younger crowd in order to find their place. Unfortunately for many of them, however, you could only tell that the population had become too dense after some of the day-care centers in that niche had begun to fail.

In a related study, Baum and Christine Oliver (1992) demonstrated that organizational legitimacy increases and uncertainty decreases as an organization develops strong and stable ties with other institutions in its environment. In this case, better-connected day-care centers have better survival rates. Comparably, at the population level, the whole niche does better, and gains greater legitimacy, when some of the organizations in the niche are "embedded" in a network of inter-organizational relations. The authors call this form of embeddedness "relational density." Among other things, this gives us some clues as to how legitimacy operates to promote survival. Once some organizational form becomes recognized and, in some sense, appreciated, more established organizations in the environment are more likely to form connections with the given type of organization. These stable and somewhat visible ties further increase the perceived legitimacy of the whole form, thereby improving prospects for the entire population. Nothing succeeds like success, to coin a phrase.

Resource dependence

One of the critiques of the density-dependence model, and all organizational ecology models by extension, is that they describe the environment as the source of change, leaving organizations to simply respond to these changes (Zucker, 1987). This does not have to be the case. Organizations can also act. Ecology models developed under the rubric of *resource dependence*, while sharing many of the features of density-dependence models, specifically study the ways in which organizations strategically alter their forms in order to take advantage of environmental features.

Consider again the basic problems of attaining resources and managing uncertainty. The availability of material resources can vary greatly over time, as can their costs (Williamson, 1981). Economic models of supply and demand suggest that any time there are more consumers of the materials, or less of the material available than before, the costs will rise. This can create unanticipated hardships for organizations, particularly for firms that produce and sell things. It is difficult enough to project profits that depend on consumer behavior. It's worse when you can't anticipate costs.

A similar uncertainty exists at the distribution side. A firm may produce certain goods, and a market may exist for those goods. Yet there are still many opportunities for delays, extra expenses, competition, and failures when trying to get those goods to market. Consider the vast fluctuations in the price of gasoline in recent years, for example, and imagine the effects of that on companies that rely on trucking.

There are ways to project or influence both supply and demand. One of the most popular ones, among those firms that can manage it, is called vertical integration (Chandler, 1962). This brings us back to our earlier example of the rise of M-form firms. With vertical integration, a corporation buys at least a controlling interest in its suppliers and distributors, bringing everything under the control of a single "multi-divisional firm" (Fligstein, 1985). We see this at work in the rise of the studio system in US film-making. At one time, producers invested money in a film while the directors and others made and sold the movie. Under the studio system, the actors, directors, and writers are under contract to the studio. Films can be made in production spaces on the studio lot, so the costs of locations and related materials are controlled. More significantly, each of the major studios came to own a nationwide and later worldwide network of theaters, broadcast and cable television stations, and even video/DVD rental businesses. As little as possible remained to be purchased or contracted out from the planning through the delivery of the product. One by-product of this investment strategy has been a far greater investment on the part of studios in a smaller number of films, searching for the few winners that can dominate their markets at each stage of distribution. Small films with modest profit margins are less attractive to studios as they project the life cycle of a project.

A second, related, approach is horizontal integration. In this strategy, an organization, typically a firm, seeks more reliable markets by extending its reach. Small, local businesses expand horizontally into larger distribution channels offering a broader range of goods and services over greater spaces. The most evident recent examples can be seen in the reorganization of traditional "bricks and mortar" models into Internet businesses. Bookstores that used to sell books, with low-profit margins, became bookstores with coffee shops in them, selling books, coffee, and snacks, offering free wireless Internet access, and possibly renting movies, selling games, and hosting meetings, readings, and performances. Expanding further, many such bookstores keep only a small portion of their inventory in their stores, and sell the rest online direct from their warehouses along with movies, electronics, toys, and gifts.

Organizational entrepreneurship represents another crucial area for strategy and innovation. Organizational leaders are conscious of the resource capacities of their environments, more or less, and have some sense of the density of the various niches within it. Whether they use ecological terms or not, founders are likely to target niches that are neither fully exploited nor over-extended (Baum and Singh, 1994). Yet, following the logic of the liability of newness, entrepreneurs benefit by targeting locations that have similar organizations already there, and by choosing organizational forms that are not too different from the existing population. If they can manage this careful balance, their particular organization will resemble others, and be able to take advantage of existing resources, including inter-organizational links with potential exchange partners. Optimally, however, their forms and self-presentation would be different enough to enable them to draw on a slightly different resource pool, with less competition.

Populations of organizations, like biotic populations, have variations. Call them sub-populations. Though each variant is similar to the others, these sub-populations do not have to occupy exactly the same niches, due to their differences. Baum and Singh refer to "niche overlap" to describe the effort to find, or define, a location in the environment that partially corresponds to the existing niche of a related sub-population, while still keeping at least one foot in another niche. If accomplished effectively, the niche overlap can create links between organizations across the boundaries of multiple niches. This overlap increases resource opportunities much more than it increases competition.

These models of population dynamics assert that organizational founders and entrepreneurs use a particular kind of logic to enact survival strategies based on density and the distribution of resources. We can't assume that individual decision-makers are familiar with exactly these concepts. But case studies and statistical analyses support the idea that the foundings and failures of organizations follow such patterns. The important contribution is to show that the organizations are not simply being selected in or out of existence by their environments. These models significantly restore agency to organizations by demonstrating that population dynamics can be strategically "played."

The neo-institutional model

Chapter 4 touched on institutional theory with regard to cultural assumptions and bureaucratic forms. Institutional theories of the 1960s and 1970s laid the groundwork for contemporary studies of environmental relations. They rediscovered and expanded upon Weber's concern for legitimacy in a rational world, and recognized the importance of familiar forms and taken-for-grantedness in the pursuit of popular legitimacy.

Where does the old institutionalism leave off and the new one begin? This question may be debated, fruitfully or otherwise; I do not offer an answer here. I will only note that the discussion in chapter 4 concerned the **institutionalization** of forms of action within an organization, whereas the current section looks at the institutionalization of organizational forms in some kind of environment. As well, I should mention that by emphasizing the connection between the old institutionalism and contemporary cultural studies, I have skimmed over several additional contributions of the first institutional approach which would be necessary if we were to draw any boundaries between that school of thought and the neo version. Instead, I will attempt to draw some boundaries between population ecology studies of organizational environments and neo-institutional perspectives on the same question.

From the neo-institutional perspective, the environment is a much bigger entity than a niche. The operative term is *organizational field*, which encompasses "those organizations that, in the aggregate, constitute a recognized area of institutional life" (DiMaggio and Powell, 1983: 148). The field is not a niche or other ecological collection of resources and constraints. It is the collection of other organizations with which any organization must interact to participate in the recognized and routine activities of some domain of activity. Organizations are thus understood to be operating within – or embedded in – an institutionalized sphere of action.

This leads naturally to the question of what a sphere of action is and what makes it institutionalized. In practical terms, an organizational field is a mostly networked set of organizations and agencies that collectively get things done in some area of life. And that area of life is usually nameable in terms of some familiar social, political or economic institution. The health-care system of any given state is an institution, and a tremendous number of organizations may make up the field of organizations within the health-care field, for example. Networks are relations and links among organizations or other entities. But the institutionalization of network relations is not about the exchanges themselves. Rather, it is about the meaning and value of them. Institutions create order and meaning. Exchanges and events in the health-care field are primarily understood in terms of what they have to do with health care. The meaning of the actions depend on the ideas, goals, and even habits that have been institutionalized in that field.

The neo-institutional concept of the environment as a field is more cultural and less mathematical than the ecology models' approaches. A field is defined by the norms, values, and expectations that develop within it. Like a society or a community, a field has conventional ideas about how things should be done or not.

The organizational field may be mapped to some degree by using network links among the organizations that define it. Through these links, organizations exchange resources, information, ideas, and personnel. As in the ecology models, resources matter. But the field is held together by the fact that the organizations within it recognize that they share some domain, or that they are in the same field in the colloquial sense. They share concerns and establish IORs because they understand that they share concerns. In such a space, resources have their place, but legitimacy matters more.

One of the early contributions of the neo-institutional approach was Meyer and Rowan's re-examination of the popularity of bureaucratic organizational forms throughout industrial society. As we saw earlier, they attributed some of the success of this form to the fact that its use had been institutionalized, rather than to the issue of how well it worked.

> In modem societies, the elements of rationalized formal structure are deeply ingrained in, and reflect, widespread understandings of social reality. Many of the positions, policies, programs, and procedures of modern organizations are enforced by public opinion, by the views of important constituents, by knowledge legitimated through the educational system, by social prestige; by the laws, and by the definitions of negligence and prudence used by the courts. (Meyer and Rowan, 1977: 343)

To a certain extent, bureaucracy works because we believe in it more than we believe in alternatives to it. It becomes the most efficient system available for doing certain things because people in organizations are less likely to recognize the advantages of other ways of doing those things.

Generalizing from this point, Paul DiMaggio and Walter Powell took on the larger question of homophyly, or the tendency for so many different organizations to take on so few organizational forms. With such an uncountable number of organizations involved in virtually every social task one can think of, why isn't there more variety?

The answer to this question has grown with the years, but the initial concept of **isomorphism** formed the base for much of what followed. Isomorphism refers to the pressures that organizations experience to change their forms to more closely resemble the organizations around them (DiMaggio and Powell, 1983). The authors distinguished among three types of isomorphism: normative, mimetic, and coercive. Each of these types helps to explain how pressure from a group's organizational field can have such power.

The first observable pressure is normative. We've seen this before. An organization that is setting up shop in some identifiable field needs to have the field perceive it as a legitimate participant. It needs to be familiar and understandable. Suppose you want to open a community center, for example. Community centers provide common spaces that community groups can use. They are usually operated by people who have ties to the community, and they have bulletin boards and newsletters where announcements of local events and services can be posted. At the very least, this means that the center needs to get other groups to send them notices to post, so that it can fulfill this portion of its mission. And for that, it needs to be an acceptable partner to those other groups in order to establish a pattern of information exchange. If your community center had no local advisory panel, and no other mechanism through which members of the community could become involved in routine operations, then other community groups might question its legitimacy. And, of course, if your center didn't even have a bulletin board, then they would really look askance at it. So you would feel a lot of pressure to adopt the forms and behaviors of the other community centers in order to be seen as legitimate by the rest of the community. Hence, normative isomorphism: the pressure to seem normal for your environment.

It is possible that you hadn't thought through the legitimacy issue when you decided to create your center. Perhaps you have never worked in that field before, and didn't know what to expect. But, if that's the case, then how would you decide what your center should be like? Without that personal experience, you would probably do what most organizational entrepreneurs do: look at other centers and mimic them. That, of course, is mimetic isomorphism. Its effects tend to occur early in an organization's founding. Continuing the center example, it might be that you and your colleagues decide that your community needs a place for neighborhood groups to exchange information about development plans, gentrification, and other such issues. It's possible that you would begin with the idea of your mission and define and build the ideal space for it. More likely, as Cohen, March, and Olsen (1972) described, you would run through the possibilities of known forms, and pick one: political club, block association, angry mob, community center, and so on. As you examined each possibility, you would consider all that goes with it. A center needs a bulletin board, but a block association can serve drinks. A mob is dynamic, but a community center can get grants. Once that choice was made, most of the rest of your organizational decisions would follow, and your community center would strongly resemble most of the others.

The last form of isomorphism is coercive. Some organizations and agencies in a field have power over others. Government agencies can regulate some kinds of activities. The rules and standards of some kinds of organizations can restrict one's ability to work with them. Rating and ranking agencies can help your group get outside funding, or they can define you as a bad risk.

A community center, for example, is likely to need to handle money, and to either own or rent property. For this, the center must have a corporate identity that is considered acceptable to a bank.

And the corporation must have officers who have legal liability for how the money is spent. And if you are going to start a corporation and open a bank account, then you must register with the state and file tax forms. So what started as a group of people in a neighborhood who wanted to create a shared space becomes a corporation with a bureaucratic structure, leaders, and officers. Depending on how the law works where you are, the group might also need by-laws specifying how the officers are to be selected and what the eligibility requirements are. Your organization may choose to adopt an alternative organizational form, but will the organizations in your field let you do it? Rather than take any chances, your group might choose to just go with the flow. That is coercive isomorphism.

Adopting a familiar organizational form is a necessary step for a new organization to acquire legitimacy in its field. But it is not enough. Organizations need to participate in exchanges and cultivate inter-organizational ties in order to prove to others that they can be reliable exchange partners. They need to participate in the normal activities of the field in order to ceremonially communicate that they are the kinds of organizations that will do that sort of thing. They need to trade favors and bank some goodwill, in case of crisis. They may need to co-opt the interests of some powerful elites who can protect them against future events. In sum, they need to embed themselves deeply into the institutional life of their field (Hager, Galaskiewicz, and Larson, 2004).

As a final word on this subject, we should note that it is also possible for an organizational form to lose legitimacy. Given the power of isomorphism, we know that there are a limited number of legitimate forms out there, and that their familiarity gives them staying power. Nonetheless, change does happen. Organizations adapt and new forms emerge in response to environmental changes. So, like organizations themselves, organizational forms may have a life cycle. Finding and studying a new organizational form, however, is an elusive goal.

Gerald Davis, Kristina Diekmann, and Catherine Tinsley found an ideal case in the partial demise of the conglomerate, the same form of multidivisional firm whose rise had been partly explained by resource-dependency theory above. Multidivisional forms, also called conglomerates, grew considerably in size and number through most of the middle of the twentieth century, as large (core) firms bought up suppliers and distributors (vertical integration), acquired competitors (horizontal integration), and diversified into unrelated areas by taking over smaller, specialized companies on the peripheries of their industries. All of this growth and acquisition was permitted, even encouraged, by changes in the regulatory environment and by the actions of investors. The rapid and radical reorganizations that followed, in which the firms in question often not only bought up rivals, but stripped them for usable parts and patents, then sold the remains on the side, created a new business metaphor: the firm-as-portfolio. These conglomerates introduced the notion that the value of a firm was based on the value of its holdings, not its work, and that executive management required frequent reassessments of those holdings.

The near end to this practice came in stages. First, there was mounting empirical evidence that the large conglomerates were not efficient and, frequently, not particularly profitable. But it was not the impracticality of the process that doomed it, Davis and colleagues argue. It was the normative shift that accompanied these new ways of valuing corporations. "Thus, we contend that the move to extreme vertical disintegration in the late 1980s arose in reaction to the firm-as-portfolio model and the subsequent deconglomeration movement" (1994: 550). The recognition that the conglomerates were unsuccessful, coupled with the newly popular way of imagining a firm as a collection of holdings, led to the non-controversial realization that the parts, the individual companies, could be worth more money if they were removed from the parent firm. Buying up and tearing apart multidivisional forms became a legitimate investment activity. More than that, it was viewed as a safe bet, and routine procedures were developed to help buyers secure bank loans to fund their raids. Almost overnight, the multidivisional organizational form switched from being a symbol of strength to a marker of vulnerability. Growing firms had to avoid acquiring too many holdings for fear of being targeted for acquisition themselves. Finally, the institutional shift that had occurred during the creation period of the conglomerate firms had broken a crucial taken-for-granted image, that of the firm as a sovereign body. It had always been possible to tear a large firm apart, but, prior to the institutionalization of the firm-as-portfolio, it would have been almost unimaginable. The fiscal error of multidivisional growth revealed a cognitive error – an organization need not be viewed as a solid object or a single body. To put that differently, "Conglomerates strained the body analogy, because they offered no credible basis for a myth of identity" (Davis et al., 1994: 566).

So it is not just fields that only exist when we believe in them. Organizations may cease to have weight, and organizational forms may disappear when the idea of them is delegitimated. Highly profitable firms can fail overnight simply because people stop believing in them. We try to create a scientific basis for the study of markets, but we still can't fully account for the role of faith.

Key Readings

Readings on Environments

Aldrich, Howard E., and Jeffrey Pfeffer 1976 "Environments of Organizations." *Annual Review of Sociology,* 2: 79–105.

Thompson, J. D. 1967 *Organizations in Action.* New York: McGraw-Hill.

These two works together establish the need for organizational theorists to understand environments. They introduce the ideas that define the "open systems" approach to organizational analysis.

Readings on Ecology Models

Baum, Joel A. C., and Jitendra V. Singh 1994 "Organizational Niches and the Dynamics of Organizational Founding." *Organization Science,* 5(4): 483–501.

Carroll, Glenn R., and Michael T. Hannan 1989 "Density Dependence in the Evolution of Populations of Newspaper Organizations." *American Sociological Review,* 54(4): 524–41.

Cohen, Michael D., James G. March, and Johan P. Olsen 1972 "A Garbage Can Model of Organizational Choice." *Administrative Science Quarterly,* 17(1): 1–25.

Hannan, Michael T., and John Freeman 1986 "Where Do Organizational Forms Come From?" *Sociological Forum,* 1(1): 50–72.

Hannan, Michael T., Glenn R. Carroll, and László Pólos 2003 "The Organizational Niche." *Sociological Theory,* 21(4): 309–40.

Singh, Jitendra V., and Charles J. Lumsden 1990 "Theory and Research in Organizational Ecology." *American Review of Sociology,* 16: 161–95.

These six articles collectively define the origins, development, and new directions in ecological models of organizational analysis. They establish the key terms, the major findings, and the conceptual underpinnings for this branch of study.

Readings on Neo-institutional models

DiMaggio, Paul J., and Walter W. Powell 1983 "The Iron Cage Revisited: Institutional Isomorphism and Collective Rationality in Organizational Fields." *American Sociological Review,* 35: 147–60.

Fligstein, Neil 1993 *The Transformation of Corporate Control.* Cambridge, MA: Harvard University Press.

Powell, Walter W., and Paul DiMaggio (eds) 1991 *The New Institutionalism in Organizational Analysis.* Chicago, IL: University of Chicago Press.

Zucker, Lynne 1987 "Institutional Theories of Organization." *Annual Review of Sociology,* 13: 443–64.

These four works collectively define the origins, development, and new directions in neo-institutional models of organizational analysis. They establish the key terms, the major findings, and the conceptual underpinnings for this branch of study.

CHAPTER
07
The Non-profit Sector

Have you ever volunteered your time to help a corporation? Perhaps you can picture yourself going into a mall and offering to help a store sell its products. Maybe you could offer to deliver orders for your local deli, or help the workers at a construction site carry heavy materials. You probably wouldn't, though. Those are jobs, and people do them for money, not out of kindness.

But consider what you have volunteered to do. Have you collected recyclables or canned food for a community group, sold Girl Scout cookies, made calls on behalf of your favorite political party, served meals to the homeless, or helped with a fund-raiser that benefited your school? If so, then you have volunteered your time to a corporation. Each of these organizations is a non-profit corporation. And, in the US alone, approximately 61 million citizens volunteer an average of about 207 hours a year to help them out (Wing, Pollak, and Blackwood, 2008).

Up to this point, a disproportionate amount of attention has been given to industry in this book. The present chapter and the following one will extend our scope somewhat. Scholars in multiple fields have found it useful to distinguish among three sectors of organizational activity: government, industry, and non-profit. Industry refers to privately held market-oriented organizations that seek to make a profit, also called the private sector. The government, or state sector, refers to public organizations including government itself and state and municipal agencies. The "third sector," also called the non-profit sector, is composed of private organizations, generally operating within public arenas. Legally and analytically, the non-profit sector is defined by the "non-distribution constraint" or requirement that no organizational profits may be distributed to owners or shareholders (Hansmann, 1980).

The third sector is the most ambiguously defined. Like government, most non-profits deal with public issues, often on behalf of an identified constituency. As in the case of for-profits, they are privately organized and not managed by the state. And, realistically, the boundaries between non-profits and the other two sectors are so blurred that it is hard to place many organizations clearly in one sector or another. Schuppert (1991) has even suggested that the three sectors are so intertwined that it is actually misleading to treat them as separate entities. In effect, each can only be defined in relation to the others. Most of this chapter will therefore examine the non-profit sector in terms of its relations with government and industry.

Defining the non-profit sector

The world of non-profits is vast. Virtually all organized entities that people create for any purpose other than business or government fits there. Most conspicuously, all of our citizens' groups, neighborhood associations, cultural associations, self-help and mutual aid societies, and the entire realm of charitable organizations operate as non-profits. Most sports activities are organized, and few teams or players are professionals. Leagues, social activities, and fan clubs are non-profit organizations. Most political associations are neither for-profits nor governmental agencies. The non-profit sector therefore provides virtually the entire organizational space in which non- professionals enter into the political realm.

Non-profit organizations, or NPOs, "are seen as protectors of both pluralism and privilege, sites of democracy and control, sources of innovation and paralysis, instruments of and competitors to states" (DiMaggio and Anheier, 1990: 153). Collectively, NPOs do not have a single personality or purpose, a particular political agenda, or a distinct organizational form. Individually, they include just about every viable agenda or form. If you wanted to start a group to pursue a totally new agenda, it would probably be a non-profit. The sector overlaps considerably with the idea of **civil society**, an equally ambiguous notion intended to indicate the organizational space in which private citizens act in the public realm. It is also sometimes imprecisely referred to as the voluntary sector, or, more optimistically, as the independent sector.

Attempts to clarify and classify the non-profit sector are further complicated by variations in their use and history across states and world regions. European definitions tend to focus on charitable activities and mutual aid societies, as reflected in the British term "public charities" or the French "service economy" (Salamon and Anheier, 1996). In the Netherlands, on the other hand, a long tradition of "pillarization" allows and encourages communities to incorporate their own cultural, political, social, and economic interest groups, most of which depend on state funding (Lijphart, 1968). Pillarization refers to the division of the public realm into several distinct civil societies, such as a Catholic community with its own schools and services, separate from the Protestant community with its organizations. The state protects the equality of citizens by supporting most of these private groups. This is a very different approach from the US or UK cases where organizations operating in the public realm are expected to serve all communities equally.

And there are more variations still. Public organizations organized independently of state agencies throughout Latin America and Africa are more frequently known as Non-Governmental Organizations, or NGOs. The term Civil Society Organizations (CSOs) also occurs frequently in the NGO literature, mostly referring to the same groups. In 2004, the UN Office of the Special Advisor on Africa catalogued nearly 3,800 NGOs operating throughout Africa (OSAA, 2004). The terms NGO and CSO indicate that the organizations in question operate in the same realm as governmental agencies, but privately. NGOs can be for-profits, but most are not for profit. A great many more NGOs are transnational and work more with, or against, governmental organizations than with local community groups. And since each nation has its own laws and classification systems for non-profits, comparing NGOs to NPOs to CSOs is fraught with opportunities for error and confusion. Let's just say there are a lot of them operating all across the world in virtually all aspects of organized society.

Non-profit organizations in the industrialized democracies may be found in great numbers in a few key areas: *cultural associations*, such as the arts and ethnic organizations that celebrate cultural histories; *service organizations*, including many hospitals, legal aid, and living assistance; *philanthropy*, including small charities and large charitable foundations; *education* from nursery schools to universities; *religious organizations*, including churches, temples, mosques, and ashrams, as well as religious education; and *political advocacy*, providing voice to communities that are not otherwise organized.

Non-profit scholarship is a dynamic and growing area of study. Even so, it is difficult to get a comprehensive sense of the whole sector. Research is divided into various specialty areas, which do not always communicate well with one another. Voluntary cultural and charitable activities are most widely recognized and discussed in the research literature, while political and religious activities are the most frequently overlooked or defined as "special" cases. Overall, it has been easier to define the non-profit sector according to its economic roles rather than its many social roles, resulting in a great deal of uncertainty about the social identity of non-profits.

For the most part, I will follow the conventions of the field in reviewing the work of the non-profit sector. The chapter will begin with some of the leading economic models of the non-profit sector's functions. My aim here, though, is to try to address some of the larger questions of the organizational identity and characteristics of NPOs. What do NPOs do? How different are they, if at all, from other organizations? What do we need to know in order to either study or work within the non-profit field? The chapter will end with a brief review of work on the social and political roles of non-profits.

Why is there a non-profit sector?

Given the size and diversity of the third sector, both within and across nations, there can't be a single answer to this question. However, several consistent and important factors can help explain the origins and growth of the sector. Foremost among these are market failure, **state failure**, trustworthiness, and flexibility. Each of these theories looks at some sector of society to ask what NPOs do better there than other forms of organizations.

The **market failure** model compares non-profit organizations with for-profit organizations that provide comparable goods or services. Non-profits can be found throughout the service industries, from education to food and housing to transportation to debt relief to tax advice and beyond. Often such organizations are set up on the assumption that for-profit firms in the same industry have failed to provide the necessary range of goods and services for all of those who need them. Given the profit motive in industry, businesses are unlikely to pursue the public good as aggressively as they pursue their own interests. Firms may calculate that it is cost-effective to serve only a limited slice of the market, ignoring the rest. As a general rule, for-profit firms tend to show more interest in people with money than in those without. For example, developers may focus their efforts in the luxury housing market because that segment is the most lucrative, with little or no interest in low-income housing. If we left the question of housing entirely to market forces, a lot of people would be left out in the cold. In response to this inability on the part of the market to cover all of a society's needs, non-profit organizations take on similar functions to the firms. Without the need to bring in a profit for investors, NPOs can concentrate on the areas of greatest need, not greatest sales potential. In fact, many NPOs spend their money on behalf of others and need grants and gifts to operate.

A similar economic calculus exists in many commercial areas. Bookstores sometimes make money, while libraries do not. But libraries maintain much larger collections. Museums purchase and display unique and highly valued works of art, for which they are not paid, while the simplest gift shop selling miniature reproductions of the same works can make money. Museums spend money to serve the public interest. The profit motive may be credited with the ongoing quest for better mousetraps, but there are large segments of public life for which this motivation is not sufficient for addressing all of public needs. If hospitals operated on a pure profit motive, for example, then many fewer medical services would be provided, and to far fewer people. Plastic surgery, for example, pays very well, while long-term care for patients with cancer, HIV/AIDS, or tuberculosis is not as profitable. (Fortunately, hospitals don't work that way.)

Market failure also applies to the quality of goods and services that are available or not. Admittedly, it's much more difficult to measure the quality of things than the quantity, but a few examples can illustrate the point. Consider popular culture. Films, plays, concerts, and other performance arts are cultural products that collectively demonstrate the triumphs of a society, not in practical terms but in the combination of art, skill, knowledge, craft, and meaning. The epic oral poetry performances of ancient Greece help us to understand the aspirations of that society, while the "Dutch master painters" of the sixteenth century or light opera under the actual direction of Gilbert and Sullivan in the late nineteenth century are remembered and studied as high points of their respective times and places. Popular, profit-driven arts, by contrast, don't usually hit the same high notes.

The motto of one of the major Hollywood film studios is *ars gratia artis*, or art for art's sake. Yet a great many of the movies that follow this lofty claim are mostly noted for the amount of stuff that they blow up. Somehow, it seems, a lot of our cultural products are not quite reaching for the highest ideals of our societies. The commercial sector is good at producing popular works for mass-market distribution, but this is not the best model with which to cultivate work that is truly daring or different.

The non-profit arts world, on the other hand, promotes work that is different, untested, or even deliberately provocative. It embodies the avant-garde, the leading edge of cultural movements. Without the profit motive to drive them, the non-profit arts world can give more attention to art.

The state failure model is similar to the market failure model, in that it assumes that non-profits will grow among communities and constituencies that are not otherwise well served. This approach compares NPOs to state agencies and asks why people would put so much energy into creating things like a non-profit service sector when there are already public agencies doing that work. As with the market failure approach, the NPOs are seen as going where no one else wishes to go. In this case, however, the non-profits are seen as the more restrictive option.

Government agencies have an obligation to treat everyone more or less equally; providing services to all who qualify and sharing the costs broadly. This works well enough for public goods such as education, transportation, and postal services. But some communities have unique needs. They don't want to be treated in the same way as everyone else. They want something that others don't need or want.

Private non-profits can raise support from communities of interest and channel their efforts in highly selective directions. The advantage of NPOs is that they can design their programs for the immediate needs and constituents. They are more deeply embedded in their target communities, more aware of what has to be done and how, and often more thorough in meeting those needs. Non-profits provide goods and services to particular groups or populations when government is unable, or unwilling, to do so.

Governments can fail constituencies in other ways, as elaborated by Burton Weisbrod (1975, 1988). Democratically elected governments must be responsive to the needs of the people, up to a point. Strategically, officials need to attend to majority groups or to the median needs. Promoting the well-being of minority groups can create electoral vulnerabilities by damaging relations with the majority without delivering a comparable boost of support from the smaller groups. In many cases, such as those involving immigrant communities, children, or the elderly, much of the minority group may not even vote. This lack of government interest in or accountability to less influential communities provides one of the motives for community organizing through non-profits. These communities form their own organizations and associations to act on their own behalf.

Of course, as Weisbrod notes, the for-profit world also competes with government. Many for-profit opportunities arise from these same limitations in government provision of goods and services, even in areas where governments are active. Consider the extensive use of private package delivery services, which compete directly with state-run postal services. Private, for-profit schools (to use the American term for them) compete with public education, and the US government itself is currently paying private security firms to supplement the armed forces in Iraq and Afghanistan. In certain respects, the entire automotive industry can be seen as private competition to public transportation, though we should note that governments pay billions of dollars to build and maintain the roads on which cars depend.

Additionally, communities with resources may choose to invest more in some goods or services than the state is able or willing to provide. Many arts and cultural organizations, as well as non-profits supporting health care, education, and social well-being are founded in this way. Even social change organizations created by and for resource-poor communities are sometimes, though not often, supported by the private contributions of wealthy donors who do not trust government to sufficiently address ongoing social ills (Bartley, 2007; Ostrander, 1995). As Dennis Young (2000) has observed, however, this tension between states and non-profits is likely to be more important in highly diverse nations, such as the US or Great Britain, and less so in nations such as Japan or France where there is greater homogeneity of communities. In such cases, the state may be better able to meet the needs of more of the population, and possibly more aware of the needs of the rest.

A further motive, called **contract failure**, introduces the notion of trustworthiness. Contract failure occurs when one of the contracting parties, typically the purchaser of a service, is unable to verify that they are paying a fair market rate for the service. This can happen when the conditions and needs are too complex for anyone to establish a fair and consistent rate, or when the purchaser does not have access to the kinds of information they would need to make that decision. You may have received great credit card offers at some point, or music club discounts or the like, only to discover much later that you had agreed to terms that you were unaware of. It is also just possible that you have clicked a virtual button marked "I agree to the terms and conditions" when you were installing some software without actually having read the terms and conditions. These are examples of contract failure as well. Presumably, if you have clicked that button, you either trusted the source of the software or were not personally responsible for whatever happened to the computer you were on.

Richard Steinberg (2006) offers the example of a nursing home. Typically, one contracts with a nursing home to provide care for someone else, such as an elderly parent. The person paying for the service will not be the one receiving it, making it difficult to judge what one gets for the money. Nor can the actual service consumer, the resident, necessarily be counted on to give a reliable evaluation of the quality of care in comparison to other facilities beyond the most basic issues. So the purchaser has to choose a facility that they feel they can trust to deliver quality care at a fair price. With little information to guide their decisions, many people tend to favor a non-profit nursing home under the assumption that, because they are not driven by a profit motive, such a facility has less incentive to cut corners or overcharge.

This assumption does not always hold, for a variety of reasons. But incentives are different for non-profits and for-profits, which does have implications for trustworthiness. In cases such as education and health care, of course, governments also attempt to address the lack of information and general trust issues through regulation and oversight. That is, even though the consumers of the services are highly unlikely to be able to tell a good school or hospital from a bad one, there are government agencies that are dedicated to doing exactly that. They regulate the industries, almost guaranteeing that all licensed service providers meet at least some minimum standard, identifying the best and worst institutions, and even shutting some places down now and then. In theory, if a school or hospital is open, then it should be safe enough.

Another aspect of trustworthiness has to do with efficiency. This is particularly a concern for service organizations. All else being equal, we tend to assume that individuals working at for-profit corporations are motivated by their wages and salaries. Indeed, one of the assumptions underlying most of the administrative theories that we have looked at is that employees cannot be trusted to do their jobs unless their performance is coercively tied to their incomes. The same assumption has been in play recently in debates about executive compensation, in which advocates have suggested that a CEO of a rich corporation might not give wholeheartedly to the job if he or she were not paid much, much more than the CEOs of smaller companies. In contrast, many non-profit corporations in the human services domain operate on tight and uncertain budgets, pay less than private industry, and offer less job security. It is easy to assume that employees who take those jobs must have a greater commitment to the missions of the organizations. Otherwise, why would they be there? If true, this would give us more reason to trust that the non-profit corporations will invest more effort and care to accomplish their challenges, and with fewer resources than comparable for-profits. We have reason to hope that the non-profits would be more efficient and effective.

Finally, there is the issue of **flexibility**. Consider the differences between a large, well-established, well-funded state agency, such as the National Institutes of Health, and a small, privately operated health clinic in a mid-sized city. Which one of these do you think would be more likely to be looking at health trends and planning for 5 and 10 years into the future? I expect you would credit the NIH with that one. Which one would you expect to be able to notice and respond to the sudden appearance of an unexpected health condition? Quite possibly it would be the clinic. A small, private organization typically has fewer tasks and a more detailed knowledge of what's going on around it. When something changes in the environment, the small organization is immediately affected. So they notice these things.

Because many non-profits are small, even transitory, and because they are typically operated by relatively small numbers of people – people who can meet together all in one room – such organizations are often able to change course quickly, reallocate resources, ask new questions, and adjust to new thinking. Great ships are used to cross oceans. Little power boats are used for emergency rescues. Sometimes the analogy works for organizations as well.

In the case of organizations reacting to changing circumstances, we would eventually want the new thinking to not only make its way from the innovative small organizations into the large institutions; we would also want it to be thoroughly studied and questioned before being accepted or rejected at the institutional level. In the immediate day-to-day operations, it is often useful to have smaller, more flexible organizations as "first responders" to shifting social phenomena. In the long run, we also need the big inflexible ships.

The flexibility argument applies to organizational sectors as well as to organizations. The state sector is notoriously slow to change. Large firms seek stable and predictable inter-organizational relations, as we have already seen. The non-profit sector is therefore perceived as the organizational space in which new groups can emerge when needed, or shut down when their work is done. It is in this sector that new or experimental organizational forms can be developed as necessary. Indeed, it is implicit in the ideas of market failure and state failure that the non-profit sector should act in response to the inflexibility of other sectors. Firms are not expected to reorganize in response to non-profit failure.

Inter-organizational relations across sectors often depend on the assumption that both individual non-profits and the sector overall are more flexible. Specifically, it is the *belief* in flexibility more than the measured reality of it that drives some of these multi-sector partnerships. State agencies and corporate philanthropy define the larger goals that they wish to support, but they increasingly rely on non-profits to make it work in practical terms, believing that the non-profits have greater flexibility to do so (Gronbjerg, 2001). The non-profit world is organized by different goals and constraints than the for-profit and government sectors. We tend to assume, therefore, that they are different kinds of entities. Let us now explore this assumption further.

How are NPOs different?

We know enough about the organizational forms, practices, and internal management of for-profits already to compare them with NPOs. Bureaucratic forms are common, though not required. Variations exist, of course. But the basic hierarchy, with or without cubicles, is so common that people come to expect them. You would have to go out of your way to explain yourself if you tried to set up some other structure for your organization. In business, strict hierarchies, clear lines of communication, accountability, and well-defined tasks provide formal organizations with legitimacy because they promise a degree of efficiency, consistency, and profitability. These characteristics are considered important to shareholders, who reap the profits, and to exchange partners, who rely on stable business environments. Many of these factors partially apply to the non-profit sector, but to a much smaller degree. So NPOs can adopt bureaucratic forms as easily as any other organization.

But they don't have to. Since NPOs do not make profits, they have no shareholders and no need to guarantee a regular and consistent income. Further, NPOs often distribute goods and services outside of the normal channels of competitive business, so their exchange partners do not have the same expectations of them. For these and other reasons, NPOs may be more concerned with the breadth of their reach than with efficiency. This difference in priorities contrasts sharply with the for-profit world.

What kinds of alternative forms can NPOs adopt? Let's work backwards from for-profits and see what we might be trying to avoid. If the stereotypical image of a for-profit corporation is that of a soulless bureaucracy driven only by its quest for profit, then we can try to imagine its opposite: an organization driven by its soul. Possibly this would mean a non-bureaucratic, mission-driven collective whose members act together because they believe in what they do. We don't need to find any real organizations that work this way in order to recognize this image as the model of what we're hoping to find when we volunteer our labor, or as the model that non-profits hope you have in mind when they ask you for donations. This is trustworthiness taken to the extreme. But does it have any relationship to actual organizations, living or dead?

In fact, there are periodic attempts to create such "alternative institutions" whose existence would improve the lives of their participants and their communities. Among the most exceptional of these are "utopian communities," where groups of people with a shared set of values and goals separate themselves from the larger social world in order to create a social system that represents and reproduces their values. In such a community, ideally, the members' social roles should align so well with their values that little formal authority is needed, and members' actions would strengthen and improve the whole system. It's hard to imagine such a system working, but that is why they call them "utopian." And in the purity of their goals and the uniqueness of their isolation, utopian communities are like natural experiments in alternative systems of social organization. As Rosabeth Moss Kanter expressed it, "The essence of such a community is in strong connections and mutual obligations. Communal life depends on a continual flow of energy and support among members, on their depth of shared relationships, and on their continued attachment to each other and to the joint endeavor" (1972: 65). Simply put, the commitment of their members is everything.

Kanter's (1968, 1972) study of 91 utopian communities formed in the US in the nineteenth century has provided the basis for much of the subsequent work on this topic. One of the big questions of the field, as we have seen, is how can organizations maintain the commitment of their members. In slightly simpler terms, how can you keep them from leaving? In jobs, you can get people to stay by paying them fairly for their work. But in a voluntary community, participating in the organization often requires the members to give something up. In some cases, members pledge to follow codes of behavior, such as not smoking or drinking. In other cases, members have to leave their homes, quit their jobs, and move into a communal space.

From a strictly rational cost-benefit analysis, one might think that organizations (and communities) can better maintain their members' commitments by lowering the cost of participation. I might give up smoking for my new community, but I'd hesitate to give up my friends. Yet, Kanter finds, this perspective would not appreciate the nature of the idea of commitment. Most of the more successful communities, in fact, demand real sacrifice from their participants. "In the eyes of the group and in the mind of the individual, sacrifice for a cause . . . makes it sacred and inviolable" (Kanter, 1968: 505). Minor inconveniences in one's lifestyle just don't have that emotional impact.

Of equal, if not greater, importance is the totality of the community in its participants' lives. A community that lives on the commitment of its members does not want to share its people with other institutions in the world. All that is needed should come from within the community, while goods from outside are devalued. Such systems have practical value of course, since they help to make the community self-sufficient. But they also help to strengthen a community's sense of "we" in contrast to the "they" who are outside. Commitment is not so much to the organization or its goals as it is to the social identity represented by participation in the group. The more strictly a community can maintain the boundary between itself and the outside world, the more its members can define themselves in terms of their membership. The power of this kind of group identification process is often visible in religious communities, competitive teams, and military units. It does not apply nearly as well to more casual groups such as block associations, some unions, or most committees.

There were utopian communities in the US during the 1960s as well. Of greater interest to us, for the purposes of this book, were the "alternative institutions" of the 1970s and beyond that deliberately sought to apply community-building principles of the utopian sort to organizations, jobs, and businesses. Joyce Rothschild (Rothschild-Whitt, 1979; Rothschild and Whitt, 1986) has studied the leadership and authority (or anti-authority) structures of "free medical clinics, free schools, legal collectives, alternative media collectives, food cooperatives, research collectives, communes" among other organizations, seeking to develop a model of "value rational" social action. Unlike instrumental rationality, value rational behavior is motivated by ideals, beliefs, and, simply put, values. Participants are motivated to contribute to such organizations because they believe in them, and often do so even at a cost to themselves.

Organizational participants in value-driven non-profits, such as community-based organizations, sometimes speak of the sense of "ownership" of their work as a crucial value. This ownership refers, in part, to the collective identities that such groups construct. A community group represents a community, and while its members act within the organization they are often acting on behalf of their own people (Stoller, 1995). Crucially, however, ownership of work also requires a degree of professional autonomy and participation in the decision-making process. For participant values to have real force within the group, participants must be able to express these values. That means each individual has to be free to express their own concerns. And yet, at the same time, the strength of the group relies on the shared sense of identity within it. They need to work toward a collective agreement in order to "own" the work together. "Only decisions which appear to carry the consensus of the group behind them, carry the weight of moral authority" (Rothschild-Whitt, 1979: 512). Such moral authority is a powerful force in the mobilization of participants' commitment, though it has its costs. One of those costs is captured in the title of Francesca Polletta's study of contemporary social movements in the United States, *Freedom is an Endless Meeting*.

Value rational commitments are an essential component of volunteerism, and often a large part of the motivation for those who work for pay at many kinds of NPOs. Since non-profits may rely on volunteer labor and private donations, or simply pay much less than comparable firms, their relationships with their workforce are often quite different from what we've seen in administrative theory. Non-profits are frequently mission driven and must engage their members' desire to contribute, as well as their belief that the organization is responsive to their concerns. Mobilizing the value-commitments of their members this way also implies that the organizations will act consistently on those values. Yet, as non-profit organizations increasingly move into areas traditionally associated with the other two sectors, or form partnerships across sectors, many non-profits are altering their forms and practices to accommodate the interests of outside groups. They try to make themselves more approachable for government and business. Volunteers and staff at mission-driven non-profits may therefore react with anger or a sense of betrayal when their organizations begin to behave like businesses or bureaucracies (Kelley, Lune, and Murphy, 2005). It violates the unspoken, but taken-for-granted, relationship between the people and the organization.

Commerce and community at an arts organization

One of the most complex and interesting contemporary analyses of participant commitment is Katherine Chen's (2009) study of the organization that produces the annual Burning Man event. The Burning Man project is a curious organization. The group's purpose is to coordinate a week-long participatory arts festival. Each year volunteers build and dismantle a temporary city in the Nevada Black Rock Desert where they create and display their own art and share in one another's projects. Almost no commercial transactions are permitted on the site; participants are encouraged to engage in a gift economy without expectation of reciprocity. Yet, given the scale of the project, its insurance and other legal requirements, and the enormous movement of resources necessary to bring it about, the Burning Man organization is actually a registered Limited Liability Company, which is a kind of for-profit firm.

In Chen's analysis, Burning Man thrives in a constant state of existential crisis. Some participants want a shared communal experience; others seek a celebration; still others want to revel in an uncontrolled experiment of just letting things happen. Yet, with nearly 50,000 event-goers, and a multimillion dollar budget from event ticket sales, as well as organized opposition, media misrepresentation, and a host of people, government agencies, and companies looking to cash in on the Burning Man cachet, people have to actually organize the event. In so doing, organizers seek to walk a fine line between chaos and excessive control, or between under-organizing and over-organizing. Too little control, and they run the risk of injuries and deaths, arrests and lawsuits, commercial exploitation, non-arts-related free-for-all, or just plain failure. Too much control, and Burning Man ceases to be the unfettered creative opportunity with a unique appeal. Organizationally, as well, the event depends on some 2,000 committed volunteers who take responsibility for building temporary shelters, installing art projects, directing traffic, fielding media requests, patrolling for emergencies, and managing Internet communications. Many volunteers dedicate months of their time to the festival for little or no pay. Too little control would squander available volunteer help and talent; too much control would discourage and chase away supporters.

By most organizational logics, Burning Man is simply too large and its coordination efforts are too complex to continue functioning without a central bureaucracy. It just shouldn't work. Yet Chen's interview subjects describe the festival as being a break from, or even an antidote to, the bureaucracies within which they spend most of their days. Some are explicit that they would rather shut it down than see it "Disneyfied," by which they seem to mean standardizing the event to pursue commercial success and tourist dollars. Despite various hurdles, Burning Man continues to run, but each year brings a new chapter in the same struggle over appropriate organizing practices and the nature of the relationship between the group and its participants. All organizations struggle to some degree with the tensions between pragmatic needs and member commitments. Few, however, are as aware of these struggles or as self-conscious about managing them as the Burning Man project.

The three sectors intersect

We know that values, culture, and feelings are important to people even in their day jobs. Material rewards matter, but participants need more than that to feel committed to their various organizations. Similarly, pay and benefits matter, even to those choosing careers in the relatively resource-poor non-profit sector. This brings us back to our earlier question: how are non-profits different? Or, to refine that question a bit, how do non-profit organizations relate to the rest of the organizational world? Theoretical work and empirical studies suggest that all organizations are both value rational and instrumentally rational, to use Weber's terms. We tend to expect, or tolerate, or demand, more instrumental rationality from for-profit firms, while looking to government or the non-profit sector for a greater, but not total, emphasis on value rationality. This expectation loosely relates to our blurry distinction between private organizations and public ones. Public organizations ought to have a public function. Private organizations need to succeed.

Defining the interrelations among the three sectors has become a growth area in non-profit scholarship during the past 10 years or so. We've reviewed the economic work that has considered the relative merits of non-profit versus for-profit service provision, including the state's preference for dealing with the non-profit sector in some areas, consumers' use of non-profits following their relative evaluations of the two sectors' "trustworthiness," and non-profit work as a response to government and market failure. Political studies have also examined the role of the non-profit sector in relation to the state. This work has raised such issues as the state's increasing reliance on NPOs for a wide array of health and human service delivery (Salamon, 1987), the increasing dependency of the non-profit sector on state funding in an urban grants economy, the influence of corporate giving in a tight market for public funds (Galaskiewicz, 1997), and the viability and autonomy of NPOs in the face of budget cutbacks and competitive block grant funding (Altheide, 1987). With those questions in mind, we will turn now to the political dimensions of the state–non-profit relationship.

The state and the non-profit sector

Non-profit organizations generally register with the state as corporations. In most industrial nations, charities and service groups qualify for tax exemptions, though this designation limits their ability to do other things beyond charity work. Non-profits whose missions involve pressuring government on policy decisions, also called "interest groups," rarely enjoy the tax benefits of charities. In US tax law, the latter group register under section 501(c)(3) and enjoy a host of financial supports for themselves and their donors, while interest groups are regulated by section 501(c)(4) which does not offer the same advantages.

Despite the fact that charities tend not to involve themselves in politics, politicians often involve them in program planning. US President George H. W. Bush's "thousand points of light" plan, for example, relied on the idea that government can most efficiently (or cost-efficiently) serve the needs of the needy by providing a supportive environment for the tens of thousands of community-based charities throughout the nation (Blau and Rabrenovic, 1991). And, indeed, it has become commonplace for non-profit service providers to depend on government support for the majority of their operating budgets (Lipsky and Smith, 1989–90: 625). As Michael Lipsky and Steven Rathgeb Smith argue, "the new relationship between government and nonprofits amounts to one of mutual dependence that is financial as well as technical; increasingly, the lines between public and private are blurred."

Nations cycle between periods in which government expands to fulfill more social roles and periods in which government prefers to hand many of those functions to private-sector organizations. The various ideas about the obligations of government to citizens in need, as well as the various public and private programs designed to meet those needs, are termed "the welfare state." This concept has ideological as well as practical meaning, and the two are often at odds. Organized interest groups hold governments accountable for their public obligations, their value-rational goals, while other interest groups pressure states to operate more efficiently in instrumentally rational terms. Thus, according to Lipsky and Smith, one of the incentives for governments to contract with non-profit service organizations is to support the welfare state while appearing to reduce it. That is, by providing grants to private service agencies instead of providing services, the state's direct investment in social welfare goes down even if the total cost may go up.

Until recently, our understanding of the development of the welfare state in advanced industrial countries assumed that the hallmark of a progressive welfare state was a large public sector that relegated the private sector to a small residual role. In this view, the United States with its smaller public sector and larger private non-profit sector compared unfavorably. The expansion of government contracting with non-profit agencies raises questions about this popular image. In the recent period, government has used non-profit agencies to expand the boundaries of the welfare state in the United States in a host of service categories. The result is a welfare state that is more expansive than would be the case if policymakers relied solely on the public sector.

As the boundaries between state and private sector weaken, it is the non-profit organizations that most come to resemble government agencies, and not the other way around. Answerable to government as a source of both funding and regulation, community-based service providers may be drawn away from their constituents' priorities and interests and into those of the agencies that support them. In value-rational matters, the service NPOs have to answer to their communities. On the other hand, in instrumental-rational matters, they have to impress the government. In return, the community groups receive relatively reliable funding for at least some of their programs.

By partnering with the state, non-profits may also develop legitimacy and credibility in policy sectors (Kramer, 1981). In this way community-based organizations can hope to influence the priorities and spending of the agencies with which they work (Lune, 2007). Governments contract local agencies both to assess needs and to do something about them. Community-based service organizations can win these contracts, thereby influencing government priorities while addressing local problems.

Working as partners with government is not without risk for community groups. Estes and Alford (1990) argue that service organizations within the third sector are losing their credibility and failing their communities by becoming more governmental and bureaucratic through contracting. As mentioned above, the influence of incentives and sanctions – grants and regulatory rules – can lead an organization to alter its priorities to match the priorities of the institutions that support it (Marwell, 2004). This is called *mission creep*. Additionally, under conditions of privatized social service delivery (meaning state support for the private organizations that do the work) governments have no particular obligation to increase funding as the cost or demand for the services increases.

In the US, support from the federal government is frequently allocated to states and municipalities, and it is these various government agencies that are responsible for funding the service agencies. All of these considerations and others, from cost-cutting pressures to the influence of party politics, create conditions under which local non-profits must compete with one another for service contracts in order to survive. This competition makes the actual delivery of services less reliable and inconsistent across regions and over time. "Which specific NPOs win contracts determine *where* services are available, *how* individuals access them, and ultimately *who* benefits from public spending for the poor" (Marwell, 2004: 267).

Studying the role of non-profits in the welfare state in Germany, Wolfgang Seibel identified a further liability for the community groups in working too closely with the state. Seibel noted that under the assumptions of a welfare state system, the state is responsible for the solution of significant social problems. But many of these problems have no clear solutions, or, worse, they have solutions that would be less politically popular than the problems. Yet elected governments cannot simply fail to address them. In this model, the state may contract with non-profit service providers to do something with the problem, even if they can't solve it. The government can therefore claim that they are addressing the problem, since they have contracted others to solve it, but they cannot be blamed if the problems are still there. Thus the NPOs serve as important "problem non-solvers" for government. In extreme cases, the state agency that funds a service group may increase their responsibilities while decreasing their grant, essentially guaranteeing that "the community" will fail. "The competitive advantage of NPOs, then, is not to do things better but to disguise better how poorly things are being done. . . . Governments can appear to be doing something about [social] problems and the failure of their success can then be blurred and if necessary, blamed on the peculiar functioning of the non-profit organizations" (Seibel, 1989: 187).

Another example of this line of inquiry concerns the "absorption" of nominally independent NPOs by state agencies to the point where the non-profits act as though they were branches of government (Wolch, 1990). Smith and Lipsky (1993) argue that so many non-profits are so deeply entrenched in state contracting that the state significantly alters the shape of the non-profit sector and influences the missions of service providers. Exploring the ways in which the grants economy and government contracting has furthered the "capture" of non-profits by state agencies, they concluded that the non-profit sector's influence in social policy has been diminished rather than expanded by its partnerships with government. Dependence on state contracting "has transformed NPOs, literally, into agents of the state" (1993: 72). This has coalesced long-standing theoretical concerns with state co-optation, the increasing bureaucratization of volunteer and community-based organizations, and the autonomy of community advocacy.

State contracts limit non-profit flexibility, mandating not only specific tasks, but staffing, division of labor, and reporting procedures (Adams and Perlmutter, 1991). Due to government funding requirements, NPOs find themselves with too many clients from outside of their traditional target community, and turning away people for whom they originally started operating. NPO efficiency, based largely on the low cost of volunteer labor, is hampered by the visible disjunction between paid professional staff and volunteers. Contracting requirements press onto NPOs the need for more professional staff and competitive salaries, which increases expenses and pits the paid management (business theory, good advertisement, growth potential, market credibility) against the interests (grassroots, community-directed) of unpaid boards of directors (Smith and Lipsky 1993: 84). The same argument has been made for changes in the state–non-profit sector relations in England during the same time period (Deakin, 1995).

Related to this work is the vast body of scholarship on social movements and attempts by non-profit collective action groups to gain influence within government (but see Jenkins, 1987). NPOs often have a political role, including both advocacy and oppositional politics. As non-profits adopt the forms and practices of their funders and partners, in order to better compete for contracts, their adversarial functions may be lost. This has considerable political implications for democratic societies. Wolch argues that "the transformation of the voluntary sector into a shadow state apparatus could ultimately shackle its potential to create progressive social change" (1990: 15).

Resistance is fruitful

This state absorption model has been criticized on several points (see especially Kramer, 1981). First, many NPOs partner with the state and maintain a critical stance towards it. They work with state agencies, receive grants, and don't pay corporate taxes, yet somehow manage to retain an independent voice. Certainly, many of the older HIV/AIDS organizations that I have studied were as vocal as they wanted to be on issues such as discrimination, access to medical care, and confidentiality issues.

Second, though less salient as a critique, NPOs clearly gain benefits from the funding systems, often providing a greater freedom than they had experienced when dependent on public fundraising. For this reason, and others, NPOs often initiate the relationship. Susan Chambré's (1997) work, also on HIV/AIDS organizations in New York, highlights many such cases. NPOs that represent communities in a political arena may be constrained in their actions, but communities without such NPOs often have little or no relation with government at all. Those groups that receive state contracts form important points of contact and information exchange that benefit both governments and the rest of the community. Reflecting this basic function, Berger and Neuhaus (1977) defined NPOs as "mediating structures," serving as a protective layer between private citizens and the state.

Dennis Young (2000) looks comparatively at the state–non-profit system of relations across several nations. Drawing on multiple sources of contemporary and historical data, he tested three models in four countries. Specifically, he asked whether state–non-profit relationships in the United States, the United Kingdom, Israel, and Japan are "supplementary, complementary, or adversarial." Interestingly, he found that all three models apply concurrently in all four nations.

Supplementary relations are consistent with the state failure model. These occur when non-profits go beyond what governments offer in terms of services, protections, and/or the well-being of communities. Complementary relations describe much of the government contracting world, in which state agencies and non-profits form partnerships in the delivery of goods and services, or in research, education, or other public goods. And adversarial relations occur when communities organize non-profits to protest, challenge, or pressure governments. We will look more at this relationship in the next chapter. In each of these models, however, state agencies are seen as the institutional centers of some area of public life, with organizations in the non-profit sector orbiting around them, responding to them, or seeking connections with them. And, in each of these cases, the legitimacy of and reliability of the NPOs is judged by the state agencies on the state's own terms, even as the state often relies on the non-profits to be "different." Both of these factors place the NPOs at a disadvantage in their relations with governments.

In many respects, it seems that Selznick's explanation of co-optation is still the most apt approach to understanding durable inter-organizational relations between large institutions, such as governments, and smaller organizations of any kind (see chapter 4). The larger partners have a lot to offer, and the smaller entities frequently seek to acquire some of those resources. Frequently, as Selznick observed, the government agency or other institution does not have to explicitly tell the other groups what it wants them to do; many organizations self-censor or otherwise change their own practices in order to be more attractive partners to the funding agencies.

Studies of the non-profit sector have shown that public funding is inconsistent with public protest. These inconsistent pulls – to work with government and also work against it – create what is known as a **role conflict**. NPOs in this situation often blunt the edge of their critiques of state policies when entering into relations with govern-ment. Seen as a "survival strategy" (Lune, 2002), or a "don't bite the hand the feeds you" way of thinking (Chaves et al., 2004), non-profits with activist or advocacy missions frequently move away from their initial role as outside agitators in order to protect their new role as partners to government. Their need for outside resources, or even their dependence on outside legitimacy, leads community-based NPOs to change their priorities. This same basic process has been seen in a wide assortment of organizational types, but is most visible in organizations that had formed in order to promote alternative forms. "As alternative approaches like neighborhood food banks, health centers, and community mediation centers increasingly cooperated with existing political institutions in the 1990s and gradually became more institutionalized, they also moderated their values, lost some of their community focus, and adapted their organizational structures" (Coy and Hedeen, 2005: 408).

There are other strategies, however, with which NPOs can respond to the incompatible pressures of community advocacy and public funding. Stone (1996) and others (Lune, 2007) have observed how some NPOs have avoided this role conflict by splitting their organizations in two. A service-oriented organization with clients and contracts can spin-off an advocacy or protest group with a different name, for example. In US politics, many 501(c)(3) service organizations share leadership and memberships with 501(c)(4) interest groups (Berry and Arons, 2003). In this case, some organizations within a given field of work choose to pursue institutionally legitimate, non-threatening activities while also fostering separate organizations in the same field to serve as pressure groups. If we study individual organizations we may well find evidence of state capture or elite channeling of activities into mainstream directions. At the same time, if we look at the organizational field, we may discover an active niche of challenger activities.

Up to a point, the expectation that NPOs will adopt more formal corporate forms in order to work with state agencies is a variation on the notion of coercive isomorphism. NPOs do not generate their incomes the way for-profits do, making them more dependent on others. If those others are frequently governmental bureaucracies, then we should expect non-profits over time to become more like that, and, therefore, more like each other. Using a national database for Australian NPOs, Jeff Leiter (2005) tested exactly that prediction. What he found, contrary to expectations, was a very diverse field of organizations of many different types and forms. Furthermore, when Leiter tested for a statistical relationship between the specific conditions that should make an organization most vulnerable to isomorphic pressures and the variety of their forms, he also found no support for the prediction. One can't help but wonder why not.

Leiter offers a couple of possible explanations. One possibility is that these organizations in the database are more independent than a lot of other NPOs that weren't included. This doesn't seem to be the case, though. It could be that Australia is just different. That could be the case, but whatever else is unique about Australia there are no obvious reasons why its non-profits would evolve differently from any others. A more convincing point, and one worth ending on, is that the non-profit sector is not by itself an organizational field. The sector, in fact, contains many fields. It's still a pretty large sector, though, so each of these fields could be quite separate from one another.

Recall that an organizational field is a space in which organizations routinely interact. They share a field of work because they think of what they do as related. So, while the organizations within some given field may all orient themselves more or less around some influential institution or crucial exchange partner, other organizations in other fields won't need to know anything about that. Therefore we should expect greater isomorphism, or similarity of forms, within known fields, not across the whole sector.

I believe that this makes sense. Nonetheless, in the following chapter, I will present research findings to suggest that heterogeneity itself is an asset to a field. That is, we should expect a lot of variety of forms within fields too.

Key Readings

Hansmann, Henry 1980 "The Role of Nonprofit Enterprises," *The Yale Law Journal*, 89: 835–98.
  Economic model of non-profit sector, centered on the "non-redistribution requirement." Hansmann studies both what is unique about non-profits, and the myriad of ways in which they overlap other organizational sectors.

Kanter, Rosabeth Moss 1972 *Commitment and Community: Communes and Utopias in Sociological Perspective*. Cambridge, MA: Harvard University Press.
  Organizational analysis of over 100 years of attempts to built separate communities within the space of modern nations. The author looks at different organizational and leadership strategies, goals, missions, and various crises in the viability of these communities.

Powell, W. (ed.) 1987 *The Non-Profit Sector: A Research Handbook*, New Haven, CT: Yale University Press.
  Though published two decades ago, the *Handbook* remains one of the best introductions to the field of non-profit studies. Both theoretically and empirically comprehensive, with attention to the history, politics, economics, and sociology of non-profits.

Salamon, Lester M., and Helmut Anheier 1996 *The Emerging Sector*. Baltimore, MD: Johns Hopkins Press.
  Comprehensively tracks the growth of the non-profit sector across multiple nations. The authors measure both consistent patterns and interesting departures from the pattern in non-profit sector funding, spending, and public roles.

Seibel, Wolfgang 1989 "The Function of Mellow Weakness: Nonprofit Organizations as Problem Nonsolvers in Germany." Pages 177–92 in Estelle James (ed.), *The Nonprofit Sector in International Perspective: Studies in Comparative Culture and Policy*. Oxford: Oxford University Press.
  An important and innovative contribution to the study of the role of the non-profit sector in service delivery and welfare policies. Seibel argues that states can contract with non-profits for service delivery in order to deflect criticism when dealing with underlying social problems that cannot be solved by the delivery of services.

Smith, Steven Rathgeb, and Michael Lipsky 1993 *Nonprofits for Hire. The Welfare State in the Age of Contracting*. Cambridge, MA: Harvard University Press.
  The authors note that, from the 1980s on, the federal government in the US has "privatized" considerable amounts of its welfare policies through direct funding of non-profit social service agencies. This book seeks to explain how that alters the organizations, the policies, and the delivery of services.

Wolch Jennifer 1990 *The Shadow State. Government and Voluntary Sector in Transition*. New York: The Foundation Center.
  Examines the changing role of the non-profit sector in relation to states in the US and the UK. Wolch finds that the expansion of privatization has increasingly reorganized the independent sector into an extension of state policies and practices.

Young, Dennis 2000 "Alternative Models of Government–Nonprofit Sector Relations: Theoretical and International Perspectives." *Nonprofit and Voluntary Sector Quarterly*, 29(1): 149–72.
  Attempts to move economic theories of the non-profit sector forward by testing the viability of several seemingly incompatible models of state–non-profit relations in different contexts.

CHAPTER
08 Organizing for Social Change

IN October, 1968, the residents of San Francisco's International Hotel received word that the building was going to be demolished and they were all being evicted. Just over 100 people rented apartments there at that time, mostly retired Filipino men who lived on their meager savings, pensions, or GI benefits. The hotel was one of the last remaining spaces of "Manilatown," a small Filipino ethnic enclave that had grown on the margins of Chinatown. The community was shrinking, the people were poor, and the neighborhood was undergoing gentrification. Without the hotel, many of the residents had nowhere to go.

The campaign to save the hotel began modestly enough, with tenants looking for ways to hang on to their home. It was about a particular space, not social change. Over the next 10 years of continuous struggle, the International Hotel campaign grew to become an international incident, a turning point in local politics, a defining issue for Asian Americans in the Bay Area, a cause for student activists, an opportunity for Maoist radicals, and a flash point in the movements for affordable housing, labor rights, and the rights of the elderly (Habal, 2007). It created social change, though the tenants were eventually evicted. How do things like that happen? What were all of those people doing there? And why would students who had no direct connection to the elderly tenants spend years working (without compensation) to protect the hotel, ultimately facing police truncheons and arrest?

Organized campaigns for social change come in many forms, from local neighborhood residents petitioning the city to preserve historic housing to transnational movements for human rights. Activists put their lives on the line to protect the things they believe in. Lawyers work behind the scenes to strengthen environmental protection laws. Citizens' groups hold rallies and collect signatures to support or oppose policy changes, student groups stand in front of tanks, and immigrant workers hold one-day strikes, all hoping to be counted and to have their voices heard. Collective efforts by relatively small groups to create change in the institutions of power or in the habits of a nation may seem hopeless and insignificant, but, as Margaret Mead observed, that's pretty much how change happens. In the United States, popular movements for social change in the twentieth century are responsible for women acquiring the right to vote, the end of legal discrimination by race, the prohibition of alcohol, the repeal of the prohibition of alcohol, the end of "separate but equal" schools, the majority of our occupational safety and health rules, child labor laws, food safety regulation, and the Clean Air Act. Social movements occur all across the political spectrum. Social protest in the US has blocked passage of an Equal Rights Amendment, introduced gay marriage laws, overturned gay marriage laws, expanded the protections of gun ownership, abolished slavery, opposed war, and removed evolution from the public schools in several states.

Campaigns for social change do not have to be life-threatening, protracted, or even confrontational. When students at Washington University in St Louis began a 2008 movement to ban bottled water on campus, they probably did not expect to be the forerunners of a national movement, or to have their university's administration bragging about them. Citing cost, sustainability issues, and environmental impact, the students created an education campaign on campus that quickly garnered support from the student community and many in the administration. In February, 2009, the ban went into effect. Change happened in time for graduation.

This chapter will explore the question of how such campaigns and movements are organized. This discussion will be limited to organizing under democracies where free speech and public protest are considered legal activities and where citizens are seen as having the right to participate in politics. Although I will briefly highlight some of the recent developments in social movement theory, my review will focus on organizational aspects and the organization of collective identities. A thorough social movement study would include such topics as the study of personal motivations and networks, cultural models of the diffusion of new ideas, the "framing" of movement identity and messages, measures of participant commitment, movement-countermovement dynamics, most of the emotional and social-psychological dimensions of movement participation, and many other issues. Still, there's a lot for us to look at.

Community-based non-profits and the state

There are many kinds of *communities*, from broadly defined ethnic communities that may be dispersed all over the world, to mostly unseen, relatively marginal groups of individuals who share a hobby or other activity. Although the term has no single, overriding definition, we can follow the neo-institutional model to say that the most basic aspect of a community is that its members see themselves as part of one. Communities are frequently seen as having some connection in both space and culture, such as a neighborhood of people with similar ethnic, religious, or socio-economic backgrounds. We can think of groups like this that share some goals or needs or other concerns as *communities of interest*. When members of a community of interest of some sort wish to press their own interests or values in some larger arena – such as politics – one option is to form a private, non-profit association through which to act. Community groups, or community-based non-profits, have a long and involved history of participation in democratic politics, particularly at the local level.

When communities of some shared interest form organizations, their ability to act collectively is increased. Of greater importance, acting collectively increases their ability to think and feel collectively, to speak as a group with a common cause. Organizing helps people with shared interests create a collective identity. When we speak of the organizational identities of social change organizations, we are talking about an ideal-type for the shared aspects of the members' identities. That is, collective identity is what allows people to say "we" when acting together.

Popular social change organizing occurs through combinations of clubs, small groups, movement organizations, private associations, and other non-profits (Galaskiewicz, 1979; Knoke, 1990). Each of these groups and organizations has its own identity, and each is related in some way to some larger shared sense of purpose. Generally, though not universally, organized action for change occurs within an organizational field that is defined within some recognized institutional domain. Campaigns to change a law, for example, operate extensively within the fields of law and law enforcement, incorporating challengers, courts, regulatory agencies, legislators, and possibly police and law breakers. Campaigns to alter consumer behavior, on the other hand, occur within fields that include producers, distributors, sellers and advertisers as well as consumers, consumer advocacy groups, and the media. The organizational field concerned with US education policy within any given state would of course include public and private schools, degree-granting universities, and teacher training programs, but also teachers' unions, parents' associations, and county school boards, all of which are linked in different ways to the state Department of Education. A campaign for changes in educational policy might operate through or against any of those organizations.

The most familiar, and ideal-typical form of organizing for change is a social movement that targets some part of the state. Prior to the waves of social movement activism of the 1960s and 1970s, activism was frequently perceived and described as a kind of irrational outburst by groups with material grievances against more powerful groups. More recently, movement scholars have come to view social movements as organized campaigns for social change, often with long histories and complex strategies. Such campaigns generally involve a broad array of social movement organizations (SMOs), linked through a variety of network ties (McAdam, 1988; Gould, 1993). These SMOs share an organizational history that might include common origins (Lune, 2007), sustained during fallow periods by non-movement organizations in the field (Taylor, 1989), and strengthened by overlapping experiences in past campaigns and coalitions (Meyer and Whittier, 1994). These networks of movement organizations occupy organizational fields that include many non-movement organizations and agencies that may contribute to, or oppose, the activist groups (Curtis and Zurcher, 1973; Klandermans, 1997). Among these, there may also be countermovement organizations (Pichardo, 1995). Further, the work of the organizations in the field will be supported, or hindered, by the actions of organizations that partially overlap the field, including research organizations, universities, charities and foundations, think tanks, unions, and media organizations.

It is not always clear how SMOs and other non-profits relate to one another in the pursuit of social change. This question has been one of my research interests. Using HIV/AIDS as a case study, I examined the origins and development of a newly emerging organizational field (Lune, 2007). Within this field, numerous, seemingly inconsistent organizational forms coexisted supportively. Furthermore, they didn't just happen to coexist. In many instances, I found that highly connected social actors in one part of the field actively fostered the growth of organized action in other parts of the field in ways that clearly did not benefit their "own" niche directly, but did alter the shape and capacity of the field overall. That is, their actions can only be considered strategic if we assume that organized social actors recognize the boundaries of their field, and recognize their shared interests, even though they are pursuing different short-term goals through different means. Following neo-institutional models, I defined the organizational field of HIV/AIDS groups to encompass all of those organizations that perceived themselves to be part of this field. This shared sense of being in the field together allowed the different organizations to interact and cooperate while maintaining their independence from one another.

In certain cases, community organizers working within "mainstream" service groups sought to meet with decision-makers in federal

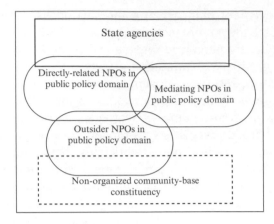

Source: Lune and Oberstein, 2001

Figure 8.1   Levels of embeddedness

agencies, while activists from different organizations condemned those same agencies and decision-makers. What was surprising was that some individuals were members of both the mainstream and activist organizations. As participants in both kinds of NPOs, they would simultaneously pursue both strategies, first helping to arrange a meeting with government officials and then protesting it when it occurred. The activists were outsiders to the policy process and wanted to pressure the government agencies to change their practices. Yet the meetings were of use to the service organizations.

The organizational field, then, can be divided into different "sites" of action according to the kind of relationship at work between the organizations in that part of the field and the key institution that they are trying to change. Not surprisingly, the distribution of different forms and types of organizations in the field correspond to the kinds of relationships they are pursuing. For the case of a broad-based field of work seeking change in state institutions, I have suggested different "levels of embeddedness" – direct, mediating, and outsider – to describe the groups' relations with the state. Organizations that are most like SMOs, engaging in protest actions, position themselves as outsiders, while service providers working with state agencies take the opposite approach. This distribution is shown graphically in figure 8.1.

While some individuals in the field believe that one approach is right and another wrong, as a collective they allow space for the whole big complicated mess, and they do so with a shared interest in the goals of the overall field. This means that many of the actors in the directly related organizations fully endorse street activism and even state that they could not do what they do as policy "insiders" if there wasn't an "outside" keeping the life and virtual power of the community growing.

Similarly, many activists recognize that activism doesn't produce tangible services and resources, but rather it alters the system of relations – the organizational environment – in which such things are allocated or mobilized by others. In many cases, individuals actively participate in both forms of work, which shows that they understand both extremes to be part of the same whole. The existence of mediating locations in the social space of the field shows that organized social actors pursue strategies that could not be defined without a comprehensive awareness of the contours of the field. That is, activism can be defined with almost no reference to any other part of the field, and service provision can be defined in terms of the state and the community. But mediating groups, including a lot of traditional advocacy organizations, broker the legitimacy of the other groups to both the state and the community. Their relationship to the state can only be explained in relation to the direct and outsider organizations. Mediating relations redefine the field.

Social change

When Rosa Parks died in 2005, her coffin was laid "in honor" in the US Capital Rotunda, and flags were lowered to half-mast throughout the country. Her heroic service to the nation is well known: she broke the law. Grade-school histories of her story often depict her as a tired old woman who just wanted a seat on the bus and who was surprised that her courageous moment of resistance led to a momentous Supreme Court decision overturning segregation laws in public facilities (Brinkley, 2000). The reality, of course, is more complex. Rosa Parks was a community activist. She was an officer in her local chapter of the National Association for the Advancement of Colored People (NAACP), an organization that had been looking for a good test case with which to challenge the seating laws. As for just wanting to sit, she famously stated that "The only tired I was, was tired of giving in."

This is a curious aspect of social protest as a strategy for social change. When you first challenge the law or commonly held beliefs, you are seen as a threat, an outlaw or a misfit. But if you succeed, you may become a hero, honored by the same state that once threatened to send you to prison. Clearly, it wasn't just the segregation laws that changed, but the whole value system that underlay them.

Social change often begins with an event or a change in the law. That's a reasonable place for change campaigns to start. For "society" to change, though, the changes have to go deeper, to reach the level of a people's values, beliefs, and aspirations. How does that occur? How do we even know when it has occurred?

We can introduce some relatively simple generalizations from social movement studies and non-profit studies that will help us to answer these questions. We can begin by assuming that the most general definition of a society encompasses an entire nation, though the concept of a society can easily be either larger or smaller than that. Social change in Canada, therefore, would be something that affects most people in Canada in some enduring manner, but not necessarily equally. And, by extension, it probably wouldn't have a direct or immediate impact on people outside of Canada.

Because we work with this assumption so often, the idea of changing society overlaps considerably with the idea of changing government. To clarify this point, we can introduce some technical jargon. Let us say that (a) societies contain different domains of organized activities, such as the political domain, the economic domain, religious domains, etc; and that (b) most recognized areas of organized social life have some sort of institutionalized system of rules, rights, and expectations at their center. "Government," for example, is the dominant institution defining a nation, although government is not a single entity and many other institutions also define the nation. Sociologists tend to refer to "the nation" when we want to include the physical space and all the people in it, and to "the state" when we are talking about those institutions that are part of government or are answerable to it. Organizing for social change, therefore, frequently involves seeking to change something within the state.

The obvious next question, then, is "How does this help?" Why is it better to refer to society as a dense network of overlapping institutional domains with more or less dominant institutions in each domain? Why not just say "society?" And the answer is that we can now define campaigns for social change as organized efforts made by members of a society to change the practices of at least one of the dominant institutions within some recognized domain of action. The clearest and most familiar example is a social movement of citizens targeting the state, though, as we've just seen, social movements occur within broader fields with many other kinds of organizations.

Many kinds of campaigns for change exist, and activists can challenge institutional domains that don't involve the state. There are also campaigns to prevent social change, preserve the status quo, or block reforms (Lune, 2002; Pichardo, 1995). And many campaigns focus on smaller, more local targets. Parents' groups challenge school boards. Neighbors organize against corporate dumping. Workers act collectively to oppose the loss of benefits, fighting to keep things from changing too much. Individuals march and demonstrate for an end to violence against women, an activity that draws needed attention to unwanted practices while leaving it to others to think about how to change those practices – which is appropriate, since social change is more about values than policies.

Social movements generally include a wide assortment of organizations, as well as many people who are not in organizations, pursuing many different claims via many different tactics. Very rarely do you find a single organization trying to do the whole work of the movement, from defining the problem to changing policies to driving the changes in how we think and feel about their issues. Any given organization may have ideas about all of those things, or contribute to some activities in each of those areas. Generally speaking, however, each group will have its own strengths and focus, its own "organizational identity" that defines its part of the larger movement.

A last note on definitions: organizational sociologists study all of the organized activities within the state, industry and the non-profit sector. But, typically, when looking at non-profits, we tend to exclude "political" organizations and action for social change as somehow a special case. Similarly, within the field of social movement studies, the focus tends to be on social movement organizations, excluding most of the other kinds of non-profit organizations with which they interact. This habit, or professional courtesy, of treating social movement groups and other community-based groups as though they were independent of one another has deprived scholars in both fields of important insights that speak directly to each other's questions, even as we invent our own terms for the same ideas. Only recently has scholarship begun to actively connect the two (Andrews and Edwards, 2004). This book partly follows this tradition by leaving SMOs out of the preceding chapter's discussion of the non-profit sector. Below, I will take a step toward "bringing them back in."

Social change organizations

Social movements are sustained and organized campaigns for social change. Though the modern social movement has been around for two centuries or thereabouts (Tilly, 1976), the sociological study of this area is quite new. The "traditional" (pre-1960s) view of movements often perceived them as chaotic and disorganized, treating activism as a threat to the social order (Le Bon, 1982; Ortega, 1994). The wave of activism that swept through much of the world through the late 1960s and into the 1970s changed the way we wrote and thought about activism. Challenging the idea that movement activists were led by their emotions and that activism itself was irrational, social movement scholars of the 1970s introduced new models to demonstrate the inherent rationality of collective action. And to do so, they focused considerable attention on the problems and processes of organizing.

Resource mobilization theory (McCarthy and Zald, 1977; Jenkins and Perrow, 1977) highlighted the question "How do you actually mobilize a mass movement?" Scholars raising this question observed that grievances and inequalities occurred throughout society, but sustained movements for social change did not. Resource mobilization studies demonstrated that effective campaigns for change generally required effective organizations. Unfortunately, the subsequent institutionalization of resource mobilization theory led to years of study and debate about which social movement organizations (SMOs) were more effective than others, with size and stability often standing in for effectiveness. From this perspective, large, professionally managed organizations with moderate goals were "better" than either small, local groups of meager means or radical movements with larger, less feasible goals.

In time, there was a backlash against this tendency to measure social movement organizations on the same terms that one would apply to for-profit firms. Civil rights scholars like Herbert Haines (1984) were able to demonstrate that both large and small, both radical and mainstream, efforts were important. More significantly, as Haines demonstrated, multiple approaches fed into one another. Responding to the use of resources as a measure of effectiveness, Haines defined the "positive radical flank effect" that occurred "when the bargaining position of moderates is strengthened by the presence of more radical groups" (p. 32). Significantly, Haines demonstrated that as the actions of newer direct-action groups became more radical, elite support for moderate and established civil rights organizations grew. Government and corporate giving to service and education programs in particular increased rapidly as "Black power" groups were taking to the streets.

Feminist scholars took this observation a bit further, noting that there were often "insider versus outsider" strategy debates in state-centered movements, and that both approaches had their place (Spalter-Roth and Schreiber, 1995). As described above, outsiders tend to fight the state while insiders collaborate with the state in pursuit of reforms. This debate was most explicit in feminist organizations that rejected top-down authority structures as a patriarchal form. Similar debates have shaped the structures of food co-ops, neighborhood medical clinics, and alternative newspapers, among others (Rothschild-Whitt, 1979). Despite the fact that many organizers recognize the usefulness of multiple approaches, many others do not. As organizers themselves grapple with the questions of how best to organize a movement, these debates can become crippling internal fights.

Movements for social change seek to energize supporters to work for change. In a sense, they have to sell their ideas to others on some combination of practical and emotional grounds. The practical side corresponds fairly well with what Weber termed "instrumental rationality." Movements for change can try to convince people that the movement goals are in their best interests. Traditional "grievance-based" movements, such as the labor movement, identify shared problems like low wages and hazardous work conditions, and propose to act collectively to solve the problem. The claim that support for the movement will result in safer conditions or better pay is an instrumental appeal. There are many forms of instrumental appeals. Following a potentially catastrophic accident at the nuclear power facility at Three Mile Island in Pennsylvania in 1979, for example, many thousands of people on the Northeast of the US suddenly realized that they had reasons to support the anti-nuclear movement (Walsh, 1981).

Emotional appeals to supporters invoke Weber's notion of "value rationality." Our values are crucial to our ideas about who we are, individually and collectively. Movements for change can appeal to people by linking their goals or priorities with shared ideas about the kind of society we want to live in.

Organized campaigns for change also have to be strategic. That is, they need to pursue tactics that can help them achieve their goals. Current approaches to the study of social change organizing emphasize a **political process** model. This approach studies movement strategies under the assumption that the driving goal of the movement is to gain influence within the political system. Some of the tactics that movements can pursue for political gain include organizing letter-writing campaigns to influence the votes of elected officials, staging media events that raise their issues so that political elites will have to address them, and raising money for candidates who support their causes. Political processes may be much more subtle as well, as campaigns seek to influence the ways in which their issues are presented in popular media, hoping to create sympathy for their causes that will open opportunities for future action.

Social change networks

Movement organizers appear to be increasingly adopting non-profit forms and collaborating across the boundaries of organizational types. Both activists for change and scholars studying them have attempted to broaden the definitions of collective action to account for these innovations. Organized advocates for change work together across great gulfs in organizational styles, despite great differences in members' goals, and over great distances. Collectively, these many different groups form an organizational field of advocacy organizations dedicated to social change (Andrews and Edwards, 2004).

As politics and economics have increasingly globalized, social change campaigns, too, have entered a transnational phase. The globalization of the economy and improvements in communications technologies have meant that the needs of relatively marginal communities are literally shared around the globe, not just in the sense of sharing the same kind of problem but as shared results of the same cause. Workers' hardships in Latin America may stem from the nature of corporate and governmental contracts signed in North America or Europe. East Asian trafficking in kidnapped girls is supported by a Western sex trade (Kyle and Dale, 2001). Economically and otherwise, we're all in this together.

In response, community activism and advocacy has been linking local welfare organizations to national-level political groups, international legal rights non-governmental organizations (NGOs), government agencies, and others acting across state borders (Lindenberg, 1999). Called "transnational advocacy networks," participants in this new organizational form have been pooling resources, sharing expertise, and challenging the legal frameworks of individual states through both institutional and extra-institutional means (Keck and Sikkink, 1998). At the same time, international development NGOs, meaning those that are based in one nation for the purpose of aiding development in others, are increasingly becoming involved in transnational advocacy (Hudson, 2002). Networks of non-profits, for-profits, NGOs, governmental organizations, local communities, and international agencies challenge our definitions of movement activism and community-based organizing. And, since these networks target states, social groups, corporations, and other organizations for the changes they would like to implement, the entire distinction between insider and outsider approaches breaks down. Indeed, one of the strengths of the transnational advocacy network as a form of organizing is its ability to quickly "externalize" local grievances beyond the borders of the nation, and then mobilize outside pressures back onto the state or local institution that is being targeted. Keck and Sikkink call this a "boomerang effect."

Transnational NGOs need to coordinate actions across multiple countries. They also need to be "on the ground" in the nations where they operate, collecting their own data, providing services, or otherwise participating in civic life. These organizations need to be as flexible as community-based organizations, and as far reaching as the major national advocacy groups. Few organizational forms can serve both needs well and simultaneously, which is why transnational NGOs frequently work as a loose network of semi-independent groups, each with its own structure and mission. The degree of independence of the local groups or chapters can vary considerably in these networks (Lindenberg, 1999).

Networking is both a powerful force and a serious threat for organizations. Above, I had indicated that each organization within some shared field has its own organizational identity and its own area of focus. Groups are freer to concentrate on their particular concerns when they are aware of other organizations out there that are picking up the slack in other, related areas. Networking among the different groups can be a way of pooling their strengths. Animal rights groups can join with environmental groups and with groups promoting sustainable development to form a powerful coalition to protect a local habitat against destruction by a shopping mall. A small, urban group promoting healthy childcare can network with a national association for women's rights to support a state-based expansion of government health insurance. The overlap of multiple interests and issues can lead to all sorts of popular campaigns.

Networking also makes demands, of course. This is where the threat comes in. Organizations whose identities are defined around a well-defined set of issues or actions may not want to spread themselves too thin or complicate their message by getting involved with other groups and campaigns. Nor would an organization that relies on popular support necessarily be comfortable joining a coalition with groups over whom they have no influence, for fear that their own image will be tainted by some future action on the part of the other groups. That was the situation within the Italian Labor Movement in the 1990s as activists in the global justice movement began to seek support from organized labor (della Porta and Mosca, 2007). Traditional labor activists had focused on local issues within geographic regions or industries. Increasingly through the 1990s, however, a more radical movement grew within the labor movement, breaking away from this vision of union identity. These groups formed alternative workers' organizations that tied their work-related issues to neo-liberalism in general, forming links with anti-war groups, transnational NGOs in support of migrant labor, human rights organizations, farmers' associations, and many others. In this broader world of collective action, the activists had to develop a shared language for describing their priorities that transcended the particular problems faced by teachers, factory workers, or the unemployed. The concepts of democracy and global justice linked each of the movements and provided a path for each to contribute to the other.

Traditional notions from social movement studies of challengers versus states are not sufficient to account for the organizational processes that occur at the transnational level. While social movement scholars have recognized and studied many different forms of activist organizing, they have tended to work with the assumption that all of the various parts of a movement act within a single nation and against a single state entity. As advocacy and activism become more global, organizations of many types around the globe seek to build collaborative connections that can bring their resources to bear against many targets in many states. The model of a network provides a means to describe and analyze the structure of these collaborative forms. At present, the organizational field may be the best notion available to us to imagine the space in which this networking takes place. By defining an organizational field as a shared space of work in which the outer limits of the field are determined by the relations among the members, we are able to study networks forming among organizations that do not meet or overlap in any physical space.

Organizational forms in social change movements

Social movement organizations (SMOs) do not simply network with non-profit organizations. Increasingly, SMOs are becoming NPOs (Cress, 1997; Jenkins and Eckert, 1986). Some of this change is motivated by the kinds of coercive isomorphism that we looked at in the last chapter. Groups that wish to grow frequently seek support from foundations, government agencies, or "elite" sponsors. Organizations that collaborate with state agencies routinely face legal and contractual constraints on their organizational forms. Often, however, organizations alter their forms by choice as their missions change. The transformation from unincorporated community group to a registered non-profit, for example, frequently reflects such changes as the move from outside agitator to service provider (Cress, 1997).

The process of organizing for social change, then, almost necessarily involves multiple organizations that operate independently from one another. Radical pressure groups and social movement organizations can create pressure for change from outside of the halls of power. Nevertheless, the institutions that are targeted for change do not like to work with pressure groups. In much of the modern industrial world, for the moment, states and other institutionalized segments of society have built-in procedures for working with non-profit organizations, non-governmental organizations (NGOs), and other advocacy groups to negotiate change. States and foundations also have partnerships and support mechanisms through which they help non-profit service organizations to provide the care and services that many communities seek, as discussed in chapter 7. At a glance, it seems that the non-protest groups are able to affect change more than the protest groups, and able to gain more public legitimacy and material support. Many community-based mobilizations for change, therefore, choose to adopt these forms. Yet successful campaigns that have strong elite support also tend to rely on the backing of a strong protest movement.

Movements for change face powerful constraints and incentives to adopt professional forms with bureaucratic leadership structures and boards of directors. Taking this route, they allow their efforts to be restricted to acceptable channels (Jenkins and Eckert, 1986) or co-opted by their institutional partners (Cress, 1997). These insider tactics can work, but the outsider tactics give them force.

All of these different ideas about the organizational forms for social change groups demonstrate the interactions among many of the major findings that we have looked at in the last few chapters. First, we see that what organizations do, how well they do those things, and how effective their actions are all depend to a large degree on how an organization relates to its environment. We had looked at exchange relationships and corporate acquisitions in the for-profit sector and found that organizations define their roles in relation to their fields of work. Among non-profits, and particularly among social change organizations, relations with their fields seem to be even more important. Links with protest groups give advocacy organizations more power to negotiate. Networking among advocacy organizations turn local conflicts into global social movements. And connections with political elites create channels of mutual influence between those in the halls of power and those furthest from them.

Second, we see that organizations choose their organizational forms, in part, as a response to their identities within a larger field. Groups are able to be more aggressive against their political targets, or more conciliatory toward them, depending on what other groups are doing.

Further, we have seen that the way in which organizations present themselves to the outside world has an effect on their ability to win the commitment of their participants. Groups that give up too much of their identities in search of outside approval may lose the approval of their own supporters. In other words, instrumental rationality has to be balanced with value rationality.

Bringing these observations together, we note that change is hazardous for organizations, even when that change involves growth. In some cases, organizations that press for social change may lose their edge, and hence much of their power, as they attempt to institutionalize their gains and form a more stable base for continued advocacy (Jenkins and Eckert, 1986). As organizations move toward "professional" models of advocacy, they often move away from, or lose, their grassroots support (Minkoff, Aisenbrey, and Agnone, 2008). These kinds of shifts are often necessary to secure tangible gains, such as legal changes. Yet they often come at a cost to the deeper goals of changing a society's values (Jalata, 2002). This shift corresponds to what I had earlier described as a move from outsider relations with the state or other institutions to insider relations.

Recall that organizations need to secure outside resources and manage environmental uncertainty in order to survive and grow. Social change organizations that lack resources and connections may be unable to press for significant change. Organizations that are more successful often reorganize to manage their success. Either way, few organizations that begin with a small, grassroots support system can continue operating like that for long.

Organizing for the long haul

Social movement studies may have hit their stride after the 1960s, but organized campaigns for political change are at least as old as the modern state (Tilly, 1976). Religious movements, including the invention and propagation of all widespread religions, are much older. Tracing the historical roots of contemporary movements reveals an assortment of organizational strategies, from network building across movements, linking campaigns to already popular concerns, and forming elite alliances, to hunger strikes, riots, and martyrdom. Conspiracies and secret societies have their place, as do churches and alehouses.

Robert Kleidman's study of contemporary US peace movements begins with a historical overview of the movement's many deep roots. He begins with the assertion that "The three intellectual traditions at the core of America's peace movement are pacifism, antimilitarism, and internationalism" (1993: 6). Pacifism in the US has its origins in "early European Christian sects" who founded their own communities here throughout the eighteenth century, though their own histories derive from the Reformation in the sixteenth century. Opposition to militarization is a second organizational strain that contributes to peace activism. This tradition, Kleidman suggests, was more extensive in the early days of the republic, but declined as the American nation grew. The third tradition, internationalism, predates "globalization" by centuries and emphasizes the connections and interdependencies among people worldwide regardless of political boundaries.

Peace activism, then, has had a fairly continuous presence for a very long time, even as the motivations, circumstances, and claims underlying the organized actions change. Yet, unless we assume that the current generation's organizing efforts for peace are unrelated to the last generation's efforts, some kind of mechanism for continuity has been a part of the system. We already know that large corporate firms and large formal government structures are designed for long-term survival even as the individuals within them come and go. But social activism is different, and activism led by volunteers working in temporary coalitions is not at all like the highly institutionalized organizational systems that governments form. How is this continuity maintained?

A thorough and proper answer to that question would be too much for these last few pages, but we have developed the tools and terms with which to offer the general outlines of an answer. To sketch out that answer, it might help to refer back to Thompson's model of three concentric levels of organizing within a firm. Here we can visualize three levels of a movement.

The inner core is formed by relatively stable organizations. These groups do not have to be activist groups, and they do not have to be committed to any given campaign. Rather, they are organizations defined by some enduring ideas or traditions. In the case of the peace movement, for example, Christian pacifists, most notably the Quakers, remain active and committed to their philosophy through times of peace and war, popularity or popular disdain, down through the generations. Unrelated to them, other organizations and societies maintain their traditions as well, including service organizations, community groups, and political associations.

At the next level, we find less enduring organizations that form in particular times and places around events of the moment. For example, during the time of slavery in the US, an abolition movement grew to encompass multiple organizations in both slave states and free states. These activist groups can form relatively quickly and define themselves effectively because they draw upon the base of existing traditions. That is to say, because there already were so many Christian groups and communities that opposed oppression in principle, the abolition groups could form as embodiments of these ideas, put into practice in this one cause. To put that into a different language, new organizations can deliberately draw on existing cultural forms in order to define their missions and reach out to others.

At the outermost level is a social movement. As we have seen, a movement is generally comprised of a great many organizations of different forms acting somewhat in concert. A movement may be built out of shifting coalitions within loosely defined networks. Or the networks can become institutionalized and fairly stable. The organizations of the movement act together out of a shared sense of the kind of social change that they would like to bring about.

We can look at any movement in its most active phase and find many coalitions and collaborations. We can recognize the shared organizational efforts as a movement for change, mostly because the participating groups will define it that way. On the other hand, if we were to look at the same field of work a few years earlier, we ought to find many of the same groups without the shared network structures. The organizational base was there, but not the movement.

If we look further back in time, before the movement began, or possibly forward to a time when the movement has died down, we should expect to see fewer of these activist organizations. This is because we are looking at a time with less organized action in a given area. Certainly, there were fewer abolitionist groups after the abolition of slavery. Even so, the core is still there. The concepts of freedom, dignity, or justice, as defined during the Enlightenment, or charity and peace, are present in the culture and the organizational background of the society.

I have outlined a kind of a visual representation of the hypothetical division of labor among organizations in movements, and distinguished between dedicated movement groups that are most active during a movement, and the supportive base out of which they grow. Verta Taylor (1989) has elaborated a far more detailed theory of social movement continuity based on empirical study of women's movement organizations that remained active in the US during the quiet, barely visible period after the successful suffrage movement in the 1920s and before the explosion of feminism in the late 1960s and early 1970s. The visible national movement that had fought for women's right to vote had disbanded by the 1930s, but there remained, at what I described as a middle layer, "a small band of feminists who, in the 1940s and 1950s, continued to remain faithful to the political vision that had originally drawn them into the suffrage movement nearly a half century earlier" (Taylor, 1989: 761–2).

It is not surprising that many activists and former supporters still believed in a greater feminist cause during this period of movement "abeyance." Taylor's research, however, documents a set of nonactivist organizations "promoting the survival of activist networks, sustaining a repertoire of goals and tactics, and promoting a collective identity" out of which the movement was reborn in later decades (Taylor 1989: 762). These organizations provide a place in which supporters of the cause can still pursue some organized action, even at a smaller or less promising scale. They sustain communities of like-minded individuals, strengthening their shared commitment in the face of opposition. They foster a focused, exclusive organizational culture. An active movement makes broad appeals for the support of many kinds of people and views. A movement in abeyance trims its mission down to a core set of principles and goals around which the dedicated few can gather. And the relatively small number of less active groups that remain during such times will network, not in the form of temporary coalitions acting together for some claim, but as a sustained web of shared resources and connections.

Recall the example with which this chapter began. Prior to the attempted eviction of the Filipino residents of the International Hotel, there was no movement to protect the housing rights of retired Filipinos in San Francisco. But there were organizations that were concerned with housing. And there were groups exploring the meaning of a "pan-Asian" heritage. And there were political groups dedicated to the rights of the poor. And there were networks of community groups and leaders in nearby Chinatown who had established working relations with the City Council and Mayor's Office. And more. The organizational base was there. A culture of change was ready. The unsuspecting owners of the hotel property who initiated the eviction provided the spark that released a wave of energy and activism that surprised even the participants. Organizations can be full of potential energy like that.

Key Readings

Edwards, Bob 1994 "Semiformal Organizational Structure among Social Movement Organizations: An Analysis of the U.S. Peace Movement." *Nonprofit and Voluntary Sector Quarterly* 23(4): 309–33.
  Demonstrates the wide assortment of organizations and organizational forms associated with a large social movement. This study also examines how such a broad and diverse set of organizations can communicate and cooperate without a centralized control structure.
Gould, Roger V. 1993 "Collective Action and Network Structure." *American Sociological Review*, 58(2): 182–96.
  Measures and models the influence of personal networks on people's decisions to join groups and act for social change. Network analysis helps explain why people take risks and volunteer their time and effort on behalf of others and the larger community.
Haines, Herbert H. 1984 "Black Radicalization and the Funding of Civil Rights: 1957–1970." *Social Problems*, 32(1): 31–43.
  Explains the "radical flank effect" whereby elites are more likely to support a non-threatening movement for social change if they see it as an alternative to a radical movement for social change.
Jenkins, J. Craig, and Chris M. Eckert 1986 "Channeling Black Insurgency: Elite Patronage and Professional Social Movement Organizations in the Development of the Civil Rights Movement." *American Sociological Review*, 51: 812–29.

This article also looks at elite support for non-radical movements, finding that elite supporters may try to build up an alternative movement in order to diminish the impact of a radical one.

Keck, Margaret E., and Kathryn Sikkink 1998 *Activists Beyond Borders: Advocacy Networks in International Politics*. Ithaca, NY: Cornell University Press.
In this age of globalization, local communities that organize against powerful states and other institutions are likely to tie into transnational inter-organizational networks. The organization environment for action, then, becomes global even as the political environment of their cause remains local.

Knoke, David 1990 "Networks of Political Action: Toward Theory Construction." *Social Forces*, 68(4): 1041–63.
Explores the effect of social networks of like-minded people on the nature of a person's political activism. Participation in voluntary associations is particularly salient in leading people to define their identities in relation to the politics of the group.

Meyer, David S., and Nancy Whittier 1994 "Social Movement Spillover." *Social Problems*, 41(2): 277–98.
The authors trace the direct influence of the ideas, people, and organizations of one movement on the emergence and growth of others. They demonstrate that social movement organizations operate within a broad field of other groups, linked through numerous ties and shared histories.

Pichardo, Nelson A. 1995 "The Power Elite and Elite-driven Countermovements: The Associated Farmers of California during the 1930s." *Sociological Forum*, 10(1): 21–49.
Demonstrates that institutions of formal power, such as governments, may sponsor and guide "community-based" movements to counter the efforts of an organized protest community.

Spalter-Roth, R., and Schreiber, R. 1995 "Outsider Issues and Insider Tactics: Strategic Tensions in the Women's Policy Network during the 1980s." In M. M. Ferree and P. Y. Martin (eds), *Feminist Organizations: Harvest of the New Women's Movement*. Philadelphia, PA: Temple University Press,.
Examines the tensions and complex negotiations among different organizations within a larger movement, regarding organizational forms, tactics, and inter-organizational relations.

Taylor, Verta 1989 "Social Movement Continuity: The Women's Movement in Abeyance." *American Sociological Review*, 54(5): 761–75.
This highly innovative study answers two questions. How do activists stay involved when a social movement is in decline? And what is the role of non-activist organizations in supporting and sustaining a movement?

What's Next for the Sociology of Organizations?

CHAPTER

09

A friend of mine used to cause me great difficulties by asking a single question of anything I wrote: "Now that we know this, what do we do with it?" This is a good challenge for any of us any time we feel that we have something to say. Now that we have reviewed the development of major schools of thought and analysis from the rise of industrialism to the present, so what? There is actually a lot that we can take from this for our work, studies, and lives. In this brief concluding chapter, I will first say a few words about where the sociology of organizations is going, or can go. Then I will address the integral connections between this work and the broader field of sociology. Lastly, I will offer some thoughts for students on how this knowledge can help you in your lives outside of school.

Which way is forward?

In this book, I have reviewed many of the major ideas and discoveries that give shape to the field of organizational sociology. There is much more going on, of course, that is beyond the scope of this introductory text. As well, there are subjects that are related to the field which have not yet been integrated into it. As we consider new directions for the field, and new configurations of organizations and the organizational society, I also want to touch on some of these questions that scholars are already asking, but which remain apart from our professional routines. The list of things we could do more of is endless, but here are some that stand out in my mind.

Beyond the three sector model

The world of organizations is highly diverse. An uncountable number of organizations participate in all spheres of social life, pursuing any number of goals and missions. Even governments and global industry have transcended the basic bureaucratic form to adopt various network forms and inter-organizational partnerships. At the same time, all kinds of organizations in all sectors adopt rational systems of command and control even when you wouldn't think they were appropriate. From day-care centers to theme parks to social movements, organizations in one sector of life model themselves on organizations from other sectors.

From a distance, we can see that formal bureaucratic forms remain as popular as ever while alternative forms appear to be fading. Up close, however, there seems to be a lot of organizational learning, much blending of forms and practices, and a fair amount of flexibility within otherwise formally defined organizations. Similarly, a look at the big picture reveals the unrestrained influence of very large institutions on all other spheres of life. Yet a close look at such institutions reveals that, in a restrained way, the smaller groups and organizations with which they interact continuously influence them as well.

A great deal of what we know about influence across industries and sectors is derived from studies of non-profits and from the three sector model in general. Dividing the organizational world into for-profit, non-profit, and public has been highly informative for studies in all sectors. Yet it now seems that the three sectors are increasingly overlapping, increasingly resembling one another, and increasingly networking. Perhaps it will be less useful in terms of going forward to talk about sectors. Instead, I believe that it would be useful to think of the sector location of an organization as something that has traditionally indicated some set of characteristics, such as structures, missions, and organizational forms. If sectors cease to serve as predictors of those factors, we can still look to forms and structures as defining attributes. Other broad differences among organizations have also emerged from comparing entities across sectors, some of which may become more important than ever as sectors become less crucial. What, then, are the relevant organizational qualities that we can measure?

Non-profit studies have revealed that "trustworthiness" is an important organizational characteristic. As I discussed in chapter 7, analysts and consumers alike often assume that non-profit organizations are more trustworthy than for-profits. This informal, mostly untested, assumption probably has some validity under some circumstances. But it does not give us a workable idea of trustworthiness in general,

or any way of testing that across sectors. We already study organizational goals and procedures. At the very least, it would be useful to ask
whether an organization's procedures are suited to deliver on their
promised goals.

Recalling that we tend to study normal cases and normative behavior routinely, as though deviant behavior were a separate field, it is
easy to see that we tend to assume organizational trustworthiness
more often than we measure it. This, upon some reflection, seems to
be an area where more work could have a considerable impact on the
study of organizations, industries, and inter-organizational relations.
Just recently, for example, much of the world was thrown into a reces-
sion due to a crisis in the global banking industry – an industry that
has been officially declared "too big to be allowed to fail." While there
is no single cause or simple explanation for this crisis, a crucial part
of it came from an industry-wide adoption of practices that appear
now to have been fundamentally irresponsible, if not actually illegal.
That is, for a variety of reasons it became highly profitable for banks
to deliberately offer very large loans to people whom they knew were
unlikely to ever pay them back. This practice is now referred to as
"predatory lending." If an analyst had compared these practices to
some set of stated goals, such as "making sound investments in home
ownership," they could have identified this as an untrustworthy
practice.

Actually, there are ratings agencies that are supposed to evaluate
trustworthiness for the banking industry. I hate to be cynical, but I
am not sure that an industry group is the best place to go for reliable
ratings of that industry. It might be more reliable for academics to
develop their own alternative ratings systems, and perhaps test their
predictions against those of industry. At present, we tend to rely on
the official industry system. Applying measures of trustworthiness
to all kinds of organizations and situations would be more work,
yielding better results, than continuing to attribute more or less
trustworthiness to an entire sector.

Similarly, we often approach non-profits with optimism based
on the hope that they will operate in a more personal, less mecha-
nistic manner than traditional for-profits or government agencies.
Identifying an organization as part of a sector implies that some
organizations will be more personable than others, or more bureaucratic. If this assumption holds at all, it is very tentative and
inconsistent. Expanding beyond the sector model, we can compare
the most "human" non-profits with the most mechanical government
agencies to create some kind of measure of organizational personality. Researchers in marketing have long paid attention to how
corporations interact with customers, but few other organizational

scholars have had much to say about the "personality" of organizations. As long as we are interested in member commitment, loyalty, and legitimacy, it seems that this is a question that we can fruitfully develop.

Organizational personality is not a well-defined concept. Yet it harkens back to Weber's concerns with the impersonal bureaucracies that were coming to dominate society in his time. The personalities of organizations in Weber's day were the personalities of the owners who created and controlled their own businesses, from small shops to large banks. With the passing of personal control, we have let go of the notion of personality. With a variety of managers, shareholders, and appointed media relations staff, one might have the impression that the apparent personal qualities of the organization would depend on which person you are interacting with. Our examination of organizational culture, however, indicates that there can be great consistency of priorities, attitudes, expectations, and ways of doing things within an organization, even over several generations of individual office holders.

I imagine that this measure would capture an organization's flexibility in dealing with clients and staff, as well as something to do with worker autonomy. We might begin the study of organizational personalities by looking at familiar issues that contribute to it, such as: the kind and extent of investment an organization makes in interpersonal contacts; characteristics of labor–management relations; relations between an organization and its physical environment; as well as various measures of control and coordination mechanisms within the organization. Organizations are social actors in the world. It would be useful to know more about how they respond to changing circumstances, special cases, and unforeseen problems. What do they do when things aren't going their way? How does any given organizational culture treat the idea of compromise? What is their definition of success?

Finally, as Rothschild observed, organizational scholars have not really picked up on Weber's "fourth" type of rationality – value rationality. Of course, even Weber was a little unclear about what to do with this characteristic. "The first three forms of social action [traditional, affectual, and instrumental rationality] correspond respectively to traditional, charismatic, and legal-rational bases of authority, with each type of authority implying a particular type of organization to implement its aims. But the last type of social action, value-rationality, has no counterpart in his typology of authority and organization" (Rothschild-Whitt, 1979: 509). As with personality and trustworthiness, organization research tends to associate the question of values with the study of non-profits, but not in a consistent manner. In many cases, we find that an organization serves a purpose that can only be explained in terms of values. Advocacy organizations, for example, seek to bring about social change on behalf of some constituency. If social change renders the organization obsolete, they sometimes declare success and disband. We can consider that an instance of value rationality. Instrumentally oriented organizations, such as most for-profits, generally treat their own growth and viability as the key indicator of their success. Nonetheless, we cannot assume that non-profits do not value their own survival, or that for-profits only seek growth. The language of corporate social responsibility may be new, but the idea that corporations serve needs that societies value is as old as capitalism itself.

As corporations seek to "go green," and political pollsters seek out "values voters," the nebulous matter of organizational values may become a fundamental characteristic by which organizations are differentiated. Indeed, given the recent US Supreme Court ruling that corporations have the same rights as individuals, particularly including the right to voice their opinions in public discourse (by running ads for or against candidates in an election), we might soon be inundated with data about what corporations value.

Technology

Up to now, we have tended to look at technology as a set of tools that are used to different effect in different settings. Some organizations or firms are highly dependent on technology, or choose to implement high-technology solutions to everyday problems, and some do not. To some extent, this approach treats technology as an afterthought, distinct from the structure and form of an organization. There is the organization, and it has some technology. I would suggest that the field overall has not fully appreciated the extent to which the technology of an organization defines that organization. This is not an original observation. Scholars who study technology have been saying as much for decades (Dickson, 1988; Ellul, 1964; Mumford, 1966). Even Karl Marx described the "technologies of production" as crucial elements in the political culture of a society. At the organizational level, I am suggesting that significant amounts of organizational behavior are led by whatever technology has been adopted. While this is certainly a general question concerning sociology and social change, I think that it is also central to the study of organizations and their social roles.

One of the insights that comes to us from the study of technology is that we often act as though we were compelled to do things simply because we can do them. If a technology allows some use, we will use it that way. Many of these uses are contrary to the original purpose of the technologies, or at least unanticipated. This observation forms the basis for most of the science-fiction films I have ever seen, but it has been noted in the real world as well (see *Jurassic Park*, *Robocop*, *Dollhouse*, or *Mimic* for some dramatized examples).

Let us consider just one example of the impact of technology, in this case an unanticipated consequence of communications technological change. Not too long ago, cell-phones were uncommon. Now they are virtually everywhere. Briefly, they were luxury items. Presently, one of my colleagues at Hunter College is looking at the use of cell-phones by homeless youths. Phones are perceived to be a communications technology, and certainly cell-phones have altered the nature of our communications. You now have the ability to instantly reach most of the people you want to call, at any hour, whether they want to be reached or not. But the social changes run much deeper than that.

Cell-phones operate by communicating with satellites, which enables global positioning systems to record the locations and movements of anyone using a phone. This might well be irrelevant to most of us most of the time, and could be useful if you find yourself trapped under a rock while hiking the Appalachian Trail. But if you have ever been under surveillance, legally or otherwise, the idea that any of us could be tracked all the time is likely to be rather disturbing. An optimistic interpretation might be that law enforcement agencies can use this power to do their jobs better. A pessimistic one would note that governments everywhere could keep tabs on their enemies, including legitimate political opponents mounting lawful challenges in a democracy (see *Enemy of the State* for an enjoyably paranoid take on this issue). More importantly, as technological change outpaces changes in the law, companies and even courts may be uncertain about which data are protected or not from what kinds of uses. In the US, at present, privacy rights organizations have raised concerns about the routine use of phone data by law enforcement agencies. Phone records have always been available to investigators with warrants and specific needs. Cell-phone records, however, are readily available, and are sometimes perceived as less private than landline data once were. In recent years, it has been reported, the call records for literally tens of millions of Americans have been voluntarily given to federal agencies by telephone companies without warrants or oversight (Nakashima, 2007). Privacy experts are having difficulty even defining what constitutes "private" information any more. Yet, if news reports about "sexting" are at all accurate, phone users continue to perceive their telephone data as private.

Computer networks are essential business tools that also allow companies to monitor the keystrokes of their employees. Cameras in elevators, lobbies, at intersections, on ATMs, around office buildings and in public transportation provide a useful security measure. They also keep most of the industrial world under near-permanent surveillance as we go about our business. As I write, parents in Philadelphia, Pennsylvania, are trying to decide what to do about one school that distributed laptops free to students, and then secretly activated the computers' cameras remotely to spy on the students. Knowledge is power, as Weber noted, and information technologies significantly alter the availability of knowledge.

Nonetheless, I don't want to merely sound the alarm against new technologies. Rather, I would like organizational studies to better integrate questions of the use of technology alongside measures of size, control structures, inter-organizational relations, and other elements that define the nature of an organization. The standard technologies of an organizational field, if we study them more rigorously, may have as much isomorphic power as the norms and practices of an industry (Shane, 2001).

Within organizations, the old question of who controls the work has resurfaced around technology. Studies of Advanced Manufacturing Technology (AMT), for example, have shown that higher-tech workplaces often adopt a much more formalized set of rules and constraints on work processes, making individuals subordinate to the efficiency of the information technology. Yet these same workplaces often rely less on centralized control mechanisms. Instead of punching time clocks or even reporting regularly to supervisors, employees sign in and out of their task databases. Work has to be prepared in particular ways because those are the only ways that the computer will recognize. The result is both more and less autonomy for workers, rather than a single pattern of either freedom or domination (Dean, Yoon, and Susman, 1992). How the next round of battles over control and freedom plays out will almost certainly depend significantly on the use of technology in the workplace. Similarly, for all of our concerns about how texting is less personal than speaking face to face, it is still more personal than neither seeing nor texting. After all, high-tech forms of communication can foster communication.

How are technologies chosen or adopted? We know from our study of rational systems that just about anything that promises more "efficiency" is likely to find an audience. We also know from our study of risk and disasters that people need to feel that risks are being managed, though they don't necessarily want to know what the risks are or how the system of managing them works. And, following neo-institutional arguments, we can expect that people in and out of organized settings often define procedures, undertake actions, or propose responses for symbolic or ritualistic purposes, whether the actions are likely to have a desirable effect or not. Together, those observations suggest that, as our organizational world becomes more complex, it will become imperative to build and distribute ever larger systems for collecting and managing information, with little consideration for which information will be most useful for what purpose.

Ross Koppel and colleagues have been studying the adoption of technological solutions to non-technological problems in healthcare settings for more than a decade. One of the cases from this work exemplifies most of the theoretical concerns listed above. Computerized Physician Order Entry systems (CPOEs) were developed to address numerous serious errors, particularly medication errors, which have been deemed responsible for hundreds of thousands of hospital deaths each year. The problem is very real, and the causes are multiple. The introduction of a computerized system for recording medication decisions, implementation, and concerns offers the promise of a technological solution to risks stemming from such diverse causes as bad handwriting, lost scraps of paper, incomplete orders, and incompatible combinations of medications. The centralized, technology-based approach promises to be efficient, more predictable than human systems, and able to "manage" the known problems. Much of this is actually true, as many kinds of errors have been greatly reduced in hospitals using CPOE systems. And yet there are significant unanticipated consequences that have hardly been noted, let alone studied. These come from the unique interactions of individuals, organizations, and technologies.

Among other findings, the researchers found that medical personnel often accepted CPOE default information, such as dosage levels, instead of making these decisions themselves. It is possible that practitioners assumed that those dosages represented a consensus on the best medical practices, although they usually came from non-medical considerations like efficient inventory control. Doctors using CPOE sometimes added new medicines to a prescription, thinking that they were replacing others, or cancelled part of a test or treatment under the impression that they were cancelling the entire procedure, when those were actually separate tasks in the computer system. They missed allergy alerts, since that information was buried in some other screen than the one for adding prescriptions. They failed to renew prescriptions that had automatically expired, because the doctors weren't aware of the expiration software. They ordered the wrong medications for patients due to misreading the complex computer display. In general, they made a lot of disturbing mistakes (Koppel, Metlay, Cohen et al., 2005). These new errors were not technical failures or simply a matter of learning a new way of doing things. The use of the technology disrupted the established practices of the hospitals that had adopted them, practices that had evolved over many years within the medical profession. The new systems have many benefits, but are guided by priorities and considerations that are different from those of the human systems that they are replacing.

Virtual organizational space and time

Organizations are less attached to specific places than ever. Changes in travel and communications technologies mean that large, diverse organizations can become more spatially diverse. People and parts do not need to be in the same state or country in order to be linked. Companies locate their large warehouses wherever real estate is cheapest, and their assembly centers wherever labor is least expensive. Corporate headquarters, meanwhile, gravitate toward those places with the least onerous tax laws.

Technological changes have led to the reorganization of space and time in organizations. Increasingly, staff are able to telecommute – to work from outside of the workplace while remaining connected to the workplace. Research in this area has shown that as workplaces lose direct supervision over staff, they seek other forms of coordination to take their place; that the collective sensibility of people working together is weakened when the people don't actually work physically together; that greater independence in work schedules may isolate some people; and that work outside of the workplace may be less visible, and therefore less rewarded than work done "on site" (Thatcher and Zhu, 2006).

Online businesses compete with "traditional bricks and mortar" firms, allowing customers to shop by computer from home without ever needing to visit an actual store. But the materials that they are shopping for still have to be stored somewhere. There are warehouses out there and people working at them. Online shopping separates customers from businesses, not staff. In the world of online commerce, labor relations and management are much less visible, but still present.

Many industries now operate around the clock. Online and by-phone service jobs can be done anywhere, any time, leading to routine encounters between workers and customers in otherwise incompatible time zones. In addition, in any given nation, workers may increasingly request or be required to work non-standard hours, such as late nights and weekends. For many employees in the "24/7 economy," work shifts may change unpredictably. This conversion of all hours into work hours places considerable stress on family life and other dimensions of one's personal life (Presser, 2003). Similarly, employees who attempt to balance work and family through flexible and reduced hours, supplemented by telecommuting, report that the demands of work do not significantly diminish while they are off the clock. The plan behind flexible hours is to allow workers with infants or other immediate home requirements to work less while still having jobs. Yet research by Pamela Stone (2007) finds the opposite frequently occurs. Between tight deadlines and "on-call" requests, work tends to expand into their home lives far beyond their scheduled (and paid) hours.

Virtual spaces and asynchronous exchanges allow a kind of "freedom" for organizational members to participate in their own time and in their own way. Naturally, there is more to it than just sleeping late. Consider two examples. First, part of my job entails research and writing. I am an employee of a university that pays my salary for doing my work. Yet most of my work does not take place at the university. I have a home office, which I, rather than my job, pay for. I have a home computer, an Internet connection, a wireless router, and a printer, all of which are considered business equipment. At a workplace, companies provide such equipment to employees so they can do their work. Since I and many other faculty work at home, we have to pay for all that ourselves, thereby saving my university a good deal of money. In my case, I have an office at the school if I choose to use it. But millions of workers in all of the large industrial nations have seen their jobs redefined from full-time in-house positions to contract work. That is, they are brought in as needed for temporary projects, and then released at the end of the job. They have no permanent positions or company space. Not only do they now have to buy their own office space and equipment to do the same work, but they do so without job security, pensions, or employer-provided insurance. The freedom for employees to work from home has included the freedom for companies to cut down on regular staff.

In a similar fashion, universities have the freedom to teach more classes with fewer classrooms. Online education allows us to offer asynchronous classes in which students work on their own and "meet" online. Of course, we can only do this by assuming that almost all of our students will buy their own computers and find their own workspaces. This freedom from the constraints of fixed scheduling also allows one to do school work in one's "spare time," and to thereby manage a full-time job or other commitments. Nonetheless, online classes require as many actual hours as any other class. Since students rarely have enough time to meet all of their commitments to begin with, it often happens that some of them choose to take an online course under the mistaken impression that this will allow them to take on additional outside commitments, such as work. I have taught many online classes, and I know that in any group of 20 students, one or two of them will simply get lost along the way, fall way behind, and fail. The virtual classroom does not cause their failure; but a live classroom might have prevented it.

Collective identity as an organized outcome

In chapter 8, I noted that organizational studies look at organizational goals, while social movement studies look at collective action and collective identity. The two fields of study inform one another, and so we are beginning to see more work that treats shared identity and shared goals as the product of organizing, rather than just as a precursor to it. I anticipate that many exciting new ideas and findings will follow from this convergence.

Identity is an elusive concept. We all belong to many categories, and others may see us or treat us as though we are part of some group that we hadn't thought of ourselves. I may define myself, or be defined by others, based on my age, gender, ethnicity, job, height, or knowledge of football. I may be perceived as "one of them" by people who fear that members of my ethnicity, occupation, or hairstyle are the cause of some problem or other. Each of us, however, has some idea in our own minds of whom we mean when we speak of people like ourselves. My people, my reference group, or my community, are the ones whom I imagine as sharing essential features with me. Whether "we are Sparta," "we are the world," or we are the new face of Hollywood, that sense of "we" is a living thing that we carry around with us.

Researchers who study topics as diverse as religion, social movements, immigration, ethnic conflict, or nationalism have derived a number of different explanations for the processes by which individuals come to identify with a particular group. Some of this work begins with those aspects of our identities that are emphasized in any given society, such as sectarian identification in Ireland or Turkey, race in the United States, or class in Great Britain. As we grow up in a society, we learn to recognize particular features of ourselves as more defining than others. Some of this research examines the symbolic processes, through language, song, and storytelling, that highlight the parts of ourselves that teach us which aspects of our histories give us bragging rights over others. A great deal of work has shown that people draw together as an "us" in the act of opposing some "them," and that shared risk or hardship in this struggle strengthens the collective bonds.

We should note that none of these shared acts or symbolic processes just happens. Groups, with a shared or named identity, create and teach these histories, act out these conflicts, and adopt the language that goes with them. Individuals are born with many identity claims.

But the collective parts, the shared ideas about who we imagine ourselves to be, are organized. Schools, teams, gangs, military units, movement organizations, ethnic associations, temples, and jobs are all major sites of identity formation and re-formation. In significant ways, collective identity formation in a mosque is different from collective identity formation in the Boy Scouts. Of greater interest to me, however, are the many ways in which they are similar.

Erving Goffman's work on total institutions, which we encountered in earlier chapters, provides one useful "ideal-type" model for examining the similarities among organizations that work on members' sense of identity. To begin with, one finds a clear distinction between those in the organization and those outside it. To help the status transition from outsider to insider, there will be entrance rituals. They may include new haircuts, as in the military, or the loss of one's personal possessions, as in jail. Uniforms are common, as seen in both of those cases, as well as teams, some schools, or some jobs. In total institutions, or strict religious communities, the dress code is law. Other communities will be less absolute. Often, instead of a uniform one will receive or adopt a membership card, lapel pin, or some very general show of uniformity, such as "the wearing of the green." Entrance rituals may involve learning the "insider" names for things, or receiving a new name or nickname.

Goffman also noted that status and power hierarchies are different within the organization or community than outside of it, and that simply recognizing and obeying the internal hierarchy is an act that defines you as one of the group. The more "total" the group or institution is, the less need or ability one has to contact those outside of it. By spending more time in the one setting than in others, one comes to defines one's peer group accordingly. As well, there are often "mortification rituals" to break down the various identity markers that one came in with, and to replace them with shared group characteristics.

Goffman's work is certainly well known and frequently referenced. Other organized aspects of our identities are less often examined, and rarely incorporated into the general study of collective identities. To take one obvious example, many organizations, including some social movement groups, ethnic and cultural associations, professional associations, and neighborhood groups, exist primarily for the purpose of defining or re-defining a shared identity. The celebration of St Patrick's Day, for example, with feasts and parades is an American invention. Specifically, Irish-born Americans and Americans of Irish descent formed their own societies with names like the Charitable Irish Society (founded 1737), the Ancient and Most Benevolent Order of the Friendly Brothers of St Patrick (1767), and the Society of the Friendly Sons of St Patrick for the Relief of Emigrants from Ireland

(1771). These groups created new songs, rituals, and celebrations through which generations of American-born Irish could come to know themselves as part of the Irish community. Over subsequent generations, these same associations inducted the children and grandchildren of the original immigrant members, forming the organizational base out of which the transnational American Irish identity was constructed.

In a more contemporary case, the "tea-party patriots" are in the process of forming a collective political identity through shared organized activities and inter-organizational relations. Initially, the so-called tea-party movement was a very loose affiliation of just about anyone who was unhappy with just about anything that the Obama administration did or might do in the future. Conservative political theorists mingled with dedicated libertarians, along with conspiracy theorists, armed survivalists, white supremacists, small business owners, insurance companies, elected officials, bloggers, and some journalists. Over time, however, through organized activities, news-letters, websites, and meetings, the movement is collectively defining its actual positions as a movement, and its members are thereby working on developing a shared identity construct as members of this movement. In the near future, some of the early supporters of the general state of protest may find that they are not really members of this movement at all, while others may find that it represents a central aspect of who they are and who they want to be.

Transnational networks

We have noted that large organizations, such as multinational firms, spread their concerns all over the globe. Governance and law are going global as well. While there are no supranational govern-ing bodies with the power to dictate national policies, nations still attempt to negotiate trade policies, environmental rules, human rights practices, and labor laws at the transnational level. Such poli-cies are affected by familiar national concerns and enacted through familiar political institutions. Additionally, however, policy outcomes are coming to depend on the relationships between national institu-tions and transnational ones.

The United Nations is one such supranational body dedicated to the pursuit of peaceful solutions to international disputes. The International Monetary Fund (IMF) is another. The IMF has been variously defined as a transnational agency that helps to stabilize the world economy, or one that helps underdeveloped nations to indus-trialize, or one that exists in order to impose a single model of global capitalism on the entire world. Which definition you get depends on whom you ask and where they have lived. But clearly the IMF is more than an organization with a mission. It is an organizational nexus among national governments and policymakers.

Organizational theory for the first half of the twentieth century was almost exclusively concerned with "closed systems," those that operated as more or less self-contained operations. It was not until late in the century that it became necessary to incorporate "open systems" approaches, looking at the interactions between organizations and their environments, in order to understand the organizations that we studied. Given the transnational environment of almost everything, it seems that it has become harder than ever for any organization to operate as a "closed" system. Our notions of organizational environments are going to have to expand to incorporate the legal systems, tax systems, education, people, and other resources of multiple nations and regions. To understand the labor practices of an electronics firm in Thailand, it becomes necessary to understand environmental policies in Great Britain. Almost no organization can isolate itself from its environment. Nor can we easily identify and explain that environment.

Textbooks, such as this one, which attempt to discuss formal organizations of the industrial world will soon become obsolete if we continue to ignore the dependencies and interactions between the industrial centers of the world and everywhere else. The different world regions are not separate. Twenty-first-century writings on organizations and culture will have to focus on multiple cultures and their interactions. Actions and expressions that are common in one place, restricted in another, and illegal elsewhere are already creating dilemmas for transnational organizations. Researchers are examining such issues, such as the recent ruling in Italy where American executives from Google were held criminally liable for allowing users to post videos that violated Italy's privacy laws, even though this particular kind of liability issue had previously been decided differently in the US and elsewhere. Students of organizational theory will need to stay up to date on this work as it develops.

People are also very much on the move in the world these days. Populations are increasing through birth and migration in most parts of the world. This increase particularly strains the already overcrowded cities where millions compete for jobs and homes. For all of the talk about the world becoming smaller and more homogeneous, however, we are still at an early stage of globalization. And, at this point, we still tend to think in terms of nations first. This means that all across the industrial world, as the flows of people increase, people are calling for national protectionism, closed borders, and job rights for natives. Those organizations that seek to ease the transitions for migrants are now coming into increasing conflict with newer organizations that seek to do the opposite. Scholars of migration have written about communities enacting this conflict, but few researchers have examined the groups and organizations through which solutions, if any, might be proffered.

Organizations are at the heart of sociology

Sociology is a vast field whose overarching purpose is to draw together the many strands of study in social, cultural, political, historical, and social-psychological research. There are specialists in all of the different sub-disciplines. Yet, when we look at the contribution of the field altogether, what makes it unique is its attention to the big picture. Clearly, the sociology of organizations is a useful sub-discipline of study on its own. Nonetheless, in an organizational society, there is little that we can learn about ourselves without a reasonable understanding of organizations.

I will not attempt to review all of sociology here. Instead, let us consider the broad areas of culture, politics, economics, and stratification. The rest I leave to the reader as an exercise.

Culture

In this book, I have treated culture as one factor among many that affect organizations or are affected by them. As I noted in chapter 4, traditional organizational studies, until recently, hesitated to get involved with questions of culture. Formal organizations had their own task-oriented cultures, and others had to accept that in order to work with them. We called that organizational culture, and mostly just left it at that.

We have learned much more about the interactions between culture and organizations in the past 20 years. Most of the major questions of organization theory relate the two. What are the optimal goals for an organization? That depends on the values of the organization's stakeholders. How can an organization get the most participation from its members? That depends on the norms and values of the people involved, the priorities of the organization, and the commitments they make to one another. How can an organization manage conflict within it and among the communities in its environment? For the organization, understanding the culture, history, and interests of the communities will help a great deal. For the organizational theorist, understanding a conflict situation often requires trying to interpret how the actions of the organization impacted the organization's perceived legitimacy from the eyes of the affected people. This problem is less about events than about the meaning of those events.

Studies of culture are also learning more from the study of organizations. Research on socialization, for example, looks at how we come to share the values, ideals, and habits that are common in our own societies. Where and how are those things learned? How are they reproduced, and how do they change? The answers to such questions most often involve the same issues that we have looked at in terms of culture in organizations. Schools and similar formal organizations for young people have their own cultures, and, like any institutionalized formal system, they transmit recognizable expectations for behavior, attitudes, and priorities. Understanding these processes requires an appreciation of schools, churches, clubs, camps, and other such bodies, both as cultural institutions and as formal organizations.

We don't want to isolate these organizations, however. Neo-institutional theories inform us that the practices and priorities found within such formal settings are shaped to a large degree by the conventional inter-organizational practices of their fields. As industrial societies shift in or out of periods of attention to things like accountability, progressive thinking, retrenchment, or other ways of explaining what's wrong with the world, schools and other public and private organizations alter their practices to go along with (or sometimes to resist) such priorities. Changes in the culture, then, lead changes in the organizational environment, which leads to changes in organizations, which in turn alters the culture of the organizations, which impacts the attitudes, expectations, and values of individual participants. Organizations may be stepping stones in the process, or they may be the incubators or even the originators of cultural change.

Politics

For a little while in recent decades, sociologists debated whether the political world of industrial democracies was dominated by individual elites or if pluralist participation really worked. This question concerns the location of power. The answers that we debated posed a false dichotomy: it was either a few individuals or the great mass of individuals. Current interest in political institutions reveals a different perspective: that the institutions through which political power is expressed are the sources of this power. They are also the guardians of it, and occasionally the amplifiers of it. The individuals who take on leadership positions within them briefly appear to hold the reins of power, but they rarely change the institutions, the relations among them, or the ways in which things happen. When these individuals move on, they may take with them a fair amount of wealth and a few bodyguards, but the real power stays behind.

To the extent that this explanation is true, we cannot hope to explain political processes, deals, coalitions, compromises, or failures unless we can explain how institutions become and remain institutionalized.

Of course, political institutions are just a part of the system. Campaigns still matter, even if they are increasingly scripted and stage-managed for TV. Speeches, debates, and even informal discussions with potential voters strongly resemble television commercials. Even so, the majority of voters have little or no direct knowledge of candidates, relying instead on media summaries and commentaries. Political organizations must therefore operate through media organizations. All of this suggests that we need to study the processes by which large, highly institutionalized organizations interact in order to understand and explain political events.

Economics

To my casual observation, the relationship between economics and sociology is most peculiar. As a field of analysis, economics is rooted in mathematical modeling. Much of this work involves using very large amounts of data on recent economic behavior to predict future behavior under different conditions. A particular goal of the field is to identify the social and economic conditions that are most likely to shift behaviors in a desired direction. In this sense, economics is a social science. The data about money and goods serve a larger purpose having to do with the organization of society. The field of economic policymaking defines which directions are desirable for a society, and applies those economic models to try to make that happen.

On the other hand, economics as a field draws on a very small number of social theories about behavior, and some economists deny that they are using theory at all. In this sense, economic models actually ignore a great deal of what is known about social processes, motivations, and human concerns. When surprises and undesired results occur in the economic realm, as they often do, we don't blame the models for failing us. Instead, we blame the groups of people who did not behave as they should have for the model to work. This is actually a pretty good explanation for why the predictions are of limited use, but the explanation itself seems to demonstrate why we need better models. We need to work sociology back into the mix.

In the case of economic studies, however, I cannot argue that they have neglected the study of organizational theory. In fact, this appears to be the one area of sociology in which economic analysts and policymakers have a strong interest. MBA programs, which educate industry leaders, policymakers, and many economists, not only teach organizational sociology, but contribute significantly to its development. One might even speculate that one of the reasons why organizational studies are not more central to sociology is the fact that they are so strongly associated with administrative theories, and, therefore, MBAs. Just as economic studies would benefit from a greater attention to sociology, so sociologists could benefit from a greater integration of economic analysis.

Stratification

A certain amount of inequality seems inevitable in any complex society. Nonetheless, the actual patterns of what resources are concentrated where depend on organized activities. We have seen that some practices in work settings can exacerbate inequalities. Comparable issues may be found in education, housing, health care, and politics, as well as in sports, popular culture, and transportation. Institutionalized inequalities shape one's encounters with police and courts, with friends and family, in stores, and on the streets. Social priorities determine where firehouses are located, which contributes to unequal insurance rates for homeowners, which affects the availability of mortgages. Unequal access to quality early education for different groups of people relate to different rates of incarceration later in life. And, of course, wealth and poverty are associated with life expectancies, infant mortality rates, and a wide assortment of indicators of health and well-being.

Wherever you go in this world, you will find dominant groups and non-dominant groups, often called minority groups, living unequally side by side. Interestingly, many of the same groups are dominant in one part of the world and minorities in another. Frequently, as well, if you speak with members of the dominant groups, those who control the most valuable land, the best jobs, and most of the political power in their societies, they will be able to explain to you what it is that's wrong with the minority groups that keeps them from improving themselves. That is, we tend to fall back on easy explanations that blame poor people for poverty and sick people for illness, no matter how consistent and predictable the patterns of these disadvantages are throughout a society.

The study of stratification – its patterns, causes, and costs – is fundamental to sociology. This study includes attention to the major social institutions that have the greatest ability to either break the patterns or to reinforce them. These, not surprisingly, are the organizations and institutions that most concern organizational sociologists. By this point, I need hardly repeat the argument of this chapter: the more we understand organizations, the better we can understand the rest of our lives and world.

Now that you know this . . .

How does this knowledge help you, today?

We can begin with the trick question that I asked in chapter 1. When in your life are you free to act, to present yourself, as you wish, outside of the bounds of organized settings? Do you have to be alone, within the walls of property that you own yourself in order to do so? Or are there still places, even public ones, where the rules and expectations are flexible? Looking at your world as a society of organizations, thinking about all of the things that just aren't done at school, or work, or on private property, or by phone or by email, you might find it worthwhile to create a bit of personal space in which to relax and explore your own nature. Maybe you could gather with a few friends in someone's home or a coffee shop and talk about how you would want to live, if you were free to choose. Your friends and family would probably enjoy the opportunity to do so as well. But, be careful. If your group becomes too popular, it might become a club, or a society. Then you would need by-laws, possibly dues, or a secret handshake. And leaders. Then where would you be?

We can flip this question around somewhat. It was, after all, a trick question. Perhaps a more useful thing to ask is whether organization is really the opposite of freedom. That is, can we distinguish between the essential, defining rules of an organized setting and the assumptions that everyone goes along with unquestioningly? Perhaps you have more individual freedom than you thought to act as you wish and express yourself honestly even in the heart of a formal organization. And, if so, what should you do with that freedom?

You can also take some time to identify and recognize the organizations and institutional settings in which your life is embedded. What common features do they share, and how does that affect you? Perhaps you divide your life between a full-time job, a full-time student schedule, and permanent family responsibilities, in which case all of your obligations equally require more of your time and attention than you can give them. On the other hand, you might have gone to the other extreme, and only entered into institutional relations that are open-ended and partial. Either way, you can use your understanding of these organizations to figure out what these relations mean for you, and why you entered into them in the first place. For example, you can ask yourself what part of school is more important to you: education, or credentials. Then you can decide whether the nature of your own participation in the institution is appropriate for these goals.

Let's move on to think about the future.

Does your school promise to help you develop job skills? Often, in my experience, that means that you are learning to be a useful employee somewhere in the corporate world, what Weber called "a cog in this bureaucratic machine." On the other hand, if you were to go through the entire course catalogue, would you find classes that could teach you how to be a leader? What would you need to know to form a new organization, to find a different way of doing things? Can you – in a word – organize?

Going along with things is one way of getting by. Sometimes, though, we would rather change things. Creating change requires a different skill set. Most often, as well, it requires collective action, and therefore some sort of organized work. If you were to join with others now in order to start a new group, organization, or association, what would it look like? With little else to go by, members of an industrial society tend to create formal bureaucracies. Only a relatively small number of people even view this as a choice that they have made, because most people have little understanding of the alternatives. With such understanding, you have choice.

Finally, let us step back from the short-term goals of working for money and working for social change. These represent only a very small number of the organizations that already shape your life. So many people fall into their places in one or another such setting, and struggle with the conflicting demands that each such organization makes against their time and commitments. If nothing else, you may find this a good time to examine your own settings, the commitments you have made, and your location within the various fields within which you move. Each location may be viewed as a node surrounded by pathways that lead somewhere else. Recognize those roads, and you can chart your own path. As Karl Marx (1867) expressed it, "Just as the savage must wrestle with nature to satisfy his wants, to maintain and reproduce life, so must civilised man, and he must do so in all social formations and under all possible modes of production."

Glossary

alienation   Marxian idea of the sense of being separate from aspects of one's life or disconnected from the world in which one lives. One can be alienated from one's job, family, culture, country, or pretty much anything else that would normally help us to define who we are.

anomie   "Normlessness," or the state of feeling that one does not fit in. The more strongly held a society's norms are, the more people who live differently will experience anomie.

authority structure   A system of rules and relations that gives some people specific and limited forms of power over others within that system. An employer has authority over employees concerning work matters in the workplace. This authority is formally attached to the job descriptions and is not supposed to carry over into other spheres of life.

bourgeoisie   In Marx's day, the bourgeoisie were seen as middle-class business owners. Today the term applies more to the upper classes. The bourgeoisie own the means of production and make a living through this ownership. In Marxian terms, this also means that they live off the work of others.

bureaucracy   An organizational system based on formal rules, strictly defined offices and responsibilities, a clear division of labor, and a chain of command. Implicitly, a bureaucracy is based on belief in rational processes and impersonal decision-making.

carrying capacity   In an organizational niche, the carrying capacity is the number of organizations with particular resource needs that can be supported. As resources become more or less available, the capacity rises or falls.

civil society   The layer of organized activity that operates "above" the level of the individual or family, and below the state or corporation. Civil society includes community groups, leisure clubs, cultural societies, political associations, religious institutions, and any other form of collective action or organizing that people enter into privately and generally by choice.

commodity   Something that exists in order to be sold or exchanged. Material goods are produced for sale from the start. Other things, including human skill, may be reduced to a commodity by their location in a system of exchange relations.

contract failure   A purchase or exchange situation in which one or more parties lacks the information they need to make a rational cost-benefit estimate prior to entering into an arrangement. The contract failure perspective treats all market exchanges as implied contracts, but recognizes that parties to such exchanges may have unequal access to the pertinent data.

co-optation   The process of convincing others that their interests are best served by working for one's own interests. Co-optation involves mutual compromises in which the group whose ideas are being co-opted comes to rely on some other group to define the priorities for both of them.

echelon   An authority system in which everyone at any given rank has authority over everyone of lower ranks, and is answerable to all those of higher ranks.

exchange value   The amount that you can get in exchange for a commodity. This is part of the item's value; the rest is use value.

exploitation   A form of exchange in which the parties involved have unequal power or need, and the more powerful party takes advantage of this to set the terms of the exchange.

flexibility   The ability of an organization to tolerate change, respond quickly to unexpected circumstances, or change its structures, actions, or goals when needed.

ideal-type   A social construct or general description of something that represents all of the most typical aspects of that thing. It isn't an ideal; it is a model of the most typical form.

institutionalization   The process by which some set of ideas or practices achieve a "taken-for-granted" status, such that it becomes difficult to imagine doing things a different way.

inter-organizational relations   All forms of regular or recognizable links among two or more organizations. Organizations may be linked by exchange relations, shared histories, overlapping personnel, material dependencies, or other forms of connection.

isomorphism   The tendency of groups, organizations, and institutions to come to resemble one another in forms and practices.

legitimacy   A cultural concept meaning that something – an act, an organization, a goal, a group of people, etc. – is seen as acceptable. There are legitimate ways of doing things, which we take for granted as valid and appropriate. Other ways may be illegitimate, possibly legal, but not seen as the right thing to do or the right way of doing it.

market failure   A partial explanation for the existence of the non-profit sector, the model suggests that non-profit organizations fill in gaps in the distribution of goods and services where for-profit firms are unable or unwilling to do so.

natural systems   A view of organizations that relies on the awareness of organizational life as a social system composed of many different people with different goals, perspectives, and feelings.

niche   The resource environment in which some population lives or functions. For an organism, the niche is the physical environment in which it seeks food, shelter, etc. An organizational niche may be a segment of the market, an organizational field, or a physical community in which the organization interacts with its environment.

norms   Expected or preferred ways of acting and being within any given culture. Norms vary from one culture to another. Alternatively, differing norms allow us to recognize that two cultures are different.

open systems   A view of organizations that recognizes that organizations' roles, actions, priorities, and forms frequently depend more on the nature of their external relations with other organizations than on the personalities or preferences of the people in the organization.

organic solidarity   A form of social solidarity wherein social actors perform limited roles in society which are functional to the whole, and, perceiving the connectedness among such roles, still feel integrated into the society at large.

organizational field   The collection of all organizations and agencies that interact with one another around some recognized area of social life. Organizational fields may overlap with markets, public policy domains, or interest-group activities.

organizational form   The internal organization of a collective entity, including how authority is defined and distributed, how decisions are made, and how activities are carried out. An organization's form determines how strictly the rules and procedures are defined or enforced, and how formal or informal the social relations within the organization might be.

piece-rate   The price a worker is to be paid for each unit of work produced, in contrast to hourly pay rates or fee-for-service pay. Piece-rates assume that each individual worker alone produces or collects some number of the item of work.

political process model   In social movement studies, the idea that collective action is significantly shaped by the nature of relations between the state and the affected community, activists'

access to political elites, and the levels of support for or opposition to movement goals among elites.

positive asymmetry   The tendency to not only expect but also
perceive desired results more often and more easily than we
imagine or perceive undesirable outcomes.

proletariat   The working class in a capitalist society. In contrast to
the bourgeoisie, the proletariat rely on the exchange value of
their labor power to live.

rational systems   A view of organizations in which decisions and
actions are assumed to be guided by cost-benefit analysis and
focused on the attainment of material goals.

resource mobilization theory   In social movement studies, the recognition that movements are organized and planned, and that
movement organizations need resources in order to grow and
thrive, just as any other organization would.

ritual   Behavior that is expected or required for symbolic reasons
rather than for its actual use. Ritual acts are typically performed
in the same manner each time, and serve to demonstrate conformity to the belief in the power of the act.

role conflict   From role theory, the idea that (1) our lives and identities are made up of multiple roles, each of which is more or
less salient in some given context; and (2) these roles may have
conflicting values, goals or needs. One's role as a member of an
organization, for example, may compel one to protect the interests of the organization in conflict with a community, while
one's role in the community may compel one to take the other
side.

social actor   Any person, group, or other entity that can be said to
act on its own behalf. Organizations, for example, have organizational goals that are different from the personal goals of the
people who make up the organization. Organizations act in
society – they produce and distribute goods, create or eliminate
jobs, collect and distribute information, etc.

stakeholder   Any social actor who has some stake in the operations or outcomes of something. Residents are stakeholders in
neighborhood events, as are property owners, planners, visitors,
vendors, and various others in and out of the neighborhood.

state failure   A partial explanation for the existence of the non-profit
sector, the model suggests that non-profit organizations fill gaps
in public functions where state agencies are unable or unwilling
to do so.

strata, stratification   Stratification is the division of society into relatively unchanging levels, or strata, based on social and economic
status.

structural-functionalism   A theoretical paradigm that begins with the idea that society is organized into various stable and enduring social structures of unequal worth and power (structuralism) and that, like a physical body, it works best when each part fulfills its own unique function. Deliberately or otherwise, structural-functionalism rejects most forms of social change.

three sector model   The classification of organizations into public (government), privately held for-profit and privately held non-profit. This model is based on the idea that organizations within any sector will tend to share interests, procedures, or forms, and that they will tend not to resemble organizational forms in other sectors.

use value   The value of something when you have it and use it instead of selling or exchanging it. An object has use value when it meets some need.

References

Adams, Carolyn, and Felice Perlmutter 1991 "Commercial Venturing and the Transformation of America's Voluntary Social Welfare Agencies." *Nonprofit and Voluntary Sector Quarterly*, 20(1): 25–38.

Adams, Gordon 1981 *The Iron Triangle: The Politics of Defense Contracting*. New York: Council on Economic Priorities.

Aldrich, Howard 2008 *Organizations and Environments*. Stanford, CA: Stanford Business Books.

Aldrich, Howard E., and Jeffrey Pfeffer 1976 "Environments of Organizations." *Annual Review of Sociology*, 2: 79–105.

Altheide, David L. 1987 "Down to Business: The Commodification of Nonprofit Social Services." *Policy Studies Review*, 6 (4): 619–30

Andrews, Kenneth T., and Bob Edwards 2004 "Advocacy Organizations in the U.S. Political Process." *Annual Review of Sociology*, 30: 479–506.

Baehr, Peter 2001 "The 'Iron Cage' and the 'Shell as Hard as Steel': Parsons, Weber, and the Stahlhartes Gehause Metaphor in the Protestant Ethic and the Spirit of Capitalism." *History and Theory*, 40(2): 153–69.

Barnard, Chester I. 1938 *The Functions of the Executive*. Cambridge, MA: Harvard University Press.

Barnetson, Bob, and Marc Cutright 2000 "Performance Indicators as Conceptual Technologies." *Higher Education*, 40(3): 277–92.

Bartley, Tim 2007 "How Foundations Shape Social Movements: The Construction of an Organizational Field and the Rise of Forest Certification." *Social Problems*, 54(3): 229–55.

Baum, Joel A. C., and Christine Oliver 1992 "Institutional Embeddedness and the Dynamics of Organizational Populations." *American Sociological Review*, 57(4): 540–59.

Baum, Joel A. C., and Jitendra V. Singh 1994 "Organizational Niches and the Dynamics of Organizational Founding." *Organization Science*, 5(4): 483–501.

Bender, Thomas 2007 *The Unfinished City: New York and the Metropolitan Idea*. New York: NYU Press.

Bendix, Reinhard 1962 *Max Weber: An Intellectual Portrait*. New York: Doubleday.

Berger, Peter L., and Richard John Neuhaus 1977 *To Empower People: The Role of Mediating Structures in Public Policy*. Washington, DC: American Enterprise Institute for Public Policy Research.

Berliner, David 2005 "The Near Impossibility of Testing For Teacher Quality." *Journal of Teacher Education*, 56(3): 205–13.

Berry Jeffrey M., and David F. Arons 2003 *A Voice for Nonprofits*, Washington, DC: Brookings Institute.

Biggart, Nicole Woolsey 1983 "Rationality, Meaning, and Self-Management: Success Manuals, 1950–1980." *Social Problems*, 30(3): 298–311.

Blau, Judith, and Gordana Rabrenovic 1991 "Interorganizational Relations of Nonprofit Organizations: An Exploratory Study." *Sociological Forum*, 6(2): 327–47.

Blau, Peter, and W. Richard Scott 1966 *Formal Organizations: A Comparative Approach*. New York: Routledge & Kegan Paul.

Boin, Arjen, Paul t'Hart, Eric Stern, and Bengt Sundelius 2005 *The Politics of Crisis Management: Public Leadership Under Pressure*. Cambridge: Cambridge University Press.

Bramel, Dana, and Ronald Friend 1981 "Hawthorne, the Myth of the Docile Worker, and Class Bias in Psychology." *American Psychologist*, 36(8): 867–78.

Braverman, Harry 1974 *Labor and Monopoly Capital: The Degradation of Work in the Twentieth Century*. New York: Monthly Review Press.

Brinkley, Douglas 2000 *Rosa Parks. A Life*. New York: Penguin Books.

Brown, Michael P. 1997 *Replacing Citizenship. AIDS Activism and Radical Democracy*. New York: The Guilford Press.

Bryman, Alan 2004 *The Disneyization of Society*. London: SAGE Publishers.

Buchanan, David A. 2008 "You Stab My back, I'll Stab Yours: Management Experience and Perceptions of Organization Political Behaviour." *British Journal of Management*, 19: 49–64.

Carroll, Glenn R., and Michael T. Hannan 1989 "Density Dependence in the Evolution of Populations of Newspaper Organizations." *American Sociological Review*, 54(4): 524–41.

Carter, Stephen L. 1992 *Reflections of an Affirmative Action Baby*. New York: Basic Books.

Cerulo, Karen 2006 *Never Saw It Coming: Cultural Challenges to Envisioning the Worst*. Chicago, IL: University of Chicago Press.

Chambré, Susan. 1997. "Civil Society, Differential Resources, and Organizational Development: HIV/AIDS Organizations in New York City, 1982–1992." *Nonprofit and Voluntary Sector Quarterly*, 26: 466–88.

Chandler, Alfred D. 1962 *Strategy and Structure*. Cambridge, MA: MIT Press.

Chandler, Alfred D. 1992 "Organizational Capabilities and the Economic History of the Industrial Enterprise." *Journal of Economic Perspectives*, 6(3): 79–100.

Chanley, Virginia A., Thomas J. Rudolph, and Wendy M. Rahn 2000 "The Origins and Consequences of Public Trust in Government: A Time Series Analysis." *The Public Opinion Quarterly*, 64(3): 239–56.

Chaves, Mark, Laura Stephens, and Joseph Galaskiewicz 2004 "Does Government Funding Suppress Nonprofits' Political Activity?" *American Sociological Review*, 69(2): 292–316.

Chen, Katherine K. 2009 *Enabling Creative Chaos: The Organization Behind the Burning Man Event*. Chicago, IL: University of Chicago Press.

Clarke, Lee 1989 *Acceptable Risk? Making Decisions in a Toxic Environment*. Berkeley, CA: University of California Press.

Cohen, Michael D., James G. March, and Johan P. Olsen 1972 "A Garbage Can Model of Organizational Choice." *Administrative Science Quarterly*, 17(1):1–25.

Coleman, James S. 1974 *Power and the Structure of Society*. New York: Norton.

COSHEP 1992 *Teaching and Learning in an Expanding Higher Education System*. Edinburgh: Committee of Scottish Higher Education Principals.

Coy, Patrick G., and Timothy Hedeen 2005 "A Stage Model of Social Movement

Co-optation: Community Mediation in the United States." *The Sociological Quarterly*, 46: 405–35.

Cress, Daniel M. 1997 "Nonprofit Incorporation among Movements of the Poor: Pathways and Consequences for Homeless Social Movement Organizations." *The Sociological Quarterly*, 38(2): 343–60.

Curtis, Jr., Russell L., and Louis A. Zurcher, Jr. 1973 "Stable Resources of Protest Movements: The Multi-Organizational Field." *Social Forces*, 52(1): 53–61.

Davis, Gerald F., and Henrich R. Greve 1997 "Corporate Elite Networks and Governance Changes in the 1980s." *The American Journal of Sociology,* 103(1): 1–37.

Davis, Gerald F., Kristina Diekmann, and Catherine Tinsley 1994 "The Decline and Fall of the Conglomerate Firm in the 1980s: The Deinstitutionalization of an Organizational Form." *American Sociological Review*, 59: 547–70.

Deakin, Nicholas 1995 "The Perils of Partnership: The Voluntary Sector and the State, 1945–1992." Pages 40–65, in Smith, Justin Davis, Colin Rochester, and Rodney Hedley (eds), *An Introduction to the Voluntary Sector*. London: Routledge.

Dean, Jr., James W., Se Joon Yoon, and Gerald I. Susman 1992 "Advanced Manufacturing Technology and Organizational Structure: Empowerment or Subordination?" *Organizational Science*, 3(2): 203–29.

della Porta, Donatella, and Lorenzo Mosca 2007 "*In movimento*: 'Contamination' in Action and the Italian Global Justice Movement." *Global Networks*, 7(1): 1–27.

Dickson, David 1988 *The New Politics of Science*. Chicago, IL: University of Chicago Press.

DiMaggio, Paul J., and Helmut K. Anheier 1990 "The Sociology or Nonprofit Organizations and Sectors." *Annual Review of Sociology*, 16: 137–59.

DiMaggio, Paul J., and Walter W. Powell 1983 "The Iron Cage Revisited: Institutional Isomorphism and Collective Rationality in Organizational Fields." *American Sociological Review*, 48: 147–60.

Dobbin, Frank 1994 "Cultural Models of Organization: The Social Construction of Rational Organizing Principles." Pages 117–41, in *The Sociology of Culture: Emerging Theoretical Perspectives*. Edited by Diana Crane. Oxford: Blackwell.

Durkheim, Émile 1964 [1893] *The Division of Labor in Society: An Essay on the Organization of Advanced Societies*. Translated by George Simpson. New York: Free Press.

Durkheim, Émile 1972 *Selected Writings*. Edited by Anthony Giddens. Cambridge: Cambridge University Press.

Durkheim, Emile 1979 [1897] *Suicide: A Study in Sociology*. Translated by John A. Spaulding and George Simpson. Edited by George Simpson. New York: Free Press.

Durkheim, Émile 1982 [1895] *The Rules of Sociological Method*. Translated by Steven Lukes and W. D. Halls. New York: Free Press.

Durkheim, Émile 1995 [1912] *The Elementary Forms of Religious Life*. Translated by Karen E. Fields. New York: Free Press.

Edwards, Bob 1994 "Semiformal Organizational Structure among Social Movement Organizations: An Analysis of the U.S. Peace Movement." *Nonprofit and Voluntary Sector Quarterly*, 23(4): 309–33.

Edwards, Richard 1979 *Contested Terrain: The Transformation of the Workplace in the Twentieth Century*. New York: Basic Books.

Ellul, Jacques 1964 *The Technological Society*. New York: Vintage.

Estes, Carroll L., and Robert R. Alford 1990 "Systemic Crisis and the Nonprofit

Sector: Toward a Political Economy of the Nonprofit Health and Social Services Sector." *Theory and Society*, 19(2): 173–98.

Fantasia, Rick 1988 *Cultures of Solidarity: Consciousness, Action, and Contemporary American Workers*. Berkeley, CA: University of California Press.

Fayol, Henri 1949 *General and Industrial Management*. Translated by Constance Storrs. London: Pitman and Sons, Ltd.

Feldman, Martha S., and James G. March 1981 "Information in Organizations as Signal and Symbol." *Administrative Science Quarterly*, 26: 171–86.

Feuer, Lewis S. 1959 *Marx & Engels: Basic Writings on Politics and Philosophy*. Garden City, NY: Anchor Books.

Fine, Gary Alan 1984 "Negotiated Orders and Organizational Cultures." *Annual Review of Sociology*, 10: 239–62.

Fligstein, Neil 1985 "The Spread of the Multidivisional Form among Large Firms, 1919–1979." *American Sociological Review*, 50(3): 377–91.

Fligstein, Neil 1993 *The Transformation of Corporate Control*. Cambridge, MA: Harvard University Press.

Foucault, Michel 1977 *Discipline and Punish: The Birth of the Prison*. Translated by Alan Sheridan. New York: Pantheon Books.

Friedland, Roger, and Robert R. Alford 1991 "Bringing Society Back In: Symbols, Practices and Institutional Contradictions." Pages 232–63, in Walter W. Powell and Paul J. DiMaggio (eds), *The New Institutionalism in Organizational Analysis*. Chicago, IL: University of Chicago Press.

Galaskiewicz, Joseph 1979 "The Structure of Community Organizational Networks." *Social Forces*, 57(4):1346–64.

Galaskiewicz, Joseph 1985 "Interorganizational Relations." *Annual Review of Sociology*, 11: 281–304.

Galaskiewicz, Joseph 1997 "An Urban Grants Economy Revisited: Corporate Charitable Contributions in the Twin Cities, 1979–81, 1987–89." *Administrative Science Quarterly*, 42(3): 445–71.

Gallant, Mary J., and Jay E. Cross 1993 "Wayward Puritans in the Ivory Tower: Collective Aspects of Gender Discrimination in Academia." *The Sociological Quarterly*, 34(2) (May): 237–56.

Garland, David 1990 *Punishment and Modern Society: A Study in Social Theory*. Chicago, IL: University of Chicago Press.

Gay, E. Greer, Jennie J. Kronenfeld, Samuel L. Baker, and Roger L. Amidon 1989 "An Appraisal of Organizational Response to Fiscally Constraining Regulation: The Case of Hospitals and DRGs." *Journal of Health and Social Behavior*, 30(1): 41–55.

Goffman, Erving 1959 *The Presentation of Self in Everyday Life*. New York: Doubleday.

Goffman, Erving 1961 *Asylums: Essays on the Social Situation of Mental Patients and Other Inmates*. New York: Anchor Books.

Goffman, Erving 1971 *Relations in Public: Microstudies of the Public Order*. New York: Basic Books.

Gould, Roger V. 1993 "Collective Action and Network Structure." *American Sociological Review*, 58(2): 182–96.

Gouldner, Alvin W. 1954 *Patterns of Industrial Bureaucracy*. Glencoe, IL: Free Press.

Greenstone J. David, and Paul E. Peterson 1973 *Race and Authority in Urban Politics; Community Participation and the War on Poverty*. New York: Russell Sage Foundation.

Gronbjerg, Kirsten A. 2001 "The U.S. Nonprofit Human Service Sector: A Creeping Revolution." *Nonprofit and Volunteer Sector Quarterly*, 30 (2): 276–97.

Gulati, Ranjay, and Martin Gargiulo 1999 "Where Do Interorganizational Networks Come From?" *The American Journal of Sociology*, 104(5): 1439–93.

Habal, Estella 2007 *San Francisco's International Hotel Mobilizing the Filipino American Community in the Anti-eviction Movement*. Philadelphia, PA: Temple University Press.

Hager, Mark A., Joseph Galaskiewicz, and Jeff A. Larson 2004 "Structural Embeddedness and the Liability of Newness among Nonprofit Organizations." *Public Management Review*, 6(2): 159–88.

Haines, Herbert H. 1984 "Black Radicalization and the Funding of Civil Rights: 1957–1970." *Social Problems*, 32(1): 31–43.

Hannan, Michael T. and John Freeman 1977 "The Population Ecology of Organizations." *American Journal of Sociology*, 82(5): 929–64.

Hannan, Michael T., and John Freeman 1986 "Where Do Organizational Forms Come From?" *Sociological Forum*, 1(1): 50–72.

Hannan, Michael T., Glenn R. Carroll, and László Pólos 2003 "The Organizational Niche." *Sociological Theory*, 21(4): 309–40.

Hansmann, Henry 1980 "The Role of Nonprofit Enterprises." *The Yale Law Journal*, 89: 835–98.

Hartley, David 1995 "The 'McDonaldization' of Higher Education: Food for Thought?" *Oxford Review of Education*, 21(4): 409–23.

Hasenfeld, Yeheskel, Jane A. Rafferty, and Mayer N. Zald 1987 "The Welfare State, Citizenship, and Bureaucratic Encounters." *Annual Review of Sociology*, 13: 387–415.

Hayes, Dennis, and Robin Wynyard (eds) 2002 *The McDonaldization of Higher Education*. Westport, CT, and London: Bergin and Garvey.

Heydebrand, Wolf, and Carrol Seron 1990 *Rationalizing Justice: The Political Economy of Federal District Courts*. Albany, NY: SUNY Press.

Hinings, C. R., and Royston Greenwood 2002 "Disconnects and Consequences in Organizational Theory?" *Administrative Science Quarterly*, 47(3): 411–21.

Hodgkinson, Virginia A., and Richard W. Lyman and Associates 1989 *The Future of the Nonprofit Sector: Challenges, Changes, and Policy*. San Francisco, CA: Jossey-Bass.

Homans, George C. 1941 *Fatigue of Workers: Its Relation to Industrial Production*. New York: Reinhold Publishing Corp.

Hudson, Alan 2002 "Advocacy by UK-Based Development NGOs." *Nonprofit and Voluntary Sector Quarterly*, 31(3): 402–18.

Hughes, Everett C. 1951 "Mistakes at Work." *The Canadian Journal of Economics and Political Science*, 17(3): 320–7.

Hughes, Everett C. 1971 *The Sociological Eye: Selected Papers*. Chicago, IL: Aldine Atherton.

Jackall, Robert 1988 *Moral Mazes: The World of Corporate Managers*. New York: Oxford University Press.

Jacobs, Ronald N., and Sarah Sobieraj 2007 "Narrative and Legitimacy: U.S. Congressional Debates about the Nonprofit Sector." *Sociological Theory*, 25(1): 1–25.

Jakubowski, F. 1990 *Ideology and Superstructure in Historical Materialism*. London: Pluto.

Jalata, Asafa 2002 "Revisiting the Black Struggle: Lessons for the 21st Century." *Journal of Black Studies*, 33(1): 86–116.

James, Estelle 1987 "The Nonprofit Sector in Comparative Perspective." Pages 43–54, in W. W. Powell (ed.), *The Nonprofit Sector: A Research Handbook*. New Haven, CT: Yale University Press.

Jenkins, C. Craig 1987 "Nonprofit Organizations and Policy Advocacy." Pages 296–318, in W. W. Powell (ed.), *The Nonprofit Sector: A Research Handbook*. New Haven, CT: Yale University Press.

Jenkins, J. Craig, and Chris M. Eckert 1986 "Channeling Black Insurgency: Elite Patronage and Professional Social Movement Organizations in the Development of the Civil Rights Movement." *American Sociological Review*, 51: 812–29.

Jenkins, J. Craig, and Charles Perrow 1977 "Insurgency of the Powerless: Farm Worker Movements (1946–1972)." *American Sociological Review*, 42: 249–68.

Kanter, Rosabeth Moss 1968 "Commitment and Social Organization: A Study of Commitment Mechanisms in Utopian Communities." *American Sociological Review*, 33(4): 499–517.

Kanter, Rosabeth Moss 1972 *Commitment and Community: Communes and Utopias in Sociological Perspective*. Cambridge, MA: Harvard University Press.

Kanter, Rosabeth Moss 1993 [1977] *Men and Women of the Corporation*, 2nd edn. New York: Basic Books.

Keck, Margaret E., and Kathryn Sikkink 1998 *Activists Beyond Borders: Advocacy Networks in International Politics*. Ithaca, NY: Cornell University Press.

Kelley, Margaret, Howard Lune, and Sheigla Murphy 2005 "Doing Needle Exchange: Prevention Point Service Providers and Organizational Transformation." *Nonprofit and Voluntary Sector Quarterly*, 34(3): 362–86.

Khurana, Rakesh 2007 *From Higher Aims to Hired Hands. The Social Transformation of American Business Schools and the Unfulfilled Promise of Management as a Profession*. Princeton, NJ: Princeton University Press.

Klandermans Bert 1997 *The Social Psychology of Protest*. Oxford: Blackwell.

Kleidman, Robert 1993 *Organizing for Peace: Neutrality, the Test Ban, and the Freeze*. Ithaca, NY: Syracuse University Press.

Knoke, David 1986 "Associations and Interest Groups." *Annual Review of Sociology*, 12: 1–21.

Knoke, David 1990 "Networks of Political Action: Toward Theory Construction." *Social Forces*, 68(4): 1041–63.

Koppel, Ross, Joshua P. Metlay, Abigail Cohen, Brian Abaluck, A. Russell Localio, Stephen E. Kimmel, and Brian L. Strom 2005 "Role of Computerized Physician Order Entry Systems in Facilitating Medical Errors." *JAMA*, 293(10): 1197–1203.

Kramer, Ralph 1981 *Voluntary Agencies in the Welfare State*. Berkeley, CA: University of California Press.

Kunda, Gideon 1992 *Engineering Culture: Control and Commitment in a High-tech Corporation*. Philadelphia, PA: Temple University Press.

Kyle, David, and John Dale 2001 "Smuggling the State Back in: Agents of Human Smuggling Reconsidered." In Kyle and Koslowski (eds), *Global Human Smuggling*. Baltimore, MD: Johns Hopkins University Press.

Lang, Kurt, and Gladys Engel Lang 1961 "Ordeal by Debate: Viewer Reactions." *The Public Opinion Quarterly*, 25(2): 277–88.

Laumann, Edward O., and David Knoke 1987 *The Organizational State: Social Choice in National Policy Domains*. Wisconsin: University of Wisconsin Press.

Le Bon, Gustave 1982 [1896] *The Crowd: A Study of the Popular Mind*. Atlanta, GA: Cherokee Publishing Co.

Leck, Joanne D., and Bella L. Galperin 2006 "Worker Responses to Bully Bosses." *Canadian Public Policy / Analyse de Politiques*, 32(1): 85–97.

Leiter, Jeffrey 2005 "Structural Isomorphism in Australian Nonprofit

Organizations." *Voluntas: International Journal of Voluntary and Nonprofit Organizations*, 16(1): 1–31.

Lijphart, Arend 1968 *The Politics of Accommodation. Pluralism and Democracy in the Netherlands*. Berkeley, CA: University of California Press.

Lindenberg, Marc 1999 "Declining State Capacity, Voluntarism, and the Globalization of the Not-for-Profit Sector." *Nonprofit and Voluntary Sector Quarterly*, 28(4): 147–67.

Lipsky, Michael 1980 *Street-Level Bureaucracy: Dilemmas of the Individual in Public Services*. New York: Russell Sage Foundation.

Lipsky, Michael, and Steven Rathgeb Smith 1989–90 "Nonprofit Organizations, Government, and the Welfare State." *Political Science Quarterly*, 104(4): 625–48.

Lorber, Judith, and Patricia Yancey Martin 2007 "The Socially Constructed Body: Insights from Feminist Theory." Pages 226–44, in *Illuminating Social Life: Classical and Contemporary Theory Revisited*, 4th edn. Edited by Peter Kivisto. Thousand Oaks, CA: Pine Forge Press.

Lukes, Steven 1972 *Emile Durkheim: His Life and Work*. New York: Harper & Row.

Lune, Howard 2002 "Weathering the Storm: Nonprofit Organization Survival Strategies in a Hostile Climate." *Nonprofit and Voluntary Sector Quarterly*, 31(4): 463–83.

Lune, Howard 2007 *Urban Action Networks: HIV/AIDS and Community Organizing in New York City*. Boulder, CO: Rowman & Littlefield.

Lune, Howard, and Hillary Oberstein 2001 "Embedded Systems: The Case of HIV/AIDS Nonprofit Organizations in New York City." *Voluntas*, 12(1):17–33.

Lune, Howard, and Miranda Martinez 1999 "Old Structures, New Relations: How Community Development Credit Unions Define Organizational Boundaries." *Sociological Forum*, 14(4): 609–34.

McAdam, Doug 1988 *Freedom Summer*. New York: Oxford University Press.

McCarthy, John D., and Mayer N. Zald 1977 "Resource Mobilization and Social Movements: A Partial Theory." *American Journal of Sociology*, 82(6): 1212–41.

McDermott, Kathryn A. 2006 "Incentives, Capacity, and Implementation: Evidence From Massachusetts Education Reform." *Journal of Public Administration Research & Theory*, 16(1): 45–65.

Mahajan, Vijay, Subhash Sharma, and Richard Bettis 1988 "The Adoption of the M-Form Organizational Structure: A Test of the Imitation Hypothesis." *Management Science*, 34(10): 1188–1201.

Marwell, Nicole P. 2004 "Privatizing the Welfare State: Nonprofit Community-Based Organizations as Political Actors." *American Sociological Review*, 69(2): 265–91.

Marx, Karl 1967 [1867] *Capital: A Critical Analysis of Capitalist Production*. Vols. 1–3, edited by Friedrich Engels. New York: International Publishers.

Marx, Karl 1976 [1849] *Wage Labor and Capital*. New York: International Publishers.

Marx, Karl, and Friedrich Engels 1972 [1845] *The German Ideology*. Translated by C. J. Arthur. New York: International Publishers.

Marx, Karl, and Friedrich Engels 1998 [1848] *The Communist Manifesto*. London: Verso.

Mayo, Elton 1960 [1933] *The Human Problems of an Industrial Civilization*. New York: Viking Press.

Merton, Robert K. 1936 "The Unanticipated Consequences of Purposive Social Action." *American Sociological Review*, 1(6): 894–904.

Merton, Robert 1968 [1957] *Social Theory and Social Structure*. New York: Free Press.

Meyer, John W., and Brian Rowan 1977 "Institutionalized Organizations: Formal Structure as Myth and Ceremony." *The American Journal of Sociology*, 83(2): 340–63.

Meyer, David S., and Nancy Whittier 1994 "Social Movement Spillover." *Social Problems*, 41(2): 277–98.

Meyer, Stephen 1981 *The Five Dollar Day: Labor, Management and Social Control in the Ford Motor Company, 1908–1921*. Albany, NY: State University of New York Press.

Michels, Roberto 1962 [1915] *Political Parties: A Sociological Study of the Oligarchical Tendencies of Modern Democracy*. New York: The Free Press.

Mills, C. Wright 1956 *White Collar: The American Middle Classes*. New York: Oxford University Press.

Mills, C. Wright 1959 *The Sociological Imagination*. New York: Grove Press.

Minkoff, Debra, Silke Aisenbrey, and Jon Agnone 2008 "Organizational Diversity in the U.S. Advocacy Sector." *Social Problems*, 55(4): 525–48.

Moahloli, Nthobi 1997 "Race, Gender and the Corporate Ethos." *Agenda*, 35: 30–34.

Mumford, Lewis 1966 *The Myth of the Machine: Technics and Human Development*. New York: Harcourt Brace Jovanovich.

Musselin, Christine 2005 "European Academic Labor Markets in Transition." *Higher Education*, 49(1/2): 135–54.

Nakashima, Ellen 2007 "Verizon Says it Turned Over Data Without Court Order." *The Washington Post*, p. A01, October 16, 2007.

NCLB 2002 *No Child Left Behind Act of 2001*, Publ. No. 107–10, 115, Stat. 1425.

Neuse, Steven M. 1983 "TVA at Age Fifty – Reflections and Retrospect." *Public Administration Review*, 43(6): 491–9.

O'Connor, Ellen 1999 "Minding the Workers: The Meaning of 'Human' and 'Human Relations' in Elton Mayo." *Organization*, 6(2): 223–46.

Ortega y Gasset, Jose 1994 [1932] *The Revolt of the Masses*. New York: W.W. Norton & Co.

OSAA 2004 *Networking: Directory of African NGOs*, 3rd edn. Office of the Special Advisor on Africa. Available for download at: <http://www.un.org/africa/osaa/ngodirectory/index.htm>.

Ostrander, Susan 1995 *Money for Change: Social Movement Philanthropy at Haymarket People's Fund*. Philadelphia, PA: Temple University Press.

Ouchi, William G. 1980 "Markets, Bureaucracies, and Clans." *Administrative Science Quarterly*, 25(1): 129–41.

Palazzo, Bettina 2002 "U.S.-American and German Business Ethics: An Intercultural Comparison." *Journal of Business Ethics*, 41(3): 195–216.

Park, Robert Ezra, E. W. Burgess, Roderick Duncan McKenzie, and Louis Wirth 1925 *The City*. Chicago, IL: University of Chicago Press.

Parsons, Talcott 1937 *The Structure of Social Action*. New York: McGraw Hill.

Parsons, Talcott 1960 *Structure and Process in Modern Societies*. Glencoe, IL: Free Press.

Perkins, Douglas. and Barbara Brown 1996 "The Ecology of Empowerment: Predicting Participation in Community Organizations." *Journal of Social Issues*, 52(1): 85–110.

Perrow, Charles 1984 *Normal Accidents: Living with High-Risk Technologies*. New York: Basic Books.

Perrow, Charles 1988 *Complex Organizations: A Critical Essay*, 3rd edn. New York: Random House.

Perrow, Charles 2000 "An Organizational Analysis of Organizational Theory." *Contemporary Sociology*, 29(3): 469–76.

Perrow, Charles 2002 *Organizing America: Wealth, Power, and the Origins of Corporate Capitalism*. Princeton, NJ: Princeton University Press.

Perrucci, Robert, and Harry R. Potter 1989 *Networks of Power: Organizational Actors at the National, Corporate, and Community Levels*. New York: A. de Gruyter.

Pichardo, Nelson A. 1995 "The Power Elite and Elite-driven Countermovements: The Associated Farmers of California During the 1930s." *Sociological Forum*, 10(1): 21–49.

Polletta, Francesca 2002 *Freedom is an Endless Meeting: Democracy in American Social Movements*. Chicago, IL: University of Chicago Press.

Powell, Walter (ed.), 1987 *The Non-Profit Sector: A Research Handbook*. New Haven, CT: Yale University Press.

Powell, Walter W., and Paul DiMaggio 1991 *The New Institutionalism in Organizational Analysis*: Chicago, IL: University of Chicago Press.

Presser, Harriet B. 2003 *Working in a 24/7 Economy: Challenges for American Families*. New York: Russell Sage Foundation.

Quinn, Beth A. 2002 "Sexual Harassment and Masculinity: The Power and Meaning of 'Girl Watching.'" *Gender and Society*, 16(3): 386–402.

Reskin, Barbara F. 2000 "Getting It Right: Sex and Race Inequality in Work Organizations." *Annual Review of Sociology*, 26: 707–9.

Ritzer, George 2000 *The McDonaldization of Society*. Thousand Oaks, CA: Pine Forge Press.

Roethlisberger, Fritz J. 1941 *Management and Morale*. Cambridge, MA: Harvard University Press.

Roethlisberger, Fritz J., and William Dickson 1964 [1939] *Management and the Worker: An Account of a Research Program Conducted by the Western Electric Company, Hawthorne Works, Chicago*. Cambridge, MA: Harvard University Press.

Roscigno, Vincent J., and Randy Hodson 2004 "The Organizational and Social Foundations of Worker Resistance." *American Sociological Review*, 69(1): 14–39.

Rothschild-Whitt, Joyce 1979 "The Collectivist Organization: An Alternative to Rational-Bureaucratic Models." *American Sociological Review*, 44(4): 509–27.

Rothschild, Joyce, and J. Allen Whitt 1986 *The Cooperative Workplace: Potentials and Dilemmas of Organizational Democracy and Participation*. Cambridge: Cambridge University Press.

Salamon, Lester M. 1987 "Of Market Failure, Voluntary Failure, and Third-Party Government: Toward a Theory of Government-Nonprofit Relations in the Modern Welfare State." *Nonprofit and Voluntary Sector Quarterly*, 16(1): 29–49.

Salamon, Lester M. 1995 *"Partners in Public Service: Government–Nonprofit Relations in the Modern Welfare State*. Baltimore, MD: Johns Hopkins University Press.

Salamon, Lester M., and Helmut Anheier 1996 *The Emerging Sector*. Baltimore, MD: Johns Hopkins University Press.

Salamon, Lester, and Wojciech Sokolowski (eds) 2004 *Global Civil Society: Dimensions of the Nonprofit Sector*. Bloomfield, CT : Kumarian Press.

Schuppert, Gunnar Folke 1991 "State, Market, Third Sector: Problems of Organizational Choice in the Delivery of Public Services." *Nonprofit and Voluntary Sector Quarterly*, 20(2): 123–36.

Scott, W. Richard 2002 *Organizations: Rational, Natural, and Open Systems*, 5th edn. Englewood Cliffs, NJ: Prentice Hall.

Scott, W. Richard 2004. "Reflections on a Half–Century of Organizational Sociology." *Annual Review of Sociology* 30:1–21.

Seibel, Wolfgang 1989 "The Function of Mellow Weakness: Nonprofit Organizations as Problem Nonsolvers in Germany." Pages 177–92, in Estelle James (ed.), *The Nonprofit Sector in International Perspective: Studies in Comparative Culture and Policy*. Oxford: Oxford University Press.

Selznick, Philip 1948 "Foundations of the Theory of Organization." *American Sociological Review*, 13(1): 25–35.

Selznick, Philip 1949 *TVA and the Grassroots: A Study in the Sociology of Formal Organization*. Berkeley, CA: University of California Press.

Shane, Scott 2001 "Technology Regimes and New Firm Formation." *Management Science*, 47(9): 1173–90.

Sherlock, Molly F., and Jane G. Gravelle 2009 CRS Report R40919, *An Overview of the Nonprofit and Charitable Sector*. Washington, DC: Congressional Research Service.

Singh, Jitendra V., and Charles J. Lumsden 1990 "Theory and Research in Organizational Ecology." *American Review of Sociology*, 16:161–95.

Smith, David Horton 1997a "The Rest of the Nonprofit Sector: Grassroots Associations as the Dark Matter Ignored in Prevailing Flat Earth Maps of the Sector." *Nonprofit and Voluntary Sector Quarterly*, 26(2): 114–31.

Smith, David Horton 1997b "Grassroots Associations are Important: Some Theory and a Review of the Impact Literature." *Nonprofit and Voluntary Sector Quarterly*, 26(3): 269–306

Smith, Stephen D. 1998 "Dress for Success: Are You Compromising Your Credibility?" *Professional Safety*, 43(2): 34–6.

Smith, Steven Rathgeb, and Michael Lipsky 1993 *Nonprofits for Hire. The Welfare State in the Age of Contracting*. Cambridge, MA: Harvard University Press.

Snow, David A., Sarah A. Soule, and Daniel M. Cress 2005 "Identifying the Precipitants of Homeless Protest across 17 U.S. Cities, 1980 to 1990." *Social Forces*, 83(3): 1183–1210.

Spalter-Roth, R., and Schreiber, R. 1995 Outsider Issues and Insider Tactics: Strategic Tensions in the Women's Policy Network during the 1980s. In M. M. Ferree and P. Y. Martin (eds), *Feminist Organizations: Harvest of the New Women's Movement*. Philadelphia, PA: Temple University Press.

Stark, David, and Balázs Vedres 2006 "Social Times of Network Spaces: Network Sequences and Foreign Investment in Hungary." *The American Journal of Sociology*, 111(5): 1367–1411.

Steinberg, Richard 2006 "Economic theories of Nonprofit Organizations." Pages 117–39, in Walter W. Powell and Richard Steinberg (eds), *The Nonprofit Sector: A Research Handbook*. New Haven, CT: Yale University Press.

Stern, Robert N., and Stephen R. Barley 1996 "Organizations and Social Systems: Organization Theory's Neglected Mandate." *Administrative Science Quarterly*, 41(1): 146–62.

Stinchcombe, A. L. 1965 "Social Structure and Organizations." In J. G. March (ed.), *Handbook of Organizations*. Chicago, IL: Rand McNally.

Stoller, Nancy 1995 "Lesbian Involvement in the AIDS Epidemic: Changing Roles and Generational Differences." In Beth Schneider and Nancy Stoller (eds), *Women Resisting AIDS: Feminist Strategies of Empowerment*. Philadelphia, PA: Temple University Press.

Stone, Melissa Middleton. 1996 "Competing Contexts: The Evolution of a

Nonprofit Organization's Governance System in Multiple Environments." *Administration and Society*, 28: 61–89.

Stone, Pamela 2007 *Opting Out? Why Women Really Quit Careers and Head Home*. Berkeley, CA: University of California Press.

Swidler, Ann 1986 "Culture in Action: Symbols and Strategies." *American Sociological Review*, 51: 273–86.

Taylor, Frederick Winslow 1967 [1911] *The Principles of Scientific Management*. New York: W. W. Norton & Co.

Taylor, Verta 1989 "Social Movement Continuity: The Women's Movement in Abeyance." *American Sociological Review*, 54(5): 761–75.

Thatcher, Sherry M. B., and Xiumei Zhu 2006 "Changing Identities in a Changing Workplace: Identification, Identity Enactment, Self-Verification, and Telecommuting." *Academy of Management Review*, 31(4): 1076–88.

Thompson, E. P. 1963 *The Making of the English Working Class*. New York: Pantheon Books.

Thompson, James D. 1967. *Organizations in Action*. New York: McGraw-Hill.

Tilly, Charles 1976 "Major Forms of Collective Action in Western Europe 1500–1975." *Theory and Society*, 3(3): 365–75.

Tucker, Robert C. 1978 *The Marx-Engels Reader*. New York: W.W. Norton & Co.

Vaughan, Diane 1999 "The Dark Side of Organizations: Mistake, Misconduct, and Disaster." *Annual Review of Sociology*, 25: 271–305.

Voss, Kim 2000 "Breaking the Iron Law of Oligarchy: Union Revitalization in the American Labor Movement." *The American Journal of Sociology*, 106(2): 303–49.

Walsh, Edward J. 1981 "Resource Mobilization and Citizens' Protest in Communities around Three Mile Island." *Social Problems*, 29(1): 1–21.

Weber, Max 1930 [1904] *The Protestant Ethic and the Spirit of Capitalism*. Translated by Talcott Parsons. New York: Charles Scribner's Sons.

Weber, Max 1958 [1946] *From Max Weber*. Translated and edited by H. H. Gerth and C. Wright Mills. New York: Galaxy.

Weber, Max 1967 [1925] *Max Weber on Law in Economy and Society*. Edited by Max Rheinstein; translated by Edward Shils and Max Rheinstein. New York: Simon & Schuster.

Weber, Max 1978 [1921] *Economy and Society: An Outline of Interpretive Sociology*. Edited by Guenther Roth and Claus Wittich. Berkeley, CA: University of California Press.

Weisbrod, Burton A. 1975 "Toward a Theory of the Nonprofit Sector in a Three Sector Economy." In Edmund Phelps (ed.), *Altruism, Morality, and Economic Theory*. New York: Russell Sage Foundation.

Weisbrod, Burton A. 1988 *The Nonprofit Economy*. Cambridge, MA: Harvard University Press.

Westhues, Kenneth 2002. "At the Mercy of the Mob. A Summary of Research on Workplace Mobbing." *OHS Canada*, 18(8): 30–36.

Whyte, William H. 1956 *The Organization Man*. New York: Simon & Schuster.

Williamson, Oliver E. 1970 *Corporate Control and Business Behavior*. Englewood Cliffs, NJ: Prentice-Hall.

Williamson, Oliver E. 1981 "The Economics of Organization: The Transaction Cost Approach." *The American Journal of Sociology*, 87(3): 548–77.

Wing, Kennard T., Thomas H. Pollak, and Amy Blackwood 2008 *The Nonprofit Almanac, 2008*. Washington, DC: The Urban Institute Press.

Wolch Jennifer 1990 *The Shadow State: Government and Voluntary Sector in Transition*. New York: The Foundation Center.

Young, Dennis 2000 "Alternative Models of Government–Nonprofit Sector Relations: Theoretical and International Perspectives." *Nonprofit and Voluntary Sector Quarterly*, 29(1): 149–72.

Zald, Mayer N., and John McCarthy 1987 *Social Movements in an Organizational Society: Collected Essays*. New Brunswick, NJ: Transaction Publishers.

Zucker, Lynne G. 1977 "The Role of Institutionalization in Cultural Persistence." *American Sociological Review*, 42: 726–43.

Zucker, Lynne 1987 "Institutional Theories of Organization." *Annual Review of Sociology*, 13: 443–64.

Zwerdling, Daniel 1984 *Workplace Democracy: A Guide to Workplace Ownership, Participation and Self Management Experiments in the United States and Europe*. New York: Harper & Row.

Index

Mayo, Elton 54, 56, 57, 58, 62, 63, 64–5
Mead, Margaret 155
media, the 11
Men and Women of the Corporation
    (Kantor) 89–90
Merton, Robert King 69–70, 84, 116
Meyer, John W. 74, 75, 103, 127
M-form (multidivisional firm or
    conglomerate) 118–20, 123–4,
    129–30
Michels, Roberto 98–9
micromanagement 45
Microsoft 77
middle class 13
    and the suburbs 13
Miller, Frank 97
Mills, C. Wright 71, 86, 88
mission creep 148
"Mistakes at Work" (Hughes) 104
modernity 22
moral mazes 92–4
mutual aid associations 11

NAACP (National Association for the
    Advancement of Colored People)
    159
NATO (North Atlantic Treaty
    Organization) 12
natural systems 55, 59, 62–3, 107, 195
neo-institutional model 125–30, 188
Netherlands, pillarization tradition in
    133–4
network analysis 111, 115–16
networks 111–14, 126, 165–6
    network structures 112, 113
    social change networks 163–6
    transnational advocacy networks
        164
    transnational networks, 185–7
    See also IOL; ION; IOR
New York Times 111
niche 5, 117, 118, 119–20, 121, 122–3,
    195
    niche overlap 125
No Child Left Behind Act (NCLB) (2002)
    50
non-governmental organizations
    (NGOs) *See* non-profit sector
non-profit organizations (NPOs) *See*
    non-profit sector
non-profit sector 132–3
    definition of 132–5
    how NPOs are different 140–4
    key areas of 134
    and the state sector 146–52
    why there is a non-profit sector
        (*see* contract failure; flexibility;

market failure; state failure,
    trustworthiness)
norms 11, 28, 195
    dysfunctional norms, 92–4
Northern states *See* advanced capitalist
    societies

OECD (Organisation for Economic
    Co-operation and Development)
    8, 12
OECD member-states *See* advanced
    capitalist, societies
office politics 94
Oliver, Christine 122–3
Olsen, Johan P. 128
open systems 106, 107, 186, 195
organic solidarity 29, 30, 195
Organization Man, The (Whyte) 71
organizational charts (org charts)
    14–16
    specification of theoretical channels
        for individual action 16
    and the structure of relationships
        among offices 16
    use of by Fayol 43
organizational dysfunctions
    built-in failures 96–9
    disasters 99–104
    everyday dysfunctions 86–96
organizational entrepreneurship
    124–5
organizational environment 107–9,
    167
    Thompson's typology of 109–11
organizational field 111, 126–7, 195
    levels of embeddedness in 158
    spheres of action in 126, 158
organizational form 17, 118, 167,
    195
organizational personality 175–6
organizational population 117
organizational society 7
organizational state 7
organizational systems 101–4
organizations 5, 72–73
    bastard organizations 94–6
    definition of an organization 2
    division of labor within 5
    and the "echo chamber effect" 87
    informal organizations 2, 5
    and in-group privilege 86
    and out-group antipathy 86
    school as 3
    semi-formal organizations 2
    See also organizations, formal
organizations, formal 2, 7
    constituents of 5